Introduction to Neurolingui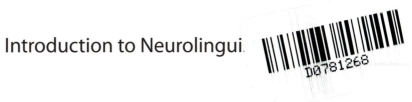

Introduction
to Neurolinguistics

Elisabeth Ahlsén
Göteborg University

John Benjamins Publishing Company
Amsterdam / Philadelphia

TM The paper used in this publication meets the minimum requirements of American National Standard for Information Sciences — Permanence of Paper for Printed Library Materials, ANSI Z39.48-1984.

Cover design: Françoise Berserik

Library of Congress Cataloging-in-Publication Data

Ahlsén, Elisabeth
    Introduction to Neurolinguistics / by Elisabeth Ahlsén
    p.   cm.
        Includes bibliographical references and index.
    1. Neurolinguistics. I. Title.

QP399.A39   2006
612.8'2336--dc22   2006042986
ISBN 90 272 3233 4 (Hb; alk. paper) / 90 272 3234 2 (Pb; alk. paper)

John Benjamins Publishing Company • P.O. Box 36224 • 1020 ME Amsterdam • The Netherlands
John Benjamins North America • P.O. Box 27519 • Philadelphia PA 19118-0519 • USA

Table of contents

Part IV: Resource chapters

Preface

It is not uncommon to search for a particular type of book, only to discover that you will have to write it yourself. The idea of this book emanates from a conversation with a representative of John Benjamins at an International Cognitive Linguistics Conference some years ago, concerning the difficulty of finding an up-to-date book of reasonable size, price and coverage for introductory courses in neurolinguistics. By then, I had been teaching such courses for students of linguistics and communication disorders for a long time. Both of us were well aware of this problem, and when it was suggested that I should write such a book, I agreed. We were also in agreement concerning the relative lack of communication between neurolinguistics and cognitive linguistics, pragmatics and communication studies at the time and the need for these areas to be better integrated into basic neurolinguistics. This discussion and further reflections on the "state of the art" led to the fairly broad selection of topics that are covered in this book and to the relative weighting given to the different chapters. One important concern has been to place the different theories, methods and studies discussed in a historical perspective, showing how different frameworks have developed, sometimes in parallel, sometimes in sequence, and left their traces on the ways we think about language and the brain and how we apply this thinking in our research and therapy. The book grew gradually out of many years' work, as preliminary versions were used in introductory courses, and chapters were revised and added.

This book is a basic introduction to neurolinguistics, intended for anybody who wants to acquire a grounding in the field. It was written for students of linguistics and communication disorders, but students of psychology, neuroscience and other disciplines will also find it valuable. It can be used as coursebook for introductory courses or as a source of information on specific topics in neurolinguistics. The only prerequisite for using it is a basic knowledge of linguistics, including linguistic terminology. Students who have no linguistic background at all should first read an introductory linguistics text. As for students who have no background in neuroanatomy and neurophysiology, some basic information about the brain is provided in Chapter 14.

The book is divided into four parts. The first is an introduction to what neurolinguistics is, what the important questions are, and how the main neurolinguistic frameworks have developed over time. This section provides an important background for understanding why the representatives of specific present-day approaches presented later in the book reason in the way they do. The second part constitutes the linguistic core of the book, in which different components or aspects of neurolinguistics (phonology, morphology, syntax, lexical semantics, and semantics and pragmatics in communication) are described. The third part contains chapters on selected topics that are of central interest to many neurolinguists and other scientists seeking to understand how language and the brain interact. The four topics are reading and writing, bilingualism, the evolution of language, and multimodality in communication, all viewed from the perspective of describing and explaining disorders of language and communication. The fourth part contains an introduction to the brain, which can read before the rest of the book or used as a reference, and two additional resource chapters on matters that are often referred to in neurolinguistics: neuroimaging (and other methods for investigating brain activity and brain damage) and modeling, especially with artificial neural networks. These chapters are not the core of the book, but should be regarded as resources to be consulted for more information.

Each chapter has a short table of contents at the beginning and a summary at the end. It also suggests further readings from the reference list that will help students learn more about the topics covered in that particular chapter. Each chapter (except the resource chapters) also has a set of assignments at the end. These assignments are not simple factual questions, but are designed to make students apply, think, reason about and discuss the contents of the chapter and what they imply. They are mainly intended for homework, group work and discussion in seminars, for example.

As mentioned above, the book's aim is to provide an up-to-date linguistic perspective, focusing especially on semantics and pragmatics, evolutionary perspectives, neural network modeling and multimodality, areas that may have been neglected by earlier introductory works. It presents theories from the 19th century, when many of our most basic ideas about language and the brain were formed (the Wernicke-Lichtheim model, Jackson's evolutionary perspective, etc., as well as more holistic views), classical frameworks that have had and still have a considerable influence on clinical practice (the neoclassical "Bostonian" and Lurian approaches), and frameworks that are in their development phase today (pragmatics and communication, multimodality, communication technology, cognitive neuropsychology and neurolinguistics), as well as some brief information on emerging topics and frameworks that are likely to influence neurolinguistics in the near future (mirror neuron findings, embodiment and alignment in communication).

Over the years, many people have contributed in various ways to the approach, contents and form of this book. I have been greatly influenced by the books that focused my interest on neurolinguistics in the 1980s: the *Studies in neurolinguistics* series published by Whitaker and Whitaker, Ruth Lesser's book on linguistics and aphasia, and the work of my supervisor in logopedics, Bibi Fex, who directed my clinical interest towards aphasia and brain damage. I am also indebted to the teachers and fellow students at the 1982 Linguistic Institute on Neuro- and Psycholinguistics at the University of Maryland, the members of Lise Menn and Loraine Obler's Cross Language Aphasia Study project and my colleagues in the Nordic Linguistic Network.

An important influence on my particular perspective on linguistics and neurolinguistics is the work of colleagues at the Department of Linguistics and the SSKKII Center for Cognitive Science, Göteborg University, especially my former supervisor Jens Allwood, whose theories on communication as cooperation and action made me look at neurolinguistics with a critical eye and relate it more to theories from semantics, pragmatics, communication and cognitive linguistics. Special thanks are also due to the research group on neurolinguistics and communication disorders, my Ph.D. students, and the numerous students of linguistics and logopedics who have been subjected to earlier versions of the book and who have given me valuable feedback.

I would probably neither have started nor finished this project without the support and encouragement I received from Benjamins, especially Kees Vaes, and the text would not have been in its present shape without the meticulous copy-editing work of Zofia Laubitz and of Shirley Nicholson for earlier versions.

This book has mainly been a project I worked on in my "spare time," but I have received some valuable support for related research projects financed by the Swedish Council for Working Life and Social Science Research, the Swedish Research Council and the Vårdal Foundation. During my time as a research fellow in the Embodied Communication group at the ZiF Interdisciplinary Center for Research, University of Bielefeld, in 2005 and 2006, I was given the possibility of finishing the manuscript at last.

I would like to express my thanks to everyone mentioned above and many others, not least the patients and research subjects who have given me new insight into the intriguing relationship between language and the brain.

Copyright acknowledgement

List of tables

List of figures

Part I

Introduction to neurolinguistics

Chapter 1

What is neurolinguistics?

In this chapter:

- *What is included in neurolinguistics?*
- *Different views of the relation between brain and language*
- *The central questions of neurolinguistics*
- *Outline of the book*

What is neurolinguistics?

Neurolinguistics studies the relation of language and communication to different aspects of brain function, in other words it tries to explore how the brain understands and produces language and communication. This involves attempting to combine neurological/neurophysiological theory (how the brain is structured and how it functions) with linguistic theory (how language is structured and how it functions). Apart from neurology and linguistics, psychology is another central source discipline for neurolinguistics. Neurolinguistics has a very close relationship to psycholinguistics, but focuses more on studies of the brain. Studies of language and communication after brain damage are perhaps the most common type of neurolinguistic studies. However, experiments, model construction, computer simulations, and neuroimaging studies are also very frequently used methods today.

In order to identify relevant models and frameworks of neurolinguistics, let us first try to delimit this research field. The main questions of interest for neurolinguistics (see the section with this title below) were first addressed very far back in history. There was a period of intensified focus in the late 19th century; since then, they have become central to researchers in many disciplines. "Neurolinguistics" became the established term for the field in the 1960s, under the influence of the Chomskyan boost to linguistics and the development of psycholinguistics as a defined field. The subject matter of neurolinguistics is described in the introduction to the series of volumes known as *Studies in Neurolinguistics*, edited by Whitaker and Whitaker in the 1970s, as follows: even though the field of neurolinguistics is frankly interdisciplinary, there is a common theme of the relationships between language and the brain (Whitaker & Whitaker, 1976, p. xi).

A similar description, although more focused on functional aspects, can be found in the introductory description of *Brain and Language*, one of the most influential journals in this field:

> human language or communication (speech, hearing, reading, writing, or nonverbal modalities) related to any aspect of the brain or brain function (*Brain and Language*: "Description")

The common problem in relating aspects of language or communication to brain function in this dynamic formulation, is posed by Luria in *Basic problems in neurolinguistics*: what are the real processes of formation of verbal communication and its comprehension, and what are the components of these processes and the conditions under which they take place (Luria, 1976, p. 3).

The interdisciplinary character of the field

The **many disciplines** dealing with neurolinguistics provide inspiration and energy to the field. They introduce many different kinds of data, theories, and models for research.

The editors of *Studies in Neurolinguistics* in the 1970s described the series as "heterogeneous both in theoretical perspective and in topical coverage" and they claimed that the discipline at the time was "not working under a uniform paradigm and there [were] not a few, narrowly defined areas of research" (Whitaker & Whitaker, 1979, p. xi). They also refer to substantial disagreements among the researchers in the field. They do, however, also mention the positive side of heterogeneity: the richness and diversity of ideas and the fact that "attempts at synthesis must take account of many different kinds of data" (Whitaker & Whitaker, 1977, p. xi). To these points, we should add that not only data, but also theories, paradigms, models, and frameworks from different disciplines need to be taken into account, that synthesis seems necessary in this diverse field, and that, at the same time, diversity necessarily increases with further specialization.

Which disciplines have to be taken into account in neurolinguistics? *Brain and Language* states that its interdisciplinary focus includes the fields of linguistics, neuroanatomy, neurology, neurophysiology, philosophy, psychology, psychiatry, speech pathology, and computer science. These disciplines may be the ones most involved in neurolinguistics, but several other disciplines are also highly relevant, having contributed to theories, methods, and findings in neurolinguistics. They include neurobiology, anthropology, chemistry, cognitive science, and artificial intelligence. Thus, the humanities, and medical, natural, and social sciences, as well as technology are all represented.

Different views on the relation between brain and language

A number of different views about the relationship between brain and language have existed and still do. Some of those that have had a considerable influence are mentioned below.

Localism tries to find locations or centers in the brain for different language functions. **Associationism** situates language functions in the connections between different areas of the brain, making it possible to associate, for example, perceptions of different senses with words and/or "concepts." **Dynamic localization of function** assumes that functional systems of localized subfunctions perform language functions. Such systems are dynamic, and thus they can be reorganized during language development or after brain damage. **Holistic** theories consider many language functions to be handled by widespread areas of the brain working together. **Evolution-based** theories stress the relationship between how the brain and language evolved over time in different species, how they develop in children, and how adults perform language functions.

The central questions of neurolinguistics

Some of the **central questions** for neurolinguistics are:

- What happens to language and communication after brain damage of different types?
- How did the ability to communicate and the ability to use language develop as the species evolved? How can we relate this development to the evolution of the brain?
- How do children learn to communicate and use language? How can we relate their acquisition of language to the development of their brains?
- How can we measure and visualize processes in the brain that are involved in language and communication?
- How can we make good models of language and communication processes that will help us to explain the linguistic phenomena that we study?
- How can we make computer simulations of language processing, language development, and language loss?
- How can we design experiments that will allow us to test our models and hypotheses about language processing?

The first of the questions above occupies a special place in neurolinguistics. **Aphasia** is defined as "language loss due to brain damage." The cause can, for example, be an infarction (blockage of blood vessels in the brain), a hemorrhage (bursting of a blood vessel), or a head trauma. The effect of the lesion is that the comprehension and/or production of language is changed. By studying these changes, we can study how functional systems related to language work and which brain structures are involved in them. People have always studied the loss of different abilities in order to map the functions of the brain. When it comes to higher cognitive abilities, such as language, this poses many problems, but the data acquired from studies of aphasia have roughly the same degree of reliability as the data obtained with other neurolinguistic methods. **Aphasiology** or **linguistic aphasiology** is the dominant branch of neurolinguistics. Aphasia is an acquired language disorder, often defined as a focal lesion (i.e., a lesion of one or more specific areas). Acquired disorders are also caused by **progressive neurological diseases,** such as **dementias**. Language and memory are closely connected and interdependent, especially in complex higher cognitive functions.

Not only acquired language disorders, but also **developmental language disorders**, that is, disorders that are found in children who have not experienced any specific lesion event, are of interest to neurolinguistics. Neurolinguistic approaches to developmental language disorders, such as **SLI** (specific language disorder), and **developmental reading and writing problems**, including **dyslexia**, typically compare these conditions to similar acquired disorders, bearing in mind the special conditions of language acquisition and the plasticity (ability to be molded) of young brains. Neurolinguists also study the language development of children with nonspecific developmental disorders affecting language.

The development of language and speech and prerequisites **for language and speech in the evolution of the species** also need to be considered by neurolinguists. The changes in the structures and function of the brain are compared to different species' ways of living. Animal communication systems are studied under natural conditions, especially those of primates, and experiments are carried out with primates that are being taught human communication systems.

For a neurolinguist, an essential source of knowledge is the possibility **of measuring brain activity** during language tasks in normal and damaged brains. Static pictures of the brain, where lesion sites can be seen, such as the **CT** scan (computer tomography scan), which constructs a three-dimensional picture of a lesion from X-rays of many planes of the brain, or the **MRI** (magnetic resonance image) are standard information in hospitals today. The measurement of dynamic activity in the brain during language tasks by methods such as **EEG** (electroencephalography), **PET** (positron emission tomography), **fMRI** (functional magnetic resonance imaging), and **MEG** (magnetic encephalography) is an important tool for research.

Psycholinguistics, often in combination with information about brain activity in different areas of the brain, provides the basis for neurolinguistic **modeling** of processes for language comprehension, linguistic memory, language production, language acquisition, and language loss. Such models can be the basis of **computer simulations** using serial (i.e., basically "box-and-arrow") models, models with parallel processes running at the same time, interconnections between processes, and feedback loops between levels of process models. Computer simulations involving so-called "artificial neural networks" (ANN) or connectionist networks are also used. The models are also the basis of **off-line** and **on-line** (i.e., with real-time measurement of processes) **experiments** on language functions.

Outline of the book

This introductory section will be followed by a historical overview, tracing the different theoretical standpoints of neurolinguistics to their roots and following the development of neurolinguistics. The models and frameworks that form the basis of today's neurolinguistic research and practice will then be presented in more detail.

In the second part of the book, we will examine different aspects of neurolinguistics, (i.e., phonetics/phonology, morphology/syntax, lexicon/semantics, and pragmatics). The interaction between the different aspects will also be stressed.

The third part covers certain specific themes and phenomena from a neurolinguistic perspective. These phenomena are reading and writing processes, multilingualism, evolutionary and developmental perspectives on brain and language, and multimodality.

The book also contains a fourth part with three resource chapters. The first chapter of part 4 briefly presents some methods for investigating the brain (neuroimaging techniques) and the second chapter introduces computer simulation using artificial neural network (ANN) models. The chapter on ANN is included, since ANN modeling is increasingly popular in neurolinguistics . It is, however, a bit more technical than the other chapters . A final resource chapter provides a short introduction to neuroanatomy and neurophysiology; this chapter can be read at the outset of the course or consulted during the reading of the other chapters.

Summary

This introductory chapter delimits the scope of neurolinguistics by defining it as the study of the relation between brain and language. It mentions some of the definitions given and central questions raised by leading researchers in the area, such as the focus on language processing, involving predictive and explanatory psycholinguistic models, experimental studies, computer simulations, and the measurement of brain activity during language tasks. The central position of studies of language pathology after brain damage — aphasia and related disorders — and the related questions of language development in the species and the human individual are also emphasized. The main contributing disciplines — linguistics, medical neurosciences, psychology, and speech-language pathology — are identified. The chapter also briefly outlines the contents of the book.

Further reading

More extensive overviews of different areas in neurolinguistics can be found in David Caplan's introductory book from 1987 and in the Handbook of Neurolinguistics, which contains short chapters on a number of topics in neurolinguistics.

Caplan, D. (1987). *Neurolinguistics and linguistic aphasiology. An introduction*. Cambridge: Cambridge University Press.

Stemmer, B., & Whitaker, H. (Eds.) (1998). *Handbook of neurolinguistics*. New York: Academic Press.

Assignments

1. Try to think of three important questions about language and brain that you would like to find an answer to. Think about the different contributing disciplines and what type of relevant investigations, methods, and potential findings they might come up with to help answer the question.

2. Imagine a study you would like to carry out on one of these questions. Try to develop an outline of the actual design using methods that the different disciplines might contribute.

3. Try to describe what you think happens when you (silently) read (a) a word, (b) a text. Which different functions are needed and in what order?

4. Now, try to describe what happens when a child reads his or her first words. How does this differ from when you read a word?

Keep your answers to these questions handy and return to them when you have read the main parts of the book.

Chapter 2

The development of theories about brain and language

In this chapter:

- *Different views of the brain–language relationship*
- *Ideas about brain and language before the 19th century*
- *The foundations of neurolinguistic theories in the late 19th century*
- *Further developments in the 20th century*

Different views of the brain–language relationship

As we saw in Chapter 1, a number of different views of the relationship between the brain and language have existed and still exist. We will first very briefly describe some that have had a relatively great influence. We will return to them later in the chapter and see how they first arose, how they developed, and what their influence is today.

Figure 2.1 below presents an approximation of different views of the language–brain relationship along the continuum from localism to holism.

Localism

Localism claims that different "higher functions" are localized in different centers of the brain, mainly the cortex. Either these centers can be seen as "sisters," being equally important, or one center, such as the prefrontal area (in front of the frontal lobes), may be seen as superordinate to the others. In this view, aphasia is seen as the result of a lesion in a language center. Well-known localists include Gall and Broca.

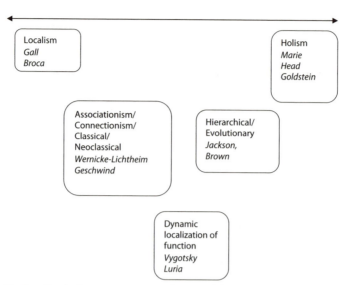

Figure 2.1. The localist–holist continuum, with a simplified placement of different views

Associationism (or connectionism)

Associationism assumes that higher functions are dependent on the connections between different centers in the cortex. Linguistic ability is seen as the relationship between images and words. Aphasia results from broken connections between the centers that are needed for linguistic function. Representatives of this view are Wernicke, Lichtheim, and Geschwind. This view is also sometimes called the classical (Wernicke-Lichtheim) or neoclassical (Geschwind) view.

Dynamic localization of function

With this type of theory, different subfunctions are seen as localized in different parts of the brain. These subfunctions must be combined in order to achieve more complex functions, which can be "put together" in a number of different ways. The relationship between a localized lesion and the functions that are disturbed becomes more complex in this case. This is the view of Luria, for example.

Hierarchical or evolution-based view

Evolution-based theories emphasize the layered structure of the brain from inner/lower and more primitive structures to the later developed and superimposed cortical layer and the role of all of these layers in language and communication. Jackson is an early representative of this view, Brown a contemporary one.

Holism

Holism is the opinion that the brain works as a whole, at least to accomplish higher functions. The cortex is said to handle, for example, "higher cognitive functions," "symbolic thinking," "intelligence," or "abstraction," and aphasia is a sign of a general cognitive loss, not a specific language loss. This view has also been called "cognitivism" and some representatives are Marie, Head, and Goldstein. Hierarchical views are also sometimes deemed to be holistic and Jackson is regarded as the founder of the "cognitive school."

Other terms: Unitarism and equipotentiality

Other terms that are used for *one unitary* function of the brain are "unitarism," the view that the soul is one and cannot be divided, and "equipotentiality," which means that all parts of the cortex have the same functional potential and that the size of a brain lesion determines the extent of the aphasia (the mass effect).

Ideas about Brain and Language before the 19th Century

Ancient Egypt, Greece, and Rome

The first reference to the brain as the center of language is found in the *Edwin Smith papyrus* from about 3500 BC. Here we find observations that damage to the head can result in symptoms in other parts of the body and that this must depend on the function of the brain. Language loss is said to be caused by an external god or death sending its spirit or breath into the brain, so that the patient becomes "silent in sadness." This condition was cured by trepanation, or drilling a hole in the skull to let the god's spirit out. The earlier view that the soul resided in the heart continued to exist.

In writings from Greek antiquity, language disorders are discussed, for example, by Hippocrates (400 BC), who described a man who lost his memory for letters; he also observed that language disorders coincided with hemiparesis (paralysis of one side of the body) in the side of the body opposite to that of the brain lesion. According to Hippocrates, the brain was the organ of the intellect (*mnemonikon*) and the heart was the organ of the senses. Around the same time, Democritus compared the brain to a guard or sentinel with two functions: the internal function of guarding the intelligence and the external function of guarding the senses. Herophilus localized intelligence in the ventricles (cavities) of the brain at about 300 BC. This view remained dominant for a long time and was still found as late as the end of the 18th century.

Plato (4th century BC) wanted to localize the different abilities of the soul in different parts of the brain, which he saw as the center of all senses. It was with Plato that

Figure 2.2. Intelligence localized in the ventricles (Herophilus)

the idea arose that a function could have a one-to-one relationship with an area in the brain. Aristotle, on the other hand, claimed that the brain was just a refrigerating system, while the heart was the center of all nerves; this opinion did not have much influence in the long run. His "flow charts" for psychological processes, from the sense organs to cognition and from cognition to motor functions — e.g., sense organ → sensation → perception → cognition → memory — did, on the other hand, influence later models of language functions.

Galen (3rd century BC) further developed the view that different abilities were localized in different ventricles. *Pneuma* in the ventricles was described as "instruments of the soul." Galen was a doctor for the Roman gladiators and found support for his theory in the brain lesions that he saw, which only seemed to disturb consciousness if they were deep enough to affect the ventricles.

From the Middle Ages to 1800

During this period, a number of case descriptions appeared, describing different types of language disorders. Theoretically, the discussion of the ventricles of the brain continued. Memory was assumed to be localized in the fourth ventricle and the Italian physician Antonio Guainerio suggested in the 15th century that word sparsity and naming errors were symptoms of a disturbance of memory, caused by too much phlegm in the fourth ventricle. In the 16th century, these theories about the ventricles

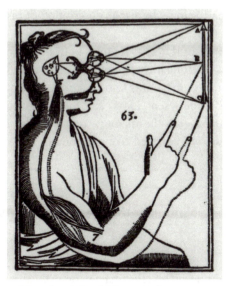

Figure 2.3. The function of the pineal gland (Descartes)

were criticized by anatomists Costanzo Varolius and Andreas Vesalius, both of whom wanted to localize psychological functions in the soft substance of the brain and to stress the importance of brain volume.

In the 17th century, the school of unitarism. René Descartes held the view that the soul was "indivisible" and had its center in the pineal gland, an organ that is located in the middle of the brain (cf. Descartes, 1974). Physician Thomas Willis (1664,1672) placed the imagination in the corpus callosum (a bundle of fibers connecting the two brain hemispheres). Memory traces of pictures were also placed in the corpus callosum. The corpus striatum (an organ inside the brain) was believed to be able to create a picture of sensory impressions, but this picture could not be complete without "help" from the corpus callosum. François de la Peyronie (1741), a French surgeon, also saw the corpus callosum as the center of the soul. Unitarian theories were criticized by the anatomist Albrecht von Haller as "theories without knowledge." They were, however, supported by the church and the monarchy at the time, since the idea of the soul as one unit, possibly located in one central brain structure, was consistent with religious dogma.

In 1770, the German physician Johann Gesner wrote a monograph called "Speech amnesia," which contained six case studies. He saw speech disorders as a type of memory disorder, caused by inertia in the connections between the different parts of the brain. These disorders were assumed to cause difficulties in associating images or abstract ideas with linguistic signs. Here, we find the first expression of an association-ism which is clearly combined with neurophysiological speculation.

Localist views were also being expressed at this time and descriptions of personal experiences of speech and language loss were published, for example, Goethe's story about his grandfather and Samuel Johnson's description of his own transient speech disturbance.

To sum up, at the turn of the 19th century, both theories and knowledge about aphasia existed. Almost all clinical types of aphasia had been described, the relation between aphasia and brain damage was known, and the hypothesis that aphasia was caused by a disconnection between "ideas" and their linguistic signs had appeared. Theories focused on damage to the memory organ or association processes, and the neurological causes were believed to be lesions in the ventricles or the brain substance.

The foundations of neurolinguistic theories in the late 19th century

Gall

The anatomist Franz Joseph Gall was the first person to localize mental faculties in the brain cortex. The cortex had earlier been considered to be an expansion of the brain membranes with the function of supplying nourishment to the brain. The brain gyri (ridges or convolutions) in humans (as opposed to in animals) were assumed to vary between individuals and to be different in the two brain hemispheres. Gall also saw the cortex as a morphologically uniform, continuous layer. He based this view on two observations: (a) cases of hydrocephalus, where the cortex had been stretched out because of too much liquid and thereby had lost its convolutions, but brain functions were unchanged; (b) the possibility of changing the structure of the convolutions by externally affecting the cortex. Gall decided to explore and map out the surface of the brain (Gall & Spurzheim, 1810–1819). He explained that the cortex was the highest level of organization of the brain and that the cortex and other areas of gray matter are connected by fibers of white matter.

Gall made several assumptions as the basis for his theory:

- that a number of innate abilities exist;
- that it is impossible to reduce these abilities to a unity and that they are independent of each other;
- that the real nature of the abilities cannot be examined, only their material conditions, which are in the organism;
- that these material conditions must be in the cortex.

The background of these assumptions was empirical. Gall started from observations of behavior, but found (unlike the pure sensationalists, who claimed that all abilities can be reduced to sensory impressions) that certain abilities had to be innate, since they could not be explained in any other way. He exemplified the view of the plurality

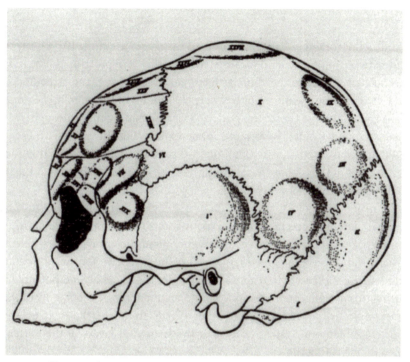

Figure 2.4. Gall's map of the cranium

of mental abilities with dreams, where certain abilities are resting, while others are active. There ought to be many abilities and they could not be too general. The role of the cortex was motivated by its importance for sensory and motor functions and for phenomena like phantom pain (in amputated limbs), its size, and the relation between the size of a brain lesion and the severity of symptoms. All of these assumptions exercised a major influence for about 150 years.

In order to find out what the abilities of the soul were, Gall started from studies of language and, first and foremost, from the biographies of well-known persons. In this way, he identified 27 human abilities. In mapping these abilities, Gall assumed that the development of the skull depended on the size of the cortex under it. Consequently, by observing the cranium, it would be "almost" possible to examine the cortex. This procedure was named cranioscopy and it was from cranioscopy that phrenology developed; phrenology, of course, later fell into disrepute. Gall studied the different abilities in a number of persons and examined their skulls. The result was that each of the 27 abilities was related to one cortical area, bilaterally. These areas included two areas for language, both in the frontal lobes, one for speech articulation and the other for word memory. This localization was based on Gall's observations of persons with frontal lobe lesions and speech disorders. To sum up, Gall's opinions were extremely localist.

After Gall

When Gall, who worked in Paris, proposed his theory (1791 and 1810), a lively debate followed between unitarists and localists. The conflict was partially political. Localists were seen as hostile to the church, the pope, and the king, and as deniers of the immortality of the soul, while unitarists were champions of the church, the pope, and the divine right of kings. Those who criticized Gall, including the philosophers Hegel, Schopenhauer, and Comte, were more influential during this period. These critics claimed that it was impossible to combine two such radically different things as behavior and parts of the cortex, that the abilities were too abstract, and that the theory had no morphological anatomical basis.

Gall's major antagonist was French physiologist Pierre Flourens (1824). He claimed that there was a certain division of functions in the brain, but that the cortex had to work as one unified whole. He made experiments on animals, mostly birds, and found that it was possible to remove large parts of the cortex without any functions disappearing. These ideas were to reappear later under the name of "equipotentiality."

During this period, extensive work was done in mapping the anatomy of the cortex, for example, by Luigi Rolando and Louis-Pierre Gratiolet (who was, surprisingly, a supporter of Flourens against Gall), and the structural layers of the cortex were examined in by histologists.

Bouillaud and Auburtin

Jean-Baptiste Bouillaud can be seen as a link between Gall and Broca. He was Gall's student and supported him. Bouillaud (1825) decided to prove that lesions in the frontal lobes caused loss of speech. He claimed, against Flourens, that limited cortical lesions cause partial muscle paralysis, which showed that there were specific centers in the cortex. He presented a series of cases where speech disorders were correlated with frontal lobe lesions and a series of cases with lesions of other lobes where there were no speech disorders. Bouillaud found two types of speech disorders connected to brain damage: disorders of "speech movements" and disorders of "word memory"; this was in accordance with the abilities assumed by Gall. The unitarists made counterarguments. They produced patients who had lesions in the frontal lobes but no speech loss, and patients who had speech loss following lesions in other lobes. Progress had been made since Gall in two respects: (a) there was a better idea of *what* to localize, after clinical observations of language loss, among other things; (b) there was also a better idea of *where* to localize, because of the mapping of the cortex.

Ernest Auburtin was Bouillaud's son-in-law and introduced his ideas to the anthropological society of Paris in 1861. He had found a patient who had attempted to commit suicide and shot away his skull bone over the frontal lobes. The frontal lobes were intact but "accessible." Auburtin had discovered that if you pressed the frontal lobes with a spatula, the patient stopped talking, and he saw this as a proof of the localization of speech in the frontal lobes. The surgeon and anthropologist Paul Broca, who was present at the meeting, shortly thereafter found a patient who was dying and who had a severe speech disorder. He decided to provide further evidence in the form of that patient's brain.

Broca

Traditionally, neurolinguistics is said to have been born in 1861, when Paul Broca presented his theory, based on a patient's symptoms and the dissection of his brain. The patient, Leborgne, had major difficulties producing speech. He was called "Tan," since this was his only speech output. At the autopsy, the oldest brain damage, which had probably caused his speech disorder (other symptoms had been added later), affected a specific area in the brain that came to be known as Broca's area, the third frontal convolution (gyrus) (pars triangularis and pars opercularis) in the left hemisphere.

After studying this patient and several others with similar symptoms, Broca presented two important hypotheses in 1865:

1. that it was possible to localize psychological functions in brain convolutions;
2. that linguistic symptoms were caused by lesions in the left hemisphere and that consequently language was lateralized, which was totally unexpected.

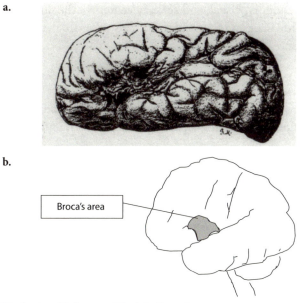

Figure 2.5. a. The brain of Leborgne (Tan), b. Broca's are

Broca called the linguistic disorder *aphémie* (inability to speak). Broca's theory led to new conflicts between unitarists (mostly conservative) and localists (mostly liberal republicans). Furthermore, an article by Marc Dax was raised, in which he had already localized language in the left hemisphere as early as 1836 (Dax, 1865). Dax's son claimed that he had presented his theory at a conference in Montpelier and that Broca was guilty of plagiarism. Broca, however, won the dispute, since it could never be proven that Dax had presented his theory and the article had never been published. Localism now became very popular and researchers worked to localize symptoms such as "agraphia," "word deafness," and "word blindness."

Meynert

Theodor Meynert (1885/1968) was an anatomist who became very influential because of his associationist theory. He examined nerve fibers in the white matter in animals and found that they were of two types: (a) projection fibers between the cortex and the spinal cord, and (b) association fibers between different convolutions within each hemisphere or between the two hemispheres. Meynert claimed that consciousness, intelligence, and memory were cortical but not localized. Inductive thinking was the result of associations between perceptions and deductive thinking was simply an external result of induction. He also compared the cortex of primates and humans and found that the human cortex was most developed around the Sylvian fissure; he therefore believed that this area ought to be related to language function.

Other researchers examined the cortex with the help of electrical stimulation and found the motor, auditory, visual, and sensory centers in the dog. A couple of these researchers, Eduard Hitzig and David Ferrier (1886), claimed that intelligence resided in the frontal lobes.

Wernicke

In 1874, neurologist Carl Wernicke presented a theory based on Broca's findings and on his own dissections of the brains of patients with problems understanding language.

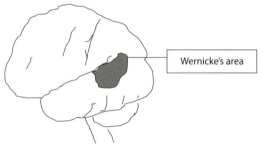

Figure 2.6. Wernicke's area

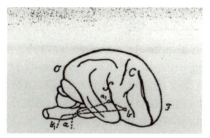

Figure 2.7. Localization of the language areas. Wernicke's area, the inferior parietal lobe, angular gyrus, Broca's area

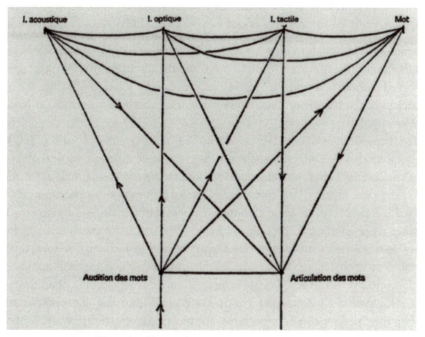

Figure 2.8. Linguistic "flow chart" according to Wernicke. (Acoustique = hearing, Optique = vision, Tactile = tactile, Mot = word, Audition des mots = word hearing, Articulation des mots = word articulation)

He further developed the idea that functions were localized in the brain convolutions (gyri). Patients with reduced language comprehension had lesions in an area that came to be known as Wernicke's area, the posterior part of the first or superior temporal gyrus and adjacent areas (parts of the angular gyrus, the supramarginal gyrus, and the second temporal gyrus are included)

Wernicke imagined that there was a specific "language gyrus" ranging from Wernicke's area (responsible for the receptive function) to Broca's area (responsible for the expressive function). Lesions in either of these areas or in the connection between them would cause aphasia.

Wernicke's theory was a more elaborate model of the relationship between linguistic functions and brain structures than had ever existed before. It should be noted that lesions in Wernicke's area or in the connection between Wernicke's and Broca's areas also cause symptoms in language production, since the input to Broca's area is disturbed. Important parts of Wernicke's theory are:

- the identification of symptom complexes,
- the idea of the flow of information (a sort of high-level "reflex arc"),
- the idea of representation. Broca's area is said to have a "motor representation" of speech, while Wernicke's area is said to have an "auditory sound representation."

By assuming that aphasia could be caused by damage to the connection between Wernicke's and Broca's areas, Wernicke predicted the discovery of the type of aphasia now called "conduction aphasia" (most likely caused by a lesion affecting the arcuate fasciculus, the bundle of fibers connecting the two areas, according to Norman Geschwind).

The theoretical viewpoint behind Wernicke's "sensory aphasia" (also called Wernicke's aphasia) is as follows: association fibers connect different cortical areas and create associations between visual, auditory, and tactile representations/conceptions/ideas of the same object. The view is that each item is born out of associations that are repeated and stabilized, so that for example the visual image alone is enough to evoke the other representations. Through the association paths, we move from "primary images" in one sensory modality to "secondary images," which combine and unite all the images of an object, and then on to "tertiary images," which are the foundations of abstract concepts and words. Consciousness of the external world is, at all times, the result of the state of all these connections. For example, the idea of causality exists in the brain and thanks to these connections. Wernicke's view is strictly associationist and

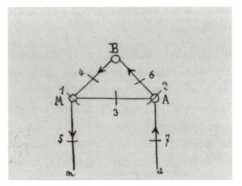

Figure 2.9. The Wernicke-Lichtheim "house" model of 1855

also idealist from the philosophical perspective. Experiences of the external world do not correspond to states in the world but to states within of the brain. Some other well-known associationists of that period were Jean Martin Charcot and Joseph Déjerine.

Lichtheim

German physician Ludwig Lichtheim(1885) found it necessary to postulate a third language center with an unspecified localization, the "concept center," in the model of language function which he theoretically constructed on the basis of Wernicke's model. The model includes auditory input and analysis into auditory word representations in Wernicke's area. Then there is either transmission to Broca's area, where motor word representations are formed and can be executed in articulation (repetition), or transmission to a concept center which can interpret the meaning of the word (understanding). Utterances can also be initiated from the concept center. In this case, concepts are transmitted to Broca's area, where motor word representations are formed and are sent on to motor commands for speech.

In Lichtheim's model, the following kinds of aphasia exist:

- Broca's aphasia: disturbed expressive function;
- Wernicke's aphasia: disturbed receptive function;
- Conduction aphasia (disrupted connection between Wernicke's and Broca's areas): normal comprehension, speech as in Wernicke's aphasia, disturbed repetition;
- Transcortical sensory aphasia (disrupted connection between Wernicke's area and the concept center): disturbed comprehension, normal spontaneous speech, normal repetition;
- Transcortical motor aphasia (disrupted connection between the concept center and Broca's area): normal comprehension, disturbed spontaneous speech, normal repetition.

The period after Broca, Wernicke, and Lichtheim

After Broca, Wernicke, and Lichtheim, localism and associationism became the dominant views. But protests had already been made in the early stages, even though they did not become very influential until the 1920s, when the holistic, so-called cognitive school started to dominate.

Armand Trousseau was the first to challenge the localist view that thinking as such was not affected by aphasia. He attacked Broca and concluded, on clinical grounds, that "intelligence is always damaged in aphasia." The term *aphasia* was borrowed from Greek antiquity, when Sextus Empiricus had used it to denote a philosophical branch which avoided making statements for or against anything. The term *aphasia* replaced *aphemia*, which could also be interpreted as meaning "bad reputation."

In England, philosophical empiricism and associationism led to a view that differed from Wernicke's associationism. Psychologist Alexander Bain claimed that there is a psycho-physical parallelism — that everything that happens psychologically also happens physically at the same time. Meanwhile, Herbert Spencer introduced evolutionary thinking, whereby repeated associations modify the nervous system in a way that is then inherited from generation to generation and forms the basis of the brain's intelligence. Both influenced the founder of the cognitive school, John Hughlings Jackson.

Jackson

Jackson was not interested in anatomical localization. Instead, he studied how stimuli evoke responses and how complex these responses are. Jackson distinguished two levels of language: automatic and propositional. The automatic level consists of stereotyped sentences, certain neologisms (newly created words), and swearing. The propositional level is defined partly by its form (sentences that express a relationship between two objects) and partly by its degree of flexibility (the fact that it can be affected by semantics and by the situation). The use of propositions is seen as a superimposed level. Speech is viewed as a part of thinking. Aphasia represents an inability to "propositionalize," that is, to use language in the service of thought, which is why intelligence is necessarily reduced. Brain damage to a given area does not cause a total loss of function; the ability to speak still exists in aphasia, but it becomes dependent on emotional conditions, since the "intellectual" level has been damaged.

Jackson applied Spencer's evolutionary principles and considered the nervous system as functioning and developing in a hierarchical way:

1. from simple to more complex,
2. from lower centers to higher centers,
3. from more organized centers to more complex centers,
4. from automatic to intentional.

He distinguished three levels of function: elementary reflexes, automatic actions, and intentional actions. These levels are not localized in any centers. Rather, localization is vertically oriented, from the low level (spinal column and brain stem) to the intermediate level (motor and sensory), and then on to the high level (frontal). Jackson's often cited warning to other researchers was that "localization of symptoms can never be identified with localization of function," which means that you cannot conclude from the fact that the loss of a certain ability is correlated with a lesion in a specific area that that function was localized in that area. He was not strictly against localization, but his

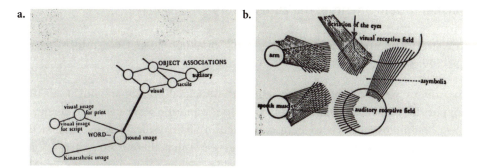

Figure 2.10. a, b. Freud's language field

ideas were taken up by the idealists as counterarguments to the materialist orientation that had been dominant in classical neurology.

Jackson was followed by David Ferrier (1886) and Karl Maria Finkelnburg (1870), who introduced the concept of *asymbolia*, or a generally decreased ability for symbolic thinking underlying aphasia, and Adolph Kussmaul (1876), who named the same disorder *asemia* (inability to use signs). Jackson's theories were presented as early as 1874 and 1875, but remained relatively unknown until they were adopted by Head in the 1920s (Jackson, 1932, Head 1926).

Freud

Sigmund Freud also attacked Wernicke's and Lichtheim's associationism in his monograph "On aphasia" in 1891. His criticism was that the syndromes that defined different types of aphasia were really only symptoms that happened to co-occur and that these symptoms must be affected by external conditions. Freud claimed that other symptom complexes were as frequent as the ones Lichtheim's model showed and that this model was therefore incomplete. He suggested that language could be represented in a "field" in the border area between the temporal, parietal and occipital lobes, where all the properties of an object were connected in a network (smell, taste, look, sound representation, etc.). Lesions in the periphery of this network were claimed to be common in aphasia.

Freud did not work out his theory in more detail. It did not attract much notice during his lifetime and had no influence on research at that time. In later years, it became popular, since it contained thoughts that pointed forward, for instance, about the pragmatic influence on linguistic symptoms.

Further developments in the 20th century

The strengthening of holism: Marie, von Monakow, Head, Goldstein, Lashley, Bay, and Brown

By around 1900, localism and associationism were totally dominant. But at this time, support for holism was increasing in philosophy and the wind started to change. In 1896, the philosopher Henri Bergson argued in favor of idealism, in which active, dynamic plans are the basis of consciousness (and thus there is no material "brain memory"). The Würzburg school of psychology claimed that abstract thoughts are primary and independent and cannot be reduced to sensory impressions and images. A return to "Platonism" (i.e., primary abstract ideas) was suggested.

A holistic school of neurologists and psychologists now claimed that "symbolic activity" is the main mental process and that brain damage results in a reduction of this function. In these researchers' view, the description of behavior and psychological analyses was more important than examinations of the brain.

Another important event occurred in 1898, when Albert Pitres described "amnestic aphasia," or difficulties in finding words in spontaneous speech and in naming objects. This type of aphasia did not fit into the localist-associationist models.

Neurologist Pierre Marie saw aphasia as a disorder that had to contain an intellectual defect. This "lack in general intelligence" was the same as Wernicke's aphasia, while Broca's aphasia constituted aphasia plus anarthria (articulatory difficulties). By "general intelligence," Marie meant the "ability to manipulate acquired knowledge." His article "The third frontal lobe convolution has no linguistic function whatsoever" in 1906 was a fierce attack on Broca and attracted a lot of attention. It contained clinical data that showed that Broca's area was not necessarily the center of speech production.

At first, Constantin von Monakow was a localist, but then he changed sides. He argued for "localization in time" instead of in space. According to von Monakow (1911, 1914), there are, on the one hand, neural mechanisms that perform primitive (sensory and motor) functions immediately; damage to these mechanisms produce defined effects. On the other hand, there are neural mechanisms that work over time and perform higher functions. Lesions in the latter mechanisms produce an inhibitory effect that affects the entire cortex. This hits the latest acquired and least automatic functions. Thus, the damage affects functions, not centers, and it is the process in time that is damaged, for instance, by a change of thresholds for nerve activation. When acquired intentional functions are destroyed, they are replaced by more automatic ones (in a regression to an earlier stage).

Henry Head, who published Jackson's work, was the most severe critic of localism and associationism, the proponents of which he called "diagram makers" and accused of having achieved "chaos" with their increasingly complex models.

Head himself was an adherent of Jackson's and von Monakow's theories about the brain as a hierarchic organization of functions as a result of evolution. In his view, brain damage caused "asymbolia" affecting both verbal and nonverbal functions. He developed a test battery where verbal tasks were supplemented by nonverbal tasks, such as imitating a body posture, drawing pictures, and setting watches. According to Head, the extent of the lesion determined the seriousness of the symbolic disturbance. He found four different types of aphasia, which he claimed represented different "aspects of symbolic thinking": verbal aphasia (motor), syntactic aphasia (agrammatism), nominal aphasia (naming disorder), and semantic aphasia (meaning disorder), and in fact he also tried to localize them.

The principles underlying Head's theory were as follows:

1. When all levels of an activity are damaged, the most complex and the most recent are damaged first and most.
2. Negative manifestations of a lesion are noticed at the damaged level.
3. A lesion causes effects that are positive and disinhibits activities that are normally controlled by functions at the damaged level.
4. The functions of the central nervous system have developed slowly in a process from lower to higher functions.
5. The integration of the function of the whole nerve system is based on competition between many physiological activities for the possibility to be expressed.

The idea of negative and positive effects of damage was a new formulation of Jackson's ideas. According to Head, aphasia was dominated by negative phenomena. On the positive side, only automatisms occurred. Head exerted a major influence on research during the first half of the 20th century.

The psychiatrist Kurt Goldstein was another holist, and one who was to become even more influential. His ideas coincided with a growing interest in holistic methods and he had a reputation as a broad-minded neurologist who produced fascinating accounts of speech disorders. Goldstein was influenced by gestalt theory and experimental rationalism. Together with the psychologist Adhemar Gelb, he examined amnestic aphasia (naming disorders). This type of aphasia seemed to coincide with an inability to sort and categorize colors and objects. In 1948, Goldstein presented his theory that an "inability to assume an abstract attitude" caused aphasia. "Abstract attitude," according to Goldstein, involves being able to:

*   take initiative,
*   change and choose aspects,
*   simultaneously keep different aspects in memory,
*   extract what is important from a totality,
*   plan symbolic use,
*   distinguish the self from the external world.

Abstract attitude is lacking in patients with anomia (inability to name), since they cannot categorize, and in patients with agrammatism (difficulties using grammatical morphemes and function words), since they cannot use elements that "have no meaning in isolation." In his description of abstract attitude, Goldstein mixes psychological factors, such as the ability to separate figure and ground, with physiological factors, like spreading and activation (i.e., the fact that stimuli can activate an abnormally large area in the cortex if thresholds of activation for neurons are changed by brain damage, which makes the patient unable to detect, for example, exactly where somebody is touching his skin). An abstract attitude is required for the fully efficient use of language and therefore the linguistic disorder arises secondarily. Words lose their function to organize the external world.

Goldstein assumed different positions with respect to localization, but he was mainly an anti-localist. He claimed that the cortex could be separated into a "peripheral part" with structural localization and a "central part" which is equipotential and constructs "dynamic structures" against a "dynamic background." Lesions in the central part cause a loss of abstract attitude.

It was Karl Lashley (1933, 1950), a physiologist, who presented the theory of cerebral equipotentiality and mass effect. Equipotentiality means that all parts of the cortex have the same "ability" and mass effect means that functions are dependent on how much of the cortex is used. Lashley claimed that studies of humans were too unreliable, due to humans' complex behavior, and therefore concentrated on experiments with rats in mazes. He accepted specified functions only for motor and sensory projection areas and objected to attempts to localize mental functions. He emphasized that psychological unity does not guarantee neurological unity; for example, many structures participate in intentional movements. Lashley tried to identify different integrative mechanisms, such as intensity, spatial orientation and serial ordering.

Inspired by Marie, Bay (1962) suggested that speech is dependent on a large number of "extralinguistic" factors, which are disturbed by brain damage. In aphasia, the transmission of information is disturbed. This disorder always involves a reduced intellect. The aphasic patient's concepts become pathologically distorted, which can be seen in tasks like drawing or sculpting. The same defect is noticed in speech: concepts become fuzzy, deformed, and poorly differentiated.

Jason Brown's theory of aphasia is inspired by Jackson, von Monakow, and Freud. It contains, among other things, evolutionary aspects and a regression hypothesis combined with a functional view of aphasia. He raises the connections between emotions, degree of consciousness and intentionality, creativity, and language. Brown's theory is presented in several books, including *Mind, brain and consciousness* from 1977. (See also Chapter 10.)

Localism and associationism

Localism continued to survive but it did not attract much attention during the first half of the 20th century. Some examples are mentioned below.

Swedish neurologist Salomon Henschen (1926) formulated a detailed model on the basis of all the clinical pathological cases of aphasia that had been described to that point. The model contained a large number of separate centers for different aspects of language function.

Korbinian Brodmann (1909), another neurologist, divided the cortex into numerous histologically defined areas, each of which had a determined physiological function. His numbering system is still used to give exact references to areas of the brain (see Figure 14.6 in Chapter 14).

Karl Kleist (1916) investigated war injuries from the First World War and tried to find a psychological explanation for each cyto- and myeloarchitectonic (related to cellular patterns and myelinated nerve cell patterns, respectively) area. Speech and language were localized according to tradition.

Johannes Nielsen (1947) devoted himself to the anatomical-physiological classification of cortical functions. He distinguished between receptive and afferent signals, and between primary identification through one sense and secondary identification via associations of different senses at a higher level. According to Nielsen, recognition means receiving impressions and comparing them to engrams (physical alterations of nerve tissue in response to stimuli). Remembering, on the other hand, is starting from the concept and identifying it with an engram, which takes place at a higher level. Two types of aphasia can then occur: (a) a type that changes the connection between language and recognition, and (b) a type that changes the "signification" (what Head called "semantic aphasia"). The latter is not localized in specific areas; rather, any lesion can affect the whole system. The destruction of a projection area causes a total loss of function, while the destruction of an adjacent zone causes agnosia (inability to recognize) and the destruction of association zones that are not localized results in memory disorders. Thus, this theory is strongly inspired by associationism.

Associationism is rediscovered by Geschwind

Associationism continues to be very influential today. It was Norman Geschwind who rediscovered associationism and made it known as "connectionism," or the neoclassical school of neurolinguistics, in his 1965 book *Disconnection syndromes in animals and man*. (For more information, see Chapter 3.)

Dynamic localization of function: Pavlov, Vygotsky, and Luria

Dynamic localization of function is a tradition originating in Russia which developed during the 20th century in parallel with the other traditions. Today, it also has considerable influence in Western Europe and the U.S.

The well-known physiologist Ivan Pavlov (1949) claimed that complex behavior could not be handled by isolated and fixed brain structures, but must emerge during the ontogenetic development of dynamic systems. These systems were said to consist of connected structures in different places within the nervous system.

Psychologist Lev Vygotsky emphasized that it is necessary to first investigate *what* is to be localized, before asking the question *where*. Functions must be analyzed with respect to ontogenetic development. Vygotsky (1970) saw a function as a complex activity whereby the whole organism adapts to a task. The activity can be performed in different ways, because of the cooperation of several organs. This dynamic cooperation is controlled by neural structures that monitor different organs and are localized in different places. Vygotsky also formulated a theory about the development of language and thinking that became very influential.

The noted psychologist and aphasiologist Alexander Luria studied aphasia within the framework of the theory of dynamic localization of function. Luria's work has been extremely influential in aphasia research, and especially in clinical work. (It will be further discussed in Chapter 3.)

The test psychological tradition

Theodore Weisenburg and Katherine McBride investigated cognitive factors in persons with aphasia, persons with right-hemisphere lesions, and control subjects, using a large test battery of verbal and nonverbal tasks. Their methodology became the model for a large number of studies. The results showed that persons with aphasia varied a great deal cognitively. In general, aphasia was associated with a cognitive disorder, but there was no necessary correlation. Certain persons with severe aphasia had excellent results on nonverbal tests. Thus, there was no support for Head's theories. Weisenburg and McBride claimed that the importance of language for thinking must differ in different individuals and that the intellect before the lesion must be determinant.

Many psychologists were inspired by Weisenburg and McBride and by Goldstein and developed experiments for testing "symbolic thinking" in aphasics. Subjects with aphasia performed classification tasks, Raven's matrices (analogy tests), and similar tests. The results most often showed considerable variability, and the general conclusion was that the cognitive disorder, where such a disorder existed, could not be attributed to the linguistic disorder. Nevertheless, certain types of cognitive disorders were often found in persons with aphasia, such as difficulties in discriminating faces and interpreting mimed actions, as well as construction apraxia (i.e., problems performing spatial construction tasks).

Linguists and the linguistic influence on aphasiology

Aphasia research was traditionally an area for neurologists, but philosophers and psychologists have also had considerable influence on the area. In the middle of the 20th century, linguists joined this group. They saw studies of aphasia as a means of testing general theories about language. By functionally analyzing different disorders using the descriptive methods of linguistics, they aimed to gain better understanding of the role of the brain in normal speech. The term *neurolinguistics* was eventually adopted for these studies. In 1941, Roman Jakobson published the book *Kindersprache, Aphasie und allgemeine Lautgesetze* ("Child language, aphasia and phonological universals"), in which he pointed out parallels between linguistic universals, children's language development, and symptoms of aphasia. At this point, he was the only linguist to systematically describe aphasia within the structuralist framework. Jakobson applied Ferdinand de Saussure's principle of paradigmatic and syntagmatic relations in language. If language consisted of two types of operations — choice of units and combination of units — then two types of aphasia should be possible: (a) a disturbance of similarity, that is, problems choosing the right unit (paraphasias and anomia), and (b) a disturbance of contiguity, or problems combining units (agrammatism) (Jakobson, 1964).

After entering into contact with Luria, Jakobson extended his theory in 1964. He now envisaged three dichotomies for aphasia:

1. encoding — decoding (problems constructing and reconstructing utterances);
2. restriction — interruption (a difference in degree of disorder);

Table 2.1. Jakobson's description of Luria's aphasia types

	Aphasia					
	efferent	sensory	dynamic	semantic	afferent	amnestic
Disturbed:						
encoding (+) or **decoding** (–)	+	–	+	–	+	–
sequence (+) or **co-occurrence** (–)	+	–	+	–	–	+
Present: **interruption** (+) **or** **restriction** (–)	+	+	–	–		

(Source: Jakobson, 1964)

3.   sequence — co-occurrence (problems combining units or performing "simultane-
     ous synthesis"; closely related to 1).

With the help of these factors, Jakobson tried to describe Luria's aphasia types within
the schema shown below. His description, however, is not completely clear. (Compare
the description of Luria's aphasia types in Chapter 3.)

Luria applied used linguistic insights in his descriptions of aphasia from quite an
early phase and extended the linguistic parts of his writings more and more.

Linguist Noam Chomsky and the theories about language he presented in 1957
and 1965 (the so-called "standard theory," transformational grammar, or generative
grammar, later minimalism) had a major influence on the linguistically oriented
aphasia research, which started to blossom, especially in the U.S., but also in other
countries. The theory described an abstract linguistic system, with an underlying "deep
structure" separate from the "surface structure" of utterances and assumed intermedi-
ary "transformations." Linguists also made a distinction between the language user's
competence and performance. Competence was the knowledge of a central language
system, while performance was the observed language use. Researchers started to
investigate how this model could be applied to aphasic symptoms. Data from aphasia
could be used to test the theory's "psychological reality." Since transformational grammar focused on syntax and morphology, these aspects of language were studied most,
but studies of phonology were also done. A general theory of the biological basis for
language, building on Chomsky's work, was presented by Eric Lenneberg in 1967 and
affected the views of linguists and psychologists many years (as it still does today). In
summary, Lenneberg claimed:

- that language is determined by innate, species-specific, biological features (species-specific cerebral function);
- that this makes certain features of human languages universal (the inner form is
  common for all languages);
- that ontogenetic development comes about through physical maturation — "language readiness" and progressive differentiation — up to the teenage years;
- that contact with the surroundings only brings the ability into play, by functioning
  as the "trigger" of an innate mechanism.

In the early 1970s, a number of neurolinguistic studies appeared, most of which applied transformational grammar to the field, for example, Harry Whitaker's (1971)
On the representation of language in the human brain. He claimed that certain types
of aphasia, such as agrammatism, pointed to a disruption of competence. He made
the assumption that "Loss of X caused by a lesion can be seen as proof that X is part
of the competence of a normal native speaker." In 1971, Whitaker emphasized that
aphasia must always constitute damage to the central language system (not the pe-

ripheral language modalities) and therefore a disorder of competence. The distinction between competence and performance would not be of any value to neurolinguistics, if both were always affected. Weigl and Bierwisch (1970), on the other hand, claimed that aphasia data showed that the difference between competence and performance was real and that aphasics had disturbed performance but intact competence. Neither Whitaker's nor Weigl and Bierwisch's arguments were watertight. Arguments about competence and performance in aphasia are still going on.

Linguistic descriptions also contributed the descriptive aspects or "levels" of language: semantic, syntactic, lexical, phonological, and phonetic (Whitaker, 1971) and researchers sought to find "neurological evidence" from aphasia that these "levels" could be separated. This is another question that is still being discussed.

The transformational grammar framework for describing aphasic symptoms is, of course, not the only possible one. It was criticized by Crystal, Fletcher & Garman (1976), who pointed out that the syntactic problems in aphasia, especially comprehension problems, could not readily be described in transformational grammar and that another theoretical framework was needed. The structuralist methods of description were, according to Crystal, Fletcher and Garman, more useful. Other, more recent, linguistic frameworks will be presented in Part 2 of this book.

Commentary

The problems of relating the brain's structures and dynamics to specific functions are many; this is especially true of the higher cognitive functions such as the use of language. To have a strictly materialist view of these functions and thus follow the same patterns as with the "simpler" motor and sensory functions means searching for centers or structures responsible for functions or parts of functions, localized cortically or subcortically. Associationism and dynamic localization of function are more sophisticated views than pure localism, but still take basically the same approach. Holism, on the other hand, has a different theoretical background, where higher cognitive abilities are seen as different in nature from simpler ones and as, in principle, impossible to localize in specific cortical areas. These theories are therefore more dependent on psychology and less dependent on anatomy and physiology.

To use data from pathological conditions in order to claim what is normal is also connected to great uncertainty. Brown (1977) summarizes these problems for a symptom like paralysis in the following way:

Given a series of stages in the production of movement A – B – C, a damage in B can either remove function B from the repertoire of performance, block function A or disinhibit function C; a damage in B can also evoke a disturbed function B, allow function A to "overflow" or fail to activate function C. This only concerns the loss effect of the damage, and a similar set of possibilities apply to the stimulation of B. Does the final symptom mirror function A, B or C, the disturbed function of the whole system ABC, or the rest of the brain sans [without] ABC? (Brown, 1977, p. 5)

These problems, of course, apply even more to language functions. This should be kept in mind when studying data from neurolinguistics and neuropsychology. "Lesion data" are fascinating and inspire many theories, but it is very hard to draw any definite conclusions about normal function from pathological findings alone.

Summary

This chapter has first taken us through the development of neurolinguistic theories, from the earliest findings and ideas up to the late 19th century. We have read about Gall's localism, about the localization of language functions in the convolutions of the cortex by Broca and Wernicke, the development of associationist frameworks by Wernicke and Lichtheim, and the opposition from researchers with more holist-cognitivist views, such as Marie and Jackson. We have also followed the developments of associationism and holism, including evolution-based theories, and of Luria's dynamic localization of function in the 20th century. We have also traced some important influences from the test psychological tradition on the methods of neurolinguistic experiments, and of linguistic theories, notably structuralism and generative linguistics, on the description and explanation of neurolinguistic phenomena.

Further reading

The historical descriptions in this chapter are based on a number of sources, mainly the original works by the classical researchers, which can be recommended to anyone who is specifically interested in going further. Good overviews can be found, for example, in Caplan's *Neurolinguistics and linguistic aphasiology* from 1987 and in Hécaen and Lanteri-Laura's *Évolution des connaissances et des doctrines sur les localisations cérébrales* from 1977. The four volumes of *Studies in neurolinguistics* edited by Whitaker and Whitaker in 1976–1979 contain examples of neurolinguistic studies from the 1970s and a good overview called *Linguistic investigations in aphasia* was provided by Ruth Lesser in 1978.

Caplan, D. (1987). *Neurolinguistics and linguistic aphasiology: An introduction*. Cambridge: Cambridge University Press.

Hécaen, H., & Lanteri-Laura, G. (1977). *Évolution des connaissances et des doctrines sur les localisations cérébrales*. Paris: Desclée de Brouwer.

Lesser, R. (1978). *Linguistic investigations in aphasia*. London: Edward Arnold.

Whitaker, H., & coeditors (1976–1979). *Studies in neurolinguistics*. New York: Academic Press.

1. Discuss the main reasons for assuming localization of language in:
    a. a central structure in the brain, such as the pineal gland or corpus callosum;
    b. the ventricles (i.e., central cavities in the brain filled with cerebrospinal liquid);
    c. the brain substance;
    d. different specified areas or convolutions of the cortex;
    e. widespread functional systems or networks of subfunctions involving large parts of the brain;
    f. hierarchical layers of brain structures.

Chapter 3

Models and frameworks in neurolinguistics today

In this chapter:

- *Influences: Linguistics, psychology, clinical work, neuroimaging, computer simulation*
- *Clusters of influence*
- *Two basic frameworks: the neoclassical and dynamic localization of function approaches*
- *Developing areas: linguistic and cognitive linguistic theories, communication research, cognitive neuropsychology*

Influences: Linguistics, psychology, clinical work, neuroimaging, computer simulation

This chapter provides an overview of the main influences on neurolinguistics at the beginning of the 21st century. We will see how the more classical influences, for example, the neoclassical and Lurian traditions, as well as more hierarchical and holistic theories developed and how they are being combined with new theories and techniques. The two basic frameworks are given a more thorough presentation here and new approaches and techniques are briefly presented with references to Parts 2, 3, and 4 of the book, where they will be examined in more detail.

Linguistics

One of the main linguistic influences has been the *structuralist* tradition (de Saussure, 1916), where languages are described in terms of the structure of systems representing different aspects of language: phonology, morphology, syntax, and the lexicon are thus treated separately. *Generative grammar*, mainly in the form proposed by Chomsky (1965), subsequently had a large impact on one branch of neurolinguistics, dealing mainly with syntax. *Cognitive semantics*, that is, attempts to make "mental models" of semantic processes, has a certain influence on the study of semantic problems in aphasia, and vice versa. In recent years, the question of whether there is any sense in studying semantics separately from pragmatics has come into focus cf. Allwood (1981). The contextual influence on language in interaction, interaction patterns, and conventional and conversational principles are considerations from pragmatics. The influence of philosophy, anthropology, and sociology is also noticeable. *Functionalism*, as opposed to structuralism, takes language functions to be the main objects of study.

Psychology and cognitive science (artificial intelligence)

In psychology, we find that the methodology of *test psychology*, as used by Weisenburg and McBride (1935) in their studies of linguistic and "nonlinguistic" cognitive ability in aphasics and control groups, had a considerable impact on neurolinguistic methodology. *Group studies* of aphasics, using *experimental design* and *statistical analysis*, were widely used in the 1960s and 1970s and indeed are still used, while a methodological discussion, leading to increased popularity for the single case study design took place in the 1980s cf. Caramazza (1984). This discussion was mainly based on the considerable heterogeneity in groups of persons with different types of aphasia according to the neoclassical typology and in general.

The use of *models* in neurolinguistics is very old (we can go back to the Wernicke-Lichtheim model and even further). The serial type of process modeling, which also mirrors the possibilities of serial computational modeling in artificial intelligence, is still widely used in this area. Parallel processing and connectionist modeling, on the other hand, are currently the most promising computational sources of inspiration (which is, of course, not unexpected, since the main principles emanate from the neural network metaphor). (You can read more on serial and ANN modeling in Chapters 6 and 13 of this book.)

Clinical work — Therapy for language disorders related to the brain

In aphasia therapy, certain methods that are used for diagnostics and training are directly related to classical frameworks, such as Luria's theory, which targets the stepwise restoration of functional systems. Such methods have, for example, been designed by Luria (1963), Christensen (1974) and Weigl & Bierwish (1970).

Other therapies are more or less specifically and directly related to the theoretical assumptions of the Wernicke-Lichtheim-Geschwind framework. Here we might mention VIC (Visual Communication) (Gardner, Zurif, Berry & Baker, 1976), VAT (Visual Activation Therapy) (Helm-Estabrooks, Fitzpatrick & Barresi, 1982), and MIT (Melodic Intonation Therapy) (Albert, Goodglass, & Helm, 1973) as examples, where activation of nondamaged centers in the brain that are not primarily used for language is attempted in order to mediate language functions.

Still other therapies are more communicatively based, for example PACE (Promoting Aphasics' Communicative Efficiency) (Carlomagno, 1994).

We also find therapies that are built on more extensive use of another sign system, such as Bliss, which uses visual signs on paper, and Amerind, which uses hand signs. These sign systems are not primarily designed for use with patients with language disorders and frameworks motivating and explaining their use seem to have developed mainly from clinical users of the systems.

If we look at current aphasia therapy, we can use the classification by Howard and Hatfield (1987). The main general frameworks for therapy are still the Reorganization of Function School (e.g., Luria) and the Neoclassical School. Although still fairly new and very much involved in current trends, the Pragmatic School, the Neurolinguistic School, and the Cognitive Neuropsychology School, which are presented later in this chapter, are now well established and increasingly influential.

Neuroimaging and studies of dynamic processes in the brain

The development of neuroimaging techniques, from static ones, such as the CT scan and MRI, to today's very popular dynamic techniques, PET, SPECT, fMRI, MEG, EEG, and evoked potentials (see Chapter 12 for these terms), constitutes a major breakthrough for neurolinguistic research. They make it possible to study brain activity during linguistic and other cognitive processes in real time in both normally functioning and lesioned brains. The activity patterns can then be compared to model-based hypotheses about the cognitive steps in the processes. The combination of neuroimaging and psycholinguistic experimental techniques is far from trivial and nor are the interpretation of results and development of models, but this is a highly interesting and informative area, which is very productive. (You can read more about this area in Chapter 12.)

Computer simulation of language and other cognitive processes

Computer simulation is a way of implementing and fine-tuning the psycholinguistic process models that neurolinguistics postulates. Simulations demand extreme explicitness and make it possible, for example, to trace the results of hypothetical "lesions" in hypothetical models of cognitive processes. Serial models of the linguistic production and comprehension processes have been used for a long time. (We should recall that this approach dates as far back as Aristotle, as we saw in Chapter 2.) They have been the frameworks for most psycholinguistic and neurolinguistic experimental studies with both normal and brain-damaged subjects in recent decades. Computer simulations have used serial modeling (box and arrow models) and parallel models since the 1980s. In later years, artificial neural network (connectionist) simulations of different types have become increasingly popular. These networks can be of many different types and can produce different types of simulations. (You can read more about this area in Chapters 6 and 13 of the book.)

Clusters of influence

We can detect certain clusters of compatible influences (here only very crudely sketched) that emanate from different disciplines, yet co-exist fairly peacefully within groups of neurolinguists.

The predominant cluster of influences in neurolinguistics during the 1970s and 1980s, and still today, combines the following parts: (a) classical influence from the Lichtheim-Geschwind models, (b) linguistic structuralism and/or generative grammar, (c) test psychology, group studies using statistics (lately also case studies), (d) serial modeling, and (e) therapy of a mainly "neoclassical" or "cognitive neuropsychology" type (in the terminology of Howard & Hatfield, 1987).

Another cluster is based on the Russian tradition in neuropsychology, in other words, ideas from Vygotsky and Luria, together with ideas from general systems theory (Bertalanffy, 1968). In linguistics, both structuralism and generative grammar have played a role in this cluster; case studies are widely used (although group studies also have their place) and serial modeling is mostly used. This cluster has a strong therapeutic tradition, as seen in Chapter 2.

A third cluster, which has fairly recently become further developed in neurolinguistics, is based on philosophical, anthropological, and linguistic ideas in the field of pragmatics. Representatives of this cluster are often influenced by holistic and/or evolutionary approaches, as well as functionalism. Connectionist modeling is seen as more promising than serial modeling. Therapy methods are pragmatically and communicatively oriented.

There are many other possible and actual combinations of influences in neurolinguistics, and this is merely an attempt to point out clusters with a substantial number of adherents. We also notice that the difference in outlook between these clusters is substantial.

The neoclassical and Lurian frameworks, which will be the focus later in this chapter, are basic frameworks underlying much of the clinical tradition today.

The hierarchical (evolution-based), cognitivist frameworks and a number of the ideas presented in more holistic theories are still around; in some cases, they are separately pursued, as in Jason Brown's structural model and theory of microgenesis, but they are also partly integrated into new approaches such as cognitive semantics, functionalist approaches, pragmatics, and embodied and/or multimodal communication. (More on these topics can be found in Parts 2 and 3 of this book.)

Two basic frameworks: The neoclassical and dynamic localization of function approaches

The two most influential "schools" in aphasia research and therapy today are Alexander R. Luria's theories and the theories issuing from the Aphasia Research Center in Boston, inspired by Geschwind and others.

The neoclassical framework — Geschwind and the Boston School

Geschwind brought associationism into today's neurology, when he presented his theory in "Disconnection syndromes in animal and man" in 1965. It is anatomically based and posits the following disconnection syndromes: aphasia, agnosia (inability to identify sensory impressions), and apraxia (inability to perform intentional actions). Aphasia is connected to sensory and motor systems. The notion of cortical center is key; it is (1) an anatomical site, and (2) a collection of linguistic representations, associated with (3) some aspect of "processing" of these representations. Geschwind gives a careful anatomical description of the connections between the right and the left hemisphere and within each of the hemispheres. When the connections are disrupted, different disconnection syndromes arise, including forms of aphasia. The theory is an extension of Lichtheim's model (see Chapter 2).

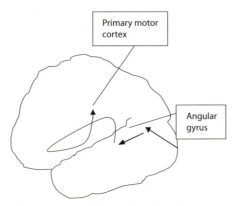

Figure 3.1. How naming happens, according to Geschwind

Geschwind identifies an area in the inferior parietal lobe, which is specific to the human brain (the angular gyrus and the supramarginal gyrus); in his view, this area is important for the ability to name, which is a prerequisite for speech (see Figure 3.1). The difference between animals and man is said to reside in this area, which makes associations between nonlimbic stimuli possible. Animals are only able to associate a nonlimbic stimulus with a limbic stimulus. (Limbic stimuli go to the limbic system deep in the brain, which deals with basic instincts, such as hunger.) Subsequent research, however, has shown naming to be more complex than Geschwind's theory claims and the argument does not hold (Caplan, 1982).

The Boston school

Geschwind was very influential in the so-called Boston school, a group of aphasia researchers connected to the Aphasia Research Center in Boston. This was the most influential group in aphasia research in the U.S., and in large parts of the western world, from the 1960s. It was also strongly influenced by Noam Chomsky's linguistic theories and by the test psychology tradition.

The Boston group developed the Boston Diagnostic Aphasia Examination (BDAE) (Goodglass & Kaplan, 1973), which is used to classify aphasics in most linguistic research. The Boston classification has been criticized by many researchers as being too crude for many research purposes, but the test and the terminology are very widely used and have been the model for many other tests.

The patients are divided into the following groups, according to their test profiles (cf. the Wernicke-Lichtheim model in Chapter 2).

This table of symptoms is only a summary of much more complex test results. We can note that the five first types of aphasia were already present in Lichtheim's model (see Chapter 2). The three new types are:

Table 3.1. Aphasia types, according to BDAE

	Fluent speech	Speech comprehension	Repetition	Naming
Wernicke's	+	–	–	–
Transcortical sensory	+	–	+	–
Conduction	+	+	–	–
Transcortical motor	–	+	+	–
Broca's	–	+	–	–
Global	–	–	–	–
Anomic	+	+	+	–
Isolated speech area	–	–	+	–

Global aphasia: the most serious type of aphasia, where the patient basically has no linguistic ability;

Anomic aphasia: inability to name;

Isolated speech area: a combination of transcortical sensory and transcortical motor aphasia.

In reality, many patients are not easy to classify into any of these groups. In any model, it is important to know whether the basis for classification is the combination of symptoms or the localization of the brain lesion. The term Broca's aphasia may, for example, be ambiguous, standing for either the syndrome defined in the table above or "aphasia after a lesion in Broca's area." These terms are usually used in the former sense, that is, based on symptoms. The two classification methods do not necessarily coincide; in fact, they often do not.

The suggested "typical lesions" for the aphasia types listed above are the following:

Table 3.2. The most typical locations of lesions for the BDAE aphasia types

Aphasia type	Most typical location of lesion
Wernicke's aphasia	Wernicke's area
Transcortical sensory aphasia	Posterior parietal lobe
Conduction aphasia	Often deep lesion between Wernicke's and Broca's areas, including white fiber bundles (the arcuate fasciculus)
Transcortical motor aphasia	Area in front of the Rolandic fissure (the supplementary motor area)
Broca's aphasia	Broca's area
Global aphasia	Large cortical and subcortical areas around the Sylvian fissure
Anomic aphasia	Often impossible to localize, traditionally said to result from lesions affecting the angular gyrus
Isolated speech area	Like transcortical sensory plus transcortical motor aphasia, in so-called "watershed areas" (borders between the areas of supply for the different arteries)

The lesions do, however, vary considerably and these types are statistically based generalizations.

Dynamic localization of function — Luria

Luria saw the brain as a functionally connected system, where a task can be performed by different mechanisms with the same result. The activity is complex and demands cooperation between several zones. It is therefore not possible to localize a language function in a certain area simply because the function is lost when that area

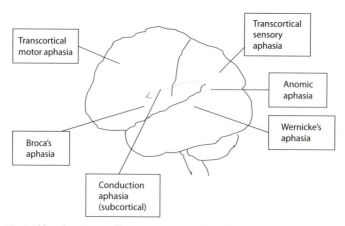

Figure 3.2. Typical localizations of lesions associated with types, according to the Boston classification

is damaged. On the other hand, different cortical and subcortical areas make specific contributions to every complex system of activity, which is why antilocalism cannot be accepted.

By starting from clinical studies of local brain damage and the changes they caused in mental processes, Luria tried to determine the contributions of different areas to these processes. He called his method "neuropsychology."

According to Luria, the brain has three functional units (blocks) and every activity demands cooperation between all three.

Block I, subcortical structures (including the limbic system) and the brain stem (including the reticular formation), has the function of regulating tone (tension) or degree of awareness. According to Pavlov, organized goal-directed activity requires sustained optimal cortical tone. This comes from three sources: (1) metabolic process-es, (2) stimuli from the external world, and (3) intentions and plans that are formed consciously with the help of speech, in block III (see below).

Damage to Block I causes a nonspecific reduction of cortical tone, which reduces the selectivity of psychological processes.

Block II, the postcentral cortex (including visual, auditory, and sensory areas in the parietal, occipital, and temporal lobes) receives, analyzes, and stores information. Primary zones are highly modality-specific (e.g., the auditory center) and handle perception. Secondary zones handle the analysis within each modality, and tertiary zones coordinate the analyses from the different modalities. The tertiary zones are in the border areas of the cortex between the occipital, temporal, and parietal lobes and are seen as specifically human.

Block II is said to be responsible for the paradigmatic organization of verbal com-munication, that is, the organization of phonematic, lexical, morphological, syntactic, and semantic units in the linguistic code.

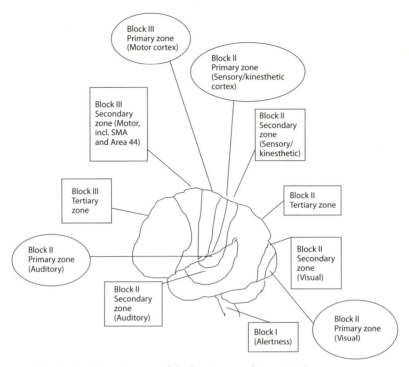

Figure 3.3. Blocks (units) and zones of the brain, according to Luria

Block III, the precentral cortex (the frontal lobes) programs, regulates, and controls mental activity. Primary, modality-specific zones are in the motor cortex, secondary zones in the premotor cortex, and tertiary zones in the prefrontal parts of the frontal lobes. The tertiary zones form intentions and programs and are seen as superordinate to all other parts of the cerebral cortex; they monitor behavior.

Block III is responsible for the syntagmatic organization of verbal communication, that is to say, the organization of connected utterances.

Three different laws apply to the blocks:

1. The law of hierarchical structure of cortical zones (primary – secondary – tertiary): Tertiary zones are superordinate to secondary zones, which are superordinate to primary zones.
2. The law of diminishing specificity in the hierarchically ordered cortical zones: primary zones are most specific, tertiary zones least so.
3. The law of progressive lateralization of function: least in primary zones, most in tertiary zones.

The types of aphasia associated with lesions in particular blocks are shown in Figure 3.4.

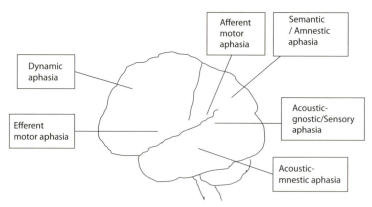

Figure 3.4. Types of aphasia, with approximate localization of main factor, according to Luria

Block II (paradigmatic organization):

Afferent motor aphasia
Lesion: Block II, sensory secondary zone
Symptoms: Phoneme exchanges (phonological paraphasias), which the patients attempts but is not able to correct, because of a lack of kinesthetic feedback about the articulatory movements to the secondary zones in Block II.

Acoustic-gnostic aphasia (or sensory aphasia)
Lesion: Block II, auditory secondary zone (including Wernicke's area)
Symptoms: Problems recognizing and discriminating phonemes. The patient speaks with severe phoneme paraphasias (substitutions) and does not react to them. The syntactic and prosodic pattern remains intact and speech is fluent. In language comprehension, the patient can interpret part of what is said with the help of these patterns.

Acoustic-mnestic aphasia
Lesion: Block II, medial zones, deep in the left temporal lobe
Symptoms: Problems in retaining series of audio-verbal traces in memory long enough, which leads to paraphasias (exchanges of phonemes and words) in naming and spontaneous speech. Syntax and prosody remain intact in this case as well.

Amnestic aphasia (or semantic aphasia)
Lesion: Block II, posterior tertiary zone (posterior and inferior parietal lobe or the border between the parietal and occipital lobes)
Symptoms: 1. Disturbances in the semantic network of words, which lead to semantic paraphasias (word substitutions), searching for words, and circumlocutions (paraphrases). 2. Difficulties handling complex grammatical relations.

Block III (syntagmatic organization):

Dynamic aphasia
Lesion: Block III, tertiary zone
Symptoms: Inability to transform a semantic plan into linearly ordered speech via "inner speech," absence of spontaneous speech. The patient repeats and names correctly.

Efferent motor aphasia
Lesion: Block III, motor secondary zone (including Broca's area)
Symptoms: Difficulties changing from one phoneme to another, perseveration (pathological inertia, repetition). (A nonspecific disturbance that also affects other movements.)

Examples of prerequisites for different linguistic processes and aphasia types caused by lesions in brain areas that are critical for these processes, according to Luria (adapted from Luria, 1973)

Speech comprehension

Input (speech)

Linguistic process	Brain area	Type of aphasia
I. Comprehension of a word		
1. Isolation of phonemes (acoustic analysis)	secondary auditory zone, left hemisphere	acoustic-gnostic aphasia
2. Identification of meaning ("image")	tertiary, posterior zone, left hemisphere	amnestic aphasia
II. Comprehension of meaning in a phrase as a whole		
1. Keeping elements in memory	secondary, auditory zone + deep medial-temporal zone, left hemisphere	acoustic-mnestic aphasia
2. Simultaneous synthesis and logical plans	tertiary, posterior zone, left hemisphere	amnestic aphasia
3. Active analysis of the most significant elements	frontal zones	

Spontaneous speech

Linguistic process	Brain area	Type of aphasia
1. Intention, plan	frontal lobes	general lack of initiative
2. Inner speech with predicative structure (linear plan)	frontal lobes	dynamic aphasia
Flexibility in nerve processes/ Articulation	premotor cortex, left hemisphere	efferent motor aphasia with perseverations

And further on to articulation/flexibility in nerve processes

Confrontation naming (naming of presented objects)

Visual "image" → Coding in words

Linguistic process	Brain area	Type of aphasia
Visual perception	parietal-occipital lobes	optic amnestic aphasia
Acoustic structure of speech	temporal lobe, secondary auditory zone, left hemisphere	acoustic-mnestic aphasia with literal paraphasias
Activation and inhibition	tertiary, posterior zone, left hemisphere	amnestic aphasia with verbal paraphasias
Flexibility in nerve processes/ Articulation	premotor cortex, left hemisphere	efferent motor aphasia with perseverations

Repetition

Linguistic process	Brain area	Type of aphasia
Phonematic hearing	temporal lobe, secondary auditory zone, left hemisphere	acoustic aphasia with literal paraphasias
Abstraction	frontal lobes	conduction aphasia
Articulation	parietal lobe, secondary sensory zone, left hemisphere	afferent motor aphasia with literal paraphasias
Flexibility in articulation/ nerve processes	Premotor cortex, left hemisphere	efferent motor aphasia with perseverations

Many people consider Luria's theory to be the most developed analysis of neuropsychological phenomena so far; it is also directly related to therapy for "restoration of language functions." His influence has been enormous in Eastern Europe and also in large parts of Western Europe and the rest of the world (Luria, 1963, 1966,1970, 1973, 1976).

Developing areas: Linguistic and cognitive linguistic theories, communication research, cognitive neuropsychology

Some areas of neurolinguistics that are currently undergoing a period of development, either in combination with one of the two basic frameworks or on their own, are introduced below.

Pragmatics, communication, and discourse, including body communication

This area is highly dynamic, both in research and in the clinical application of neu-rolinguistics. It follows from the development of pragmatics and communication research within linguistics, with inspiration from anthropology and sociology as well. While mainstream neurolinguistics has been rather late in adopting pragmatics as a branch, neurolinguistic research in this area has been going on since the 1980s. Some of the influential theories concern speech acts and language games, context, activity, conversational principles, conversation patterns, body communication, gesture, and picture communication. One approach used for interaction analysis is Conversation Analysis: microanalysis of recorded interaction sequences. The social approach to therapy has also led to a number of suggested procedures for handling aphasia. (This area is examined in the chapters about pragmatics and evolution in Parts 2 and 3: Chapters 7, 10, and 11.)

Cognitive neuropsychology: Model-based research

This approach was developed in Britain and has considerable influence on research and clinical applications. It involves working from models of linguistic processes and hypotheses about disorders and therapy related to these models. It now has a strong clinical tradition, including, for example, the PALPA investigation (Kay, Lesser & Coltheart, 1992; Whitworth, Webster, & Howard, 2005), the Pyramids and Palm Trees test (Howard & Patterson, 1992), and the documentation of model-based clinical work (Byng, Pound, Lindsay, & Swinburn, 2001). Examples of research areas studied extensively in this framework are lexical semantics and reading. (This approach is involved in many of the studies discussed in Parts 2, 3, and 4). A typical model used in an analysis applying cognitive neuropsychology is the one shown in Figure 3.5. By using this model to interpret aphasic symptoms, the researcher or therapist establishes a hypothesis concerning where and how the process of language comprehension is disturbed and can then test this hypothesis and apply it in therapy.

Linguistics-based research: The application of recent linguistic theories

Pragmatics is an aspect of linguistics that has been singled out for specific treatment in this book, since it is developing rapidly in a context of interdisciplinary cooperation, and since it has traditionally not been the focus of neurolinguistics, although it should by now be integrated, following the development of linguistics in general (cf. Joanette & Ansaldo, 1999). But apart from pragmatics, other aspects of linguistics — phonol-ogy, morphology, lexical semantics, and syntax — are in constant development and the most recent theories in these areas also have to be integrated into neurolinguistics.

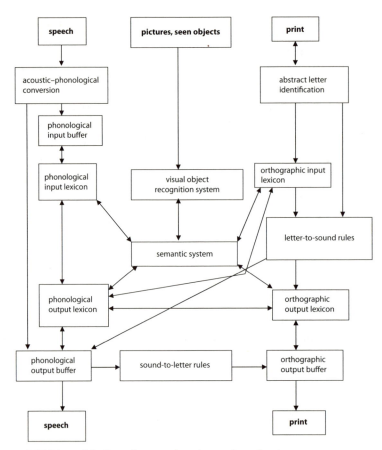

Figure 3.5. PALPA model of word comprehension and production

Some examples include the integration of nonlinear phonology, different theories about syntax, and theories from cognitive semantics. (These approaches are specifically covered in Part 2, but are also discussed in Part 3.)

Neuroimaging results: Integration, application

The application and integration of neuroimaging techniques in neurolinguistic research is a very dynamic, rapidly developing area. New interdisciplinary centers and networks with the combinations of competences needed for this research are being established and the challenge of combining activation patterns with neurolinguistic models is the main occupation of many neurolinguists. Interesting findings concern mirror neurons, that is, neurons that are activated by both performing and observing an action and that might be very important in evolution (e.g., Jeannerod, 1997). (This area is specifically covered in Chapter 12.)

Computer simulation

The focus in this area is currently on artificial neural network modeling of linguistic processes, language learning, and language loss. The combination of simulation techniques with neurolinguistic theories and models is challenging but provides interesting new possibilities. The results of neuroimaging and computer simulation should, ideally, also be compatible in terms of their neurolinguistic interpretation. (This issue is discussed in Chapter 13.)

Documentation and evaluation of therapy

One influence on neurolinguistics from clinical work in many of the areas presented above is the need for evaluation of aphasia therapy. The cognitive neuropsychology and linguistic — including pragmatic — approaches, as well as neuroimaging techniques, are used in so-called efficacy studies. The aim is to study the effect of specified and well-documented therapies over time.

Summary

This chapter has presented an overview of the different models and frameworks that are applied today in neurolinguistic research and clinical applications. Influences from different disciplines, such as linguistics and psychology, and different techniques, such as neuroimaging and computer simulation, are summarized, as are interdisciplinary clusters of influence. Two main "schools" applied in both clinical work and research are the "dynamic localization of function" and "classical–neoclassical" frameworks, which are described more in detail, with schemas presenting their classifications of aphasia. We then turned to areas which are under development today and becoming very influential. Two such areas are pragmatics/communication analysis, including the analysis of body language, picture communication, etc., and cognitive neuropsychology, providing a model-based process analysis.

Further reading

The literature below includes general overview as well as more specific readings on dynamic localization of function (Christensen Kagan & Saling, Luria), classical–neoclassical frameworks (Caplan, Goodglass & Kaplan), and cognitive neuropsychology (Kay et al, Whitworth et al.). (As mentioned above, pragmatics /communication analysis will be presented further in Chapters 7, 10 and 11.)

Caplan, D. (1987). *Neurolinguistics and linguistic aphasiology*. Cambridge: Cambridge University Press.

Christensen, A.-L. (1974). *Luria's neuropsychological investigation*. Copenhagen: Munksgaard.

Goodglass, H., & Kaplan, E. (1973). *The assessment of aphasia and related disorders*. Philadelphia: Lea & Febiger.

Howard, D., & Hatfield, F. M. (1987). *Aphasia therapy: Historical and contemporary issues*. London: Lawrence Erlbaum Associates.

Kagan, A., & Saling, M. (1988). *An introduction to Luria's aphasiology: Theory and application*. Johannesburg: Witwatersrand University Press.

Kay, J., Lesser, R., & Coltheart, M. (1992). *Psycholinguistic assessment of language processing (PALPA)*. Hove, Lawrence Erlbaum.

Lesser, R., & Milroy. L. (1993). *Linguistics and aphasia: Psycholinguistic and pragmatic aspects of intervention*. London: Longman.

Luria, A. R. (1973). *The working brain: An introduction to neuropsychology*. Hove: Basil Haigh.

Stemmer, B., & Whitaker, H. (Eds.) (1998). *Handbook of neurolinguistics*. San Diego: Academic Press.

Visch-Brink, E., & Bastiaanse, R. (Eds.) (1998). *Linguistic levels in aphasia*. London: Singular Publishing Group.

Whitworth, A., Webster, J., & Howard, D. (2005). *A cognitive neuropsychological approach to assessment and intervention in aphasia. A clinician's guide*. Hove: Psychology Press.

Assignments

Four descriptions of typical linguistic symptoms or combinations of symptoms (syndromes) in aphasia follow:

1. Anomia, or word-finding problems in language production
2. Severe language comprehension problems
3. Inability to repeat words or sentences
4. Perseveration, that is, "getting stuck" in what you have just said and repeating it when you want to move on to something new

Try to apply to each one of them what this chapter has taught you about:

a. Dynamic localization of function (Luria)
b. The classical–neoclassical model (Wernicke-Geschwind-Boston)
c. Cognitive neuropsychology (the model in Figure 3.5)

Try to describe and explain the type of aphasia associated with each symptom or syndrome. Apply the figures, tables, and schemas used by the different frameworks.

Part II

Neurolinguistics for different components of language

Chapter 4

Phonology in neurolinguistics

In this chapter:

- *Frameworks in phonology*
- *Phonological paraphasias and neologisms —*
  classical questions and investigations
- *Phonology in theories of agrammatism*
- *Units and features of analysis in phonology*
- *Frameworks and models in the analysis of*
  phonological disorders

Frameworks in phonology

Today, there is no one generally accepted framework for phonological studies. The older and more established frameworks are most frequently used in basic education and clinical application. This means a *structuralist* framework, where *phonemes* and *distinctive features* are the basic units, although they are also critically discussed. More segmentally oriented phonology is supplemented by prosodic features. Most studies done in neurolinguistics have applied this type of framework, and we will first report some well-known neurolinguistic studies in this tradition. There are also studies that rely mainly on syntactic theories in explaining agrammatism as a syntactic-phonological phenomenon, some of them in the Chomskyan tradition, and we will take a look at some examples. But *nonlinear phonology* is now firmly established in phonological research, and also to some extent in neurolinguistic studies. We will therefore also look at the basic units and features of nonlinear phonology and examples of how they have been used in neurolinguistic studies.

Phonological paraphasias and neologisms — Classical questions and investigations

Phonemic (and to some extent semantic) *paraphasias* (substitutions, etc., of phonemes) and *neologisms* (newly made-up words) are produced especially often in Wernicke's aphasia, but also in other forms of aphasia (see below). Some researchers have also proposed that agrammatism has its phonological aspects (mainly in Broca's aphasia). We will first consider some "classical" questions and studies. Then we will move on to present-day units, features, and frameworks of analysis in phonological neurolinguistic studies and discuss some examples of their use.

Questions that researchers have tried to answer are:

- How are neologisms created?
- Are paraphasias similar in all types of aphasia?
- Are paraphasias of persons with aphasia similar to slips of the tongue in normal speakers?
- Do paraphasias follow universal rules?
- What physiological, phonetic, and phonological aspects play a role in causing paraphasias?
- How can paraphasias and neologisms be related to models of speech production?

Different terms are used for phonological paraphasias:

Paraphasias	Phonological or phoneme (phonemic) paraphasias = literal	Addition Deletion Substitution	Form-based
	Semantic or word paraphasias = verbal	Substitution	Form-based Meaning-based Unrelated

Examples:

Phoneme paraphasia:

- addition: *butcher → butchler*
- deletion: *butcher → buter*
- substitution: *butcher → betcher*

Word paraphasia:

- form-based: *butcher → bitch*
- meaning-based: *butcher → grocer*

- unrelated: *butcher → train*

Some phoneme paraphasias, of course, give rise to another word, thereby becoming word paraphasias as well.

Paraphasias can be paradigmatically and/or syntagmatically affected. In a paradigmatic (choice-based) substitution, one item that can fill a particular slot in speech or writing is substituted by another that can fill the same slot; for example, *b* (/b/) fills the slot instead of *c* (/k/) when a person says *bat* instead of *cat*.

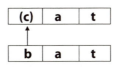

Figure 4.1. Paradigmatic substitution

In a syntagmatic (combination-based) substitution, another sound in the environment affects the production, so that it is repeated (or appears too early), for example, in *a big bog* instead of *a big dog*, where the *b* of *big* comes back instead of the *d* in *dog*.

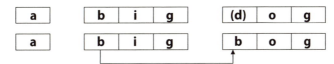

Figure 4.2. Syntagmatic substitution

We can see that the categories *paradigmatic* and *syntagmatic* are not mutually exclusive; in other words, a paraphasia that takes the form of substitution can be both at the same time. The *big bog* example is syntagmatically influenced by its surroundings but the *b* also replaces the *d* in a particular slot. Other types of paraphasias can, however, be more purely syntagmatic; for example, when an extra phoneme is inserted, as in *blue blook* for *blue book*. Exchanges (or metathesis) take place where two phonemes or words change places, such as *god* for *dog*, where *g* and *d* are exchanged.

Neologisms

People have tried to explain neologisms in different ways, for example as a word paraphasia directly followed by a phoneme paraphasia, which together make the relation between the target word and the produced word unrecognizable (the so-called two-step hypothesis of Lecours & Lhermitte, 1979; cf. Brown, 1981). This hypothesis presumes that there is some degree of access to a target word, which is then distorted.

Example: *cat → dog* (semantic word paraphasia) *→ rog* (phoneme paraphasia)

Butterworth (1979) analyzed pause lengths before neologisms and paraphasias and then suggested that there is a specific "generating device," that is, a mechanism that creates words according to the phonotactic rules of the language in question (i.e., rules for how phonemes can be combined). This mechanism comes into play if a target word is not found within a specific time. This hypothesis presumes that there is an underlying anomia. Buckingham (1981) supported this theory in his article "Where do neologisms come from?" where he raised the possibility that a neologism that has been generated by the mechanism is then perseverated (repeated) when there are word-finding problems. This could explain the fact that neologisms often have certain recurring phonological patterns.

Example: Utterance by a person with Wernicke's aphasia/jargon aphasia containing many neologisms:

a frog frock frossy that is fro that is frabbing is fog is frob

A good reason for assuming that the target word is not accessible is that when the patients get better, they often become anomic, that is, the neologisms disappear but are not initially replaced by the target words.

Phoneme paraphasias

A careful case study including a linguistic classification of jargon aphasic symptoms and a description of the progression of jargon aphasia was made by Green (1969). Green's patient first produced an abundance of neologisms and unrelated word paraphasias. According to Green, both these phenomena were examples of the same type of error — unrelated word paraphasias were neologisms that happened to be words. Later, the patient's speech came to be dominated by anomia (difficulties in finding content words), circumlocutions, and semantic paraphasias. These observations have been confirmed in other case studies and provide the basis for the hypothesis that anomia underlies the neologisms in persons with jargon aphasia.

Lecours and Lhermitte' (1979) systematically described the errors of two patients with a purely phonematic jargon aphasia from a paradigmatic and syntagmatic point of view.

Examples: [parabol] → [parapol]
                 paradigmatic influence: [b] → [p]
                 syntagmatic influence: initial [p] is repeated medially

Paradigmatic substitutions were made between phonologically similar phonemes and similar or identical phonemes in the context increased the risk of substitutions. Lecours and Lhermitte claimed that the cause of paraphasias is purely phonological, that they affect whole words or a "superordinate articulatory unit." Apart from phonological similarity and contiguity (temporal closeness), this theory also requires consideration of phonotactic rules (i.e., rules for combining phonemes). According to Lecours and Lhermitte, similar errors occur in writing and speech. The study only dealt with repetition and reading of single words. Thus, all the target words were also known.

Blumstein (1973) analyzed phonological paraphasias in different types of aphasia. (She used theories of markedness and distinctive features in the tradition of Roman Jakobson — see below in this chapter.) Her conclusion was that phonological paraphasias were of the same type in different types of patients. Some objections were raised, for example, that the selection of patient groups was not accounted for and the analysis only concerned paradigmatic substitutions, with no consideration of the influence of context. Blumstein used spontaneous speech, which made it hard to control which target words were intended. Many paraphasias were omitted from the analysis for this reason and this may also have affected the result.

Blumstein's results inspired many researchers in the field. If a single mechanism causes the errors made by all types of aphasics, is it also the same mechanism that causes slips of the tongue in normal speech?

This question was addressed by, among others, Fromkin (1971), Buckingham (1980), and Garrett (1982a), all of whom claimed that the answer to the question above was "yes." Models of speech planning and speech production in normal speakers were applied and were found to adequately explain all or most aphasic paraphasias. Examples of similarities that were pointed out are:

• that the same elements are affected, that is, stressed content words, mostly nouns and verbs, and the initial phonemes of these words;
• that phonotactic rules and prosodic structure are followed.

Other researchers pointed out the differences between speech errors produced by persons with normal speech and paraphasias produced by persons with aphasia, and assumed that the underlying factors were different. They therefore wanted to answer "no" to the question above. This applies to, among others, Butterworth (1979, 1981) and Nespoulous, Lecours, and Joanette (1982). These researchers also claimed that there are clear differences between paraphasias produced by persons with different types of aphasia (contrary to Blumstein's claim).

Nespoulous et al. (1982) found several differences between paraphasias produced by Broca's aphasics and conduction aphasics, which indicate that they should not be explained in the same way. They claimed that paraphasias in Broca's aphasia can be seen as phonetic, whereas those in conduction aphasia can be seen as phonematic (or phonological).

An investigation by Söderpalm (1979) also showed clear differences between paraphasias in aphasia and ordinary speech errors. In aphasia, there were more paradigmatic errors and less awareness of one's own errors.

So-called "blends," or mixtures of two words or expressions, indicating that two alternative plans are involved, are produced by persons with and without aphasia. Butterworth (1981) pointed out that these errors cannot be explained by serial top-down models of speech production of the type most widely used at that time. In these models, the lexicon is accessed first and phonology later. He suggested an alternative model, where lexicon, syntax, and phonology were accessible simultaneously and could affect each other. This is necessary to avoid the over-generation of errors that never occur.

Phonology in theories of agrammatism

Agrammatism, or sparseness of grammatical structure, typically involving short or incomplete sentences and omission or substitution of syntagmatic (function) words and grammatical morphemes, is covered in Chapter 5. Some of the suggested explanations of agrammatism are, however, phonological and will be presented briefly here.

Goodglass (1976) claimed that agrammatic persons primarily have difficulties initiating speech and need a phonologically salient (stressed) element to start with. This makes categorematic (content) words easier than unstressed articles in utterance-initial position, which according to Goodglass is why articles are often omitted. Syllabic suffixes are also easier to produce than nonsyllabic ones, so that the plural suffix –es in *horses* is less likely to be omitted than the plural suffix –s in *dogs*.

Another claim about phonological influence on agrammatism was made by Kean in 1977. She hypothesized that phonological clitics (elements that do not contribute to the stress pattern unless emphatically stressed) tend to be omitted in agrammatism. Such elements include articles, some prepositions, and inflectional suffixes (in other words, the class of "closed-class items" or syncategorematic (function) words, according to Kean). This hypothesis, however, turned out to be hard to apply to languages like Italian or Hebrew, and was therefore not a candidate for a universal explanation.

Units and features of analysis in phonology

The phoneme has been the classical unit of study in analyzing phonological disorders. There are several reasons for this, one being the general "written language bias" in earlier linguistic analyses (Linell, 1982) and another, related, one being the relative ease of handling "everyday" phonological analysis in terms of phonemes. Phonemic repertoires, systems, processes, and features are fairly "handy" for some types of analysis. In more recent years, however, the awareness of phonemes' being based on letters and perhaps not being the most natural units for phonological analysis in general has influenced phonological studies in neurolinguistics as well.

The units that are used today are, apart from segments, *features, syllables (syllable structure: onset, nucleus, and coda), sonority,* and prosodic features such as *stress, tones,* and *intonation contours.* In nonlinear phonology, *prosody* (including syllabic features) and *melody* (including articulatory features) are the central dimensions of analysis. Source features, such as the *voicing* feature and *voice onset time* (VOT) are also examined.

Features: Distinctive features, such as place and manner of articulation
Syllables: A syllable consists of an onset and a rhyme (sometimes spelled *rime*), which further consists of a nucleus and a coda.

```
        Syllable
       /    \
   Onset Rhyme
   / \        / \
        Nucleus Coda
   ||  ||
   X X X X
   g l æ d
   glad
```

A syllable is a string of sounds organized in such a way that sonority rises from the beginning to a peak and then falls (vowels correspond to peaks, since they have the highest sonority).
Sonority: The higher the sonority, the higher the salience.
The higher the sonority, the more open the vocal tract.
Prosody: Includes syllabic features (see above).
Melody: Includes articulatory features, such as place and manner of articulation (also some tonal features in some languages).
(Note that the terms *prosody* and *melody* are used differently here from their more conventional senses.)

Other useful concepts in phonological analysis are *underspecification* and *markedness. Underspecification* can, for example, mean that not all features have to be specified at all levels of planning, since different principles interact to "fill in" specifications in the production or perception/comprehension processes. *Markedness* is related to the fact that some features are more frequent, "natural," or in other ways "expected" and can be considered as default (unmarked) features, while a more unusual alternative may be considered as "marked" when it occurs; for instance, an unvoiced final stop would be less marked than a voiced stop for articulatory reasons (final devoicing).

These units and features of analysis are examined in a number of neurolinguistic studies and arguments that we shall now briefly consider.

The discussion of whether phonological errors are the same or different in all types of aphasia did not abate (e.g., Blumstein, 1994; Kohn, 1993). Kohn claimed that the phonological behavior of different types of aphasia can be distinguished by phonological analysis, while Butterworth (1992) criticized this view. The suggestion was that the phonological errors Wernicke's aphasics make are caused by an impairment in their access to underlying phonological representations, while those of conduction aphasics are caused by problems in constructing phonemic representations, and those of Broca's aphasics by a phonetic disturbance (cf. Gandour, 1998). This is a discussion of errors in terms of *segments* or possibly *features*.

Features are the basis of the discussion of different "tiers," such as an independent laryngeal "tier," which may be disturbed in some types of aphasia (e.g., Dogil, 1989; Gandour, 1998).

The *syllable* unit or constituent is used in many studies of language disorders. For instance, different parts of the syllable are differentially sensitive to disturbance. A study of neologistic Wernicke's aphasia by Stark and Stark (1990) revealed that the coda is more sensitive than the onset and that the nucleus is the least vulnerable part. A syllable-based analysis can also explain why consonants adjacent to vowels are more sensitive to errors than other consonants in a cluster. If the leftmost consonant in the cluster of the example word below (Figure 4.3) is interpreted as the "head," or dominant one, it will take the *onset* place if the two consonants compete for a single place on the onset node (Harris, 1998). In order to save both consonants, a vowel sound could be inserted between them, thus making an initial syllable of *p* plus a vowel, which also often happens in language disorders. We would then get something like /peley/, that is, a CVCV sequence word-initially.

This is, in other words, an account of "omission" and possible compensation for this in terms of *prosody*.

Sonority is the relative degree of perceptual prominence of a phoneme (also secondarily defined as articulatory openness of the vocal tract). Obstruents have very low sonority, while vowels have the highest. Sonority sequencing rules have been used to explain neologisms (e.g., Christman, 1992); for example, sonority should rise in the syllable until the vowel peak, then fall again, and this would affect which phonemes are produced. A case study by Romani and Calabrese (1998) applies the Sonority Dispersion Principle (Clements, 1990), which states that the sharper the rise in sonority

```
Onset Nucleus        Onset Nucleus
 |\   | \             |   || \
 x x  x x             x   x x
 p l  a y             p   a y
 play                 pay
```

Figure 4.3. Syllable structure and vulnerability of consonants in the word *play* (from Harris, 1998, p. 97)

between the beginning of the syllable and the nucleus, the better-formed the syllable, in explaining the phonological errors of a subject with aphasia. As an alternative to the phonological simplification or repair strategies suggested by other researchers, they suggest that syllabic markedness with respect to sonority dispersion accounts for a number of errors.

Stress has been used in investigating hemispheric specialization for prosody, in its traditional sense (cf. Gandour, 1998). Stress has been found to be impaired in patients with left-hemisphere damage (LHD), especially with regard to duration, which means that their linguistic prosodic problems could be due to timing problems.

Tones have been investigated in tone languages, such as Mandarin Chinese, as well as in Norwegian for pitch accent. For example, linguistically significant F0 (fundamental frequency) contrasts were found to be selectively vulnerable to LHD in Norwegian (e.g., Moen & Sundet, 1996).

Intonation can also be affected by LHD (even more than by right-hemisphere damage), most severely in Broca's aphasia, but also in Wernicke's aphasia (Danly, Cooper, & Shapiro, 1983). Some cross-linguistic findings point to an underlying timing deficit here as well (cf. Gandour, 1998).

Melody is affected by "substitution" and "distortion" of phoneme quality. These processes usually affect classes of sounds by affecting one subsegmental property, that is, a feature, such as place of articulation.

Voicing disorders, detectable as effects on *VOT* (Voice Onset Time), are also found in aphasia. VOT paraphasias where the VOT differences between phonemes are retained, but are incorrectly placed in words are often found in Wernicke's, conduction, and transcortical motor aphasia. VOT paraphasias where the contrasts between phonemes are collapsed are, on the other hand, more often found in Broca's aphasics.

Frameworks and models in the analysis of phonological disorders

The theoretical frameworks that are employed in phonology research are, on the one hand, the Chomskyan Minimalism framework and, on the other hand, Optimality Theory, processability ranking, etc., which consider vulnerability in terms of aspects of processing conditions, that is, by ranking and making hierarchies of phonological complexity, which can be used for predicting errors.

(In clinical practice, the structuralist systems and operations based on phonemes, features and phonological processes are probably still the most frequently used, but parts of the more recent frameworks are gaining in influence.)

The traditionally used serial models of speech production and perception have, as we have seen above, been criticized for a long time. (See, for example, the discussion of blends in the section on word production data in Chapter 6.) Today, there are many alternative modeling frameworks with both local and distributed neural network models being popular in applications where phonological and other disorders are simulated. (See Chapters 6 and 13 for more about models.)

Summary

This chapter has tried to capture the state of the art concerning phonology in neurolinguistics. We have seen how traditional structuralist phonology has been applied in a number of studies of phonological paraphasias and neologisms and we have also presented examples of studies where the framework of non-linear phonology has been used.

Further reading

The works below give overviews and examples of phonology in neurolinguistics. For non-linear phonology, Blevins gives a summary of the relevant features to consider in relation to the syllable, and Nespoulous and Moreay provide an example of how such features are applied to the study of aphasia.

Blevins, J. (1995). The syllable in phonological theory. In J. A. Goldsmith (Ed.), *The handbook of phonological theory* (pp. 206–235). Cambridge: Blackwell.

Gandour, J. (1998). Phonetics and phonology. In B. Stemmer & H. A. Whitaker (Eds.), (1998). *Handbook of neurolinguistics* (pp. 207–219). San Diego: Academic Press.

Harris, J. (1998). Phonological universals and phonological disorders. In E. Visch-Brink & R. Bastiaanse (Eds.) *Linguistic levels in aphasia* (pp. 91–118). London: Singular Publishing Group.

Nespoulous, J.-L., & Moreay, N. (1998). Repair strategies and the production of segmental errors in aphasia. In E. Visch-Brink & R. Bastiaanse (Eds.), *Linguistic levels in aphasia* (pp. 133–146). London: Singular Publishing Group.

Assignments

1. Make or simply listen to a recording of the speech production of a person with aphasia including a phonological disorder (or read a careful transcription) and try to find examples of as many relevant symptoms as possible involving the types of units and features discussed above in describing the phonology of the person's speech.

2. Consider a model of speech production and a model of speech comprehension and try to explain the phenomena found in your analysis in part 1 in relation to the model. A model of speech comprehension and production is presented in Figure 3.5 and models of speech production in Figures 6.5. and 6.6.

Chapter 5

Morphology and syntax
in neurolinguistics

> **In this chapter:**
>
> - *Disturbances of grammar in aphasia: syndromes, agrammatism, and paragrammatism*
> - *The role of the verb in grammar and disturbances of grammar*
> - *Morphology, grammar, and cross-linguistic findings*
> - *Three frameworks for describing agrammatism*
>   - *The mapping hypothesis*
>   - *The adaptation hypothesis*
>   - *The trace deletion hypothesis (TDH)*

Disturbances of grammar in aphasia: Syndromes, agrammatism, and paragrammatism

Disturbances of grammar have attracted many linguists, since many linguistic theories consider grammar to be especially central to the language system. This fact has nourished debates and encouraged research related to grammar in aphasia.

The traditional view of grammatical disorders in aphasia was linked to two main syndromes. One of them is Wernicke's aphasia, which results from posterior lesions (i.e., posterior to the central fissure, affecting the temporal and parietal lobes) and is characterized by fluent speech. The grammar of these patients was characterized as *paragrammatism* and did not really attract much attention from researchers. The fluent speech of these patients is characterized by frequent self-interruptions, restarts, and circumlocutions, caused by their anomic problems (word-finding difficulties). This makes it contain more "grammatical frames" or parts of grammatical frames, with a relative lack of nouns in particular, but also of adjectives and main verbs and with substitutions of grammatical morphemes. Since paragrammatism was interpreted as possibly being a secondary phenomenon to word-finding problems and since these patients often have comprehension problems, making their participation in experimental studies difficult, their grammar was not the best starting point for traditional research into this issue.

The second main syndrome was Broca's aphasia, which results from frontal lesions and is characterized by nonfluent speech. The grammar of these patients is often very sparse, and they have even been characterized as *agrammatic*. They tend to speak in very short, simple sentences or even shorter structures mainly containing nouns, main verbs and adjectives, but omitting most grammatical morphemes (such as noun and verb inflections) and so-called function words (conjunctions, articles, etc.). Agrammatism has been the main object of studies of grammar and aphasia.

The basic description of agrammatism in Broca's aphasia above, however, is much too simple to do justice to the grammatical disturbances in aphasia. The status of the traditional division of grammatical disorders into agrammatism and paragrammatism has also been called into question by cross-linguistic research into aphasia and grammatical disorders.

Studies of agrammatism are the main basis for theories about morphology and syntax in neurolinguistics. There is an extensive body of research on agrammatism in relation to specific hypotheses about the grammatical features of structures and processes.

Some of the questions that have been discussed are:

1. **The relationship between comprehension and production**. Are disorders of grammar central, thus affecting both comprehension and production, or can production be selectively disturbed while comprehension is maintained? Although many patients with aphasia show disturbances of both comprehension and production, there are clear cases of dissociation, where only production is affected (e.g., Miceli, Mazzuchi, Menn, & Goodglass, 1983). It has also been shown (Linebarger, Schwartz, & Saffran, 1983) that there are persons who show disorders of comprehension as well as production in tests of grammar, but can still make metalinguistic judgments about whether a sentence is correct or not, which indicates that some grammatical ability remains.

2. **The relationship between agrammatism and paragrammatism**. Are agrammatism and paragrammatism really two fundamentally different phenomena or are they different surface manifestations of grammatical problems that are basically similar but are accompanied by different sets of additional symptoms in Broca's

and Wernicke's aphasia? Cross-linguistic studies have pointed to difficulties with the traditional definitions of agrammatism and paragrammatism. These definitions can only partially be applied to languages with a rich morphology, such as Italian (Miceli, Silveri, Romani, & Caramazza, 1989) and languages where grammatical morphemes are not segments that can be omitted, such as Hebrew (Grodzinsky, 1984, 1986). Examples of necessary modifications include the findings that substitutions of grammatical morphemes seem to be just as common as omissions and that main verbs are often omitted. The borderline between agrammatism and paragrammatism might thus have been more due to their occurrence with certain aphasic syndromes than to any neurolinguistic motivation.

The role of the verb in grammar and disturbances of grammar

The role of the verb in grammar is a central topic for research on disorders affecting grammar. As we have seen above, for a long time there was a fairly strong belief in the classical aphasiological tradition about the localization of "word meanings." Word meanings, concepts, the mental lexicon, or whatever term was used to capture the semantic representation and/or processes associated with words (especially nouns, verbs, and adjectives) were strictly posterior left-hemisphere phenomena. On the other hand, more holistic, cognitively oriented theories often claimed that a more distributed representation, requiring widespread networks or functional systems, was more likely. However, we have seen a change and nowadays the right hemisphere is considered to play an important role with respect to semantics. We have also seen that, especially for the activation of at least certain verbs of motion and action, frontal lobe activity seems to be essential. This development is partly a result of brain activation imaging studies. Disturbances of grammar have traditionally been linked to left-hemisphere frontal lesions. We can now see that the role of verb semantics and the structural constraints used in the formation of grammatical structures and sequences can become central and link semantics and syntax, which opens the way for different hypotheses about grammatical disturbances. A recent suggestion of a link between mirror neurons for goal-directed grasping in the monkey and schemata for handling verb-argument structures is made by Arbib (2005).

Morphology, grammar, and cross-linguistic findings

In the last 20 years, a large number of studies of grammatical disturbances (usually defined as agrammatism) in typologically different languages and comparative studies using several languages have increased our knowledge of grammatical disorders in aphasia. In this section, some of the main findings from multi- and cross-linguistic studies of agrammatism (e.g., Bates & Wulfeck, 1989; Menn & Obler, 1990ab) will be mentioned and their potential interpretations discussed. We will start with morphology.

Morphology
1. Free grammatical morphemes (e.g., function words) tend to be omitted, but they are sometimes substituted as well.
2. Bound grammatical morphemes (e.g., inflectional endings) are rarely omitted, but are often substituted.

There seems to be a difference between free and bound grammatical morphemes. Both types can be substituted, but only free morphemes are omitted. Forms such as infinitives and verb stems (if they can occur as words) are produced and different inflections are substituted.

Depending on the type of language, the border between morphology and syntax can vary. Some syntactic phenomena characterizing aphasia are listed below, but some of them can also be seen as morpholexical.

Syntax
1. Agrammatism (defined only by short phrase length and slow speech rate) seems to exist in most languages and is usually combined with reduced variety in syntax.
2. There is great variation between languages, but a selective vulnerability of grammatical inflections and function words can be found in all aphasics, according to Bates and Wulfeck (1989) (who advocate a type of morpholexical interpretation of agrammatism).
3. A substantial number of main verbs are omitted. Many studies give verbs a central role in the formation of the syntactic structure of utterances (see below, for example under "The Mapping Hypothesis").

Since languages vary a great deal in grammatical structure, it has been a matter of discussion whether agrammatism of some kind can be found in all languages. (Chinese with its very sparse grammar has been a test case.) So far, some phenomena that have been considered to be comparable have been found in all the languages studied, even though this makes the definition very short and unspecific. The division between syndromes that are mainly linked to anterior lesions with nonfluent speech or to posterior lesions with fluent speech is, as we have already seen, oversimplified from a neurolinguistic point of view. Bates and Wulfeck's claim about the general vulnerability of grammatical inflections and function words is interesting in this context and can be compared to the widespread occurrence of anomia in aphasia. Whether problems affecting main verbs should be considered as mainly lexical, morphological, syntactic, or all of these is a matter for both semantic and syntactic theory that we will return to below. It does, however, seem clear that the role of verbs is especially interesting in relation to disorders of grammar. This was not really in focus in earlier definitions of grammatical disorders. Further observations of the effects of syntactic complexity add to the argument for considering morpholexical and syntactic factors as interacting.

Morphological and syntactic complexity interact
Morphological and syntactic complexity interact in making a grammatical structure hard to process. Processing conditions seem to matter in that
a.   simplification is attempted, and
b.   complex structures tend to break down and contain many errors.
This points to "access problems" as a likely underlying cause.

Finally, the role of semantic-pragmatic factors in what we have called grammatical disorders has to be considered. Depending on the theoretical framework, semantic-pragmatic factors can be considered as fundamental to, interacting with, or adding to surface manifestations of grammatical disorders. Some of the observations relating to semantic and pragmatic influence are listed below.

Interaction with semantics-pragmatics
Semantic-pragmatic aspects also interact with grammatical disorders:
1.   Bates and Wulfeck (1989) state that pragmatic aspects are involved in agrammatic speech production.
2.   Menn and Obler (1990a) also point to the interplay between strategies and grammar in producing speech, which is reflected in the output.
3.   Kolk and colleagues (e.g., Kolk, 1987; Kolk & Heeschen, 1992) emphasize adaptation as the main factor behind agrammatism (see below, under "The Adaptation Hypothesis").

Three frameworks for describing agrammatism

The Mapping Hypothesis

The Mapping Hypothesis was proposed by Saffran, Schwartz, and Marin in 1980 and by Linebarger, Schwartz, and Saffran in 1983. This group of researchers has shown that persons with agrammatism can still make judgments about the correctness of a given complex sentence, for example, a reversible passive, such as *The dog was chased by the cat*. In their view, the main problem in agrammatic comprehension is the *mapping* of syntactic representations into semantic representations, whereas syntactic parsing is not affected. Examples of thematic roles are *agent, patient, experiencer, instrument, goal,* and *theme* of the event given by the central verb (cf. Fillmore 1968). The subjects and objects of the syntactic structure must be mapped onto such roles to achieve a semantic interpretation. Grammatical judgment requires only syntactic parsing, and can therefore be performed even when mapping is disrupted. These researchers also leave open the possibility that agrammatism could be a processing limitation, which allows parsing to take place, but not parsing and mapping at the same time. This means that thematic roles cannot be assigned and certain features cannot be checked and, thus, semantic processing is prevented. In this situation, a variety of heuristics influence performance. Apart from *the syntactic route*, the *lexico-inferential route*, and the *canonical order route* are two alternatives that come into play in agrammatic sentence comprehension. (Accounts of these three routes can be found in Slobin, 1966, and Caplan, 1992.)

Use of the *syntactic route* can be simplified with respect to parsing, by the use of a simple canonical order strategy, such as N V N order, and with respect to mapping, by the use of a thematic hierarchy with principles like *first noun = agent*.

Using the *canonical order route* means using the linear order of nouns in the event process to determine their thematic roles. The sequence of nouns or noun phrases is, therefore, simply mapped onto a sequence of thematic roles without considering the semantics of the particular verb.

The *lexico-inferential route* uses semantic constraint-checking predictively and assigns thematic roles to nouns based only on whether they satisfy the selection constraints of the verb. Thus, it is the meaning of the component words that is used without regard to syntactic structure or linear order.

Let us consider an example:

The man was eaten by the frog.

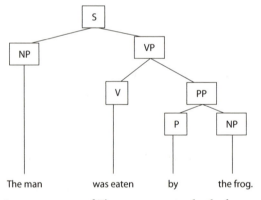

Figure 5.1. Syntactic tree structure of *The man was eaten by the frog*

The **full use of the syntactic route** involves a structural analysis into a representational tree structure, [The man [NP] [was eaten [V] [by [P] [the frog [NP]PP]VP]S]]; the relation of this tree structure to the corresponding active sentence *The frog ate the man*; and the assignment of subject and object roles as a basis for mapping onto thematic roles, where the subject is *the frog*, which is the agent, and the object is *the man*, who is the patient. (See Figure 5.2.)

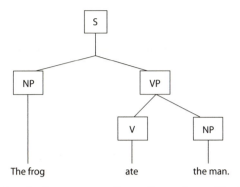

Figure 5.2. Syntactic tree for the corresponding active sentence, *The frog ate the man*

The use of **the canonical order route** would make the first noun phrase into the agent and the second noun phrase into the patient; in other words, *the man* = agent, *the frog* = patient.

The lexico-inferential route would apply the semantic constraints of the verb in combination with the semantic features of the noun phrases. In this case, it might well determine that *the man* was the *agent* and *the frog* was *the patient*, since it would be semantically more plausible that a man would eat a frog than that a frog would eat a man.

The claim of the mapping hypothesis is that all three routes interact in normal processing.

In agrammatic comprehension, we also see an interplay between syntactic processing and the other routes representing heuristics, which sometimes help, but sometimes do not. The canonical order and lexico-inferential routes, and possibly other heuristics, are abnormally influential, according to Linebarger (1998).

Mapping therapy. The mapping hypothesis is applied in *mapping therapy.* In short, mapping therapy involves, for example, using strategies to map thematic roles onto parts of speech of sentences. This can be done, for example, by color-coding subjects as red slots, verbs as blue slots, and objects as green slots and then determining which word goes in which slot, given a picture of a specific event (Schwartz, Saffran, Fink, Myers, & Martin, 1993)

The Adaptation Hypothesis

The idea that agrammatic speech production takes the form it does as the result of a strategy has been around for a long time. As early as the beginning of the 20th century, the *economy of effort* hypothesis existed; it claimed that the articulation difficulties of many agrammatic persons led to their reduced grammar because of adaptation to their need to speak more slowly and in a more reduced way. (The main argument against this hypothesis was that agrammatism also often affects language comprehension. A central disorder of "representation" or "competence" was hypothesized by, for example, Caramazza and Zurif, 1976).

The present-day adaptation hypothesis, put forward by Kolk (e.g., Kolk, 1987; Kolk & Heeschen, 1992) and others, focuses on agrammatism as a *processing disorder* rather than a central representational disorder. The underlying disorder is seen as a disorder affecting the *timing of activation* of sentence information, either by delay or by too rapid decay of activation. This allows us to see agrammatism as a disorder characterized by variations in severity. The basis is the Capacity Model of language processing (Just & Carpenter, 1992). According to the Capacity Model, reduced efficiency or maintenance can result from a shortage of capacity (e.g., slow activation and fast decay of activation). One effect of this timing disorder may be that syntactic tree constructions disintegrate prematurely (Kolk, 1987) in sentence generation. The disorder also affects the activation of lexical items, since the synchrony between the generation of syntactic slots and lexical items is disturbed. This leads to more complex structures having more errors, resulting in both paraphasias and paragrammatism (Kolk, 1987, 1998ab).

In this framework, agrammatism involves adaptation to the timing deficit. This adaptation to the "reduced temporal window" leads to three types of strategies:

1. simplification: reduced variety, isolated phrases (as a result of preventive adaptation or economy of syntactic computation);
2. restart: faster activation by restarting and profiting from the activation of the first attempt (corrective adaptation);
3. slow rate of speech.

The claim is that the operations underlying adaptation are parts of the normal process, which are just used more often as the result of learning and controlled selection. This involves awareness of the problems and selection of subsentential syntactic structures. Furthermore, adaptation is optional, which can be seen in differences between different types of talk, for instance, test situations and informal conversation.

Syntactic simplification therapy. The type of therapy that builds on the adaptation hypothesis is called syntactic simplification therapy and involves training aphasic persons to consciously use adaptation strategies, such as the choice of shorter grammatical structures. The claim is that the conscious application of such strategies makes communication more efficient.

The trace deletion hypothesis (TDH) or trace based account and the tree pruning hypothesis

The trace deletion hypothesis of language comprehension disorders in agrammatism was presented by Grodzinsky in the mid-1980s. It directly relates to Chomsky's

Minimalist Program, which builds on earlier Chomskyan frameworks; it assumes an autonomous syntax and describes agrammatism as a specific type of disorder affecting the syntactic tree structure. For a deeper understanding of this view, Chomsky's (1992) *A minimalist program* describes the theory, and articles by Grodzinsky (1986, 1990, 1995, 1998) describe the TDH.

The main suggestion of this hypothesis is that the disturbance specifically affects *traces,* or the empty positions that are left when movement transformations are performed.

What is a transformation and what is a trace? The notion of transformation rests on the theory that a more basic syntactic structure is changed into another form for output; for example, a transformation can make a basic active declarative sentence like *The dog chases the cat* into a passive sentence like *The cat is chased by the dog.* In this account, sentence construction starts with the most basic forms and some parts of the sentence are moved by the transformation. When this happens, traces of the parts that have been moved are left behind in a mental representation of the sentence structure. These traces are also used in the interpretation of a sentence. When they are not available, a passive sentence, for example, cannot be interpreted. More specifically, the parts of the sentence cannot be assigned their so-called *theta-roles* for semantic interpretation. Theta-roles are comparable to thematic roles in an argument structure; thus, *agent* is a thematic role that is typically assigned to a *subject* in a basic active sentence (cf. the thematic structures in the section on the mapping hypothesis above).

The trace deletion hypothesis was originally phrased as follows.

The Trace Deletion Hypothesis (Grodzinsky, 1986, 1990):
    Delete all traces.
    Link every NP in non-theta position to a theta-role by default (mostly NP1 = agent)

(Grodzinsky, 1998)

When an NP has been moved to another position, it is not interpreted semantically, because the trace is deleted. It then has to be interpreted by some other strategy and a default strategy is assumed.

The TDH was revised into the trace based account in 1995, in response to some points of criticism and some findings that were not easily accounted for by the earlier TDH.

Revised TDH — Trace Based Account (Grodzinsky, 1995):
1.   Trace-Deletion: Traces in theta-positions are deleted from agrammatic representation.
2.   R(eferential)-strategy: Assign a referential NP a role by its linear position if it has no theta-role.

(Grodzinsky, 1998)

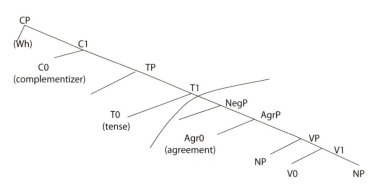

Figure 5.3. "Minimalist" syntactic tree, showing tense and agreement nodes (the curved line marks the site of agrammatic "pruning")

Another hypothesis based on the Minimalist framework is the Tree Pruning Hypothesis (TPH), which was originally proposed as an account for dissociations between tense and agreement inflections. (Friedmann, 2001). In a study of speakers of Hebrew and Arabic, Friedmann and Grodzinsky (2000) found a dissociation between tense and agreement inflection in agrammatic sentence production. Tense was more vulnerable than agreement and it was suggested that this was a result of their different positions in the Minimalist syntactic tree. The tense node was suggested to be impaired, while the agreement node was not. It was also suggested that more severe agrammatism would be caused by an impairment at a lower node in the tree than milder forms. The TPH then states that when a node is impaired, the tree is "pruned" upward, so that all nodes above it become inaccessible. See Figure 5.3 (from Pollock, 1989).

Compatibility of Approaches

The three approaches discussed above are clearly in competition with each other. They put different emphasis on agrammatic language comprehension, as opposed to production, and they differ in focus. Nevertheless, some of their proponents (Kolk, 1998b; Linebarger, 1998) also point to their similarities, and they are probably not completely incompatible.

Summary

We have discussed disturbances of grammar in aphasia, especially the use of the terms *agrammatism* and *paragrammatism* and how the study of agrammatism in different types of languages has affected the definition and view of grammatical disturbances. The role of the verb in grammatical structures was emphasized as a central question in aphasiology. Cross-linguistic findings were summarized and similarities were discussed. Three main types of hypotheses about agrammatism — the mapping hypothesis, the adaptation hypothesis, and the trace deletion hypothesis/tree pruning hypothesis — were then presented.

Further reading

There are many studies of morphology and syntax in neurolinguistics. Most studies concern agrammatism and theories of grammar applied to data from aphasia. Cross-linguistic studies that are comprehensive and often cited are the Menn and Obler volume from 1990 and Bates and Wulfeck's chapter from 1989. The three main hypotheses about agrammatism are described by Linebarger, Kolk, and Grodzinsky and good overviews are provided by chapters in Visch-Brink and Bastiaanse (1998) and in the *Handbook of neurolinguistics*. Articles about agrammatism from *Brain and Language* are collected in Whitaker (1999).

Bates, E., & Wulfeck, B. (1989). Crosslinguistic studies of aphasia. In B. McWhinney & E. Bates (Eds.), *The crosslinguistic study of sentence processing* (pp. 328–371). New York: Cambridge University Press.

Grodzinsky, Y. (1998). Comparative aphasiology: Some preliminary notes. In E. Visch-Brink & R. Bastiaanse (Eds.), *Linguistic levels in aphasiology* (pp. 175–192). London: Singular Publishing Group.

Kolk, H. (1998a). Disorders of syntax in aphasia. In H. Whitaker & B. Stemmer (Eds.), *Handbook of neurolinguistics* (pp. 249–260). San Diego: Academic Press.

Kolk, H. (1998b). The malleability of agrammatic symptoms and its implications for therapy. In E. Visch-Brink & R. Bastiaanse (Eds.), *Linguistic levels in aphasiology* (pp. 193–210). London: Singular Publishing Group.

Linebarger, M. (1998). Algorithmic and heuristic processes in agrammatic language comprehension. In E. Visch-Brink & R. Bastiaanse (Eds.), *Linguistic levels in aphasiology* (pp. 153–174). London: Singular Publishing Group.

Menn, L., & Obler, L. (Eds.) (1990). *Cross-language agrammatic source book*. Amsterdam: John Benjamins.

Schwartz, M., Saffran, E., Fink, R.., Myers, J., & Martin, N. (1993). Mapping therapy: A treatment program for agrammatism. *Aphasiology, 8,* 19–54.

Visch-Brink, E., & Bastiaanse, R. (Eds.) (1998). *Linguistic levels in aphasia*. London: Singular Pub-
    lishing Group.

Whitaker, H. (Ed.) (1999). *Agrammatism*. New York: Academic Press.

Assignments

Study the following text transcribed from the speech of a person with agrammatism and try to
answer the following questions.

Agrammatism has sometimes been called "telegraphic style."

1. What are the similarities between the transcribed speech and a typical "telegraphic" mes-
    sage (telegram, SMS or short note for memory, e.g., a "to-do list")?

2. What are the differences?

3. Try to explain the similarities and differences.

4. Try to rewrite the transcription, applying the strategy of only using short sentences of
    simple Subject-Verb or Subject-Verb-Object types. Discuss the possible advantages and
    disadvantages of such a strategy.

Example of agrammatic speech (Little Red Riding Hood)

Red Riding Hood–pretty girl. Mother grandmother /stik/ … um home, uh forest … uh wolf ..
um eat … us . Grandmother … uh. Eat . g-grandmother . uh wolves–wolf eat grandmother, Uh
Riding Hood, pretty girl, basket, uh uh (sighs) you know? "Pretty girl" … Uh … likes grandmother's voice, uh noodles … (laughs).

'n likes uh Riding Hood–uh memory–uh–looks uh voice, looks . uh dress, looks, bed, uh looks
… uh … uh … Riding Hood … Riding Hood …

(Extracted and adapted from Menn & Obler, 1990a, p. 168)

Chapter 6

Lexical semantics

In this chapter:

- *What is meaning and how is it linked to word forms and to larger linguistic units?*
- *Word semantics*
  - *Prototype theory*
  - *Semantic distinctive features*
  - *Semantic fields*
  - *Semantic features and operations in aphasia*
- *Sources of data and theories*
  - *Deep dyslexia*
  - *Category-specific anomia*
  - *Right-hemisphere lesions and lexical-semantic problems*
  - *Semantic dementia*
- *Methodological considerations*
  - *Group studies versus case studies*
  - *Central or access disorder*
  - *Mapping of form and meaning*
- *Types of process models*
  - *Word comprehension*
  - *Word production*
- *Simulation*
- *Links to therapy*

What is meaning and how is it linked to word forms and to larger linguistic units?

There are many different theories of meaning. One classical distinction divides theories in three main types. *Nominalism* is the stance that there are objects and phenomena in the world and words to denote them; nothing else (i.e., no intermediate representation) is needed. *Conceptualism* is the opinion most often found in neurolinguistic studies: that there are concepts in our minds that link words to objects and phenomena in the world. What concepts are, how they are formed, and how they can be disturbed are some of the main objects of study for cognitive linguistics, neurolinguistics, and semantics. A third possible position is that of *conceptual realism*, which claims that concepts exist in themselves, independently of human minds (e.g., so-called Platonic ideas).

There are also different opinions about what is or can be the basic units of meaning. Are words, parts of words, or even smaller features basic, or are sentences, utterances, contributions, longer texts, monologues, or dialogues basic for meaning in use? Or could they all be? And what is the relationship between the meanings of linguistic units and their context of use?

We will start by looking at word semantics or lexical semantics, since this is the area that has been studied by far the most in neuro- and psycholinguistics.

Word semantics

Anomia (difficulties in finding "content words") is a symptom shared by almost all persons with aphasia. (In the type of aphasia called "anomic aphasia," this is the only symptom; while in the other types of aphasia, it is one of several symptoms.) Anomia creates problems in tasks such as naming objects (visually displayed, from verbal descriptions, or from memory). Aphasic ways of searching for words and aphasic semantic word substitutions (semantic paraphasias) have been used to test different hypotheses about how a "mental lexicon" can be organized. A basic question is whether the "lexicon" can be disturbed in itself — that is, can its organization be affected? — or whether only the ways of accessing the lexicon can be disturbed. Since we are dealing with patterns of activation in the brain, this is really a pseudo-question, or rather a question regarding the quality, degree, or variation in activation patterns. An example of anomic speech is presented below. (The person with anomia (A) is trying to name the object in the picture presented by a therapist (T).)

Picture naming by person with anomia

Target word: LADDER

A: yes there we have it there… he had one of those yesterday the one who picked apples I know so well what it's called we have one over there by the shed no cannot

Target word: SHOEMAKER

A: carpen … no it isn't that shoebake … shoebaker, no carpen carpen

T: shoemake …

A: shoebaker

T: no shoemake …

P: shoemaker

The example shows that the target word is hard to "find" and how associations and words related to the target are activated.

The phenomenon of word-finding problems in language production and comprehension has been studied from different perspectives. Below we will describe three frameworks that have been used to describe word-finding problems and illustrate them with some "classical" studies of lexical semantics in aphasia (mostly from the 1970s).

Prototype theory

Prototype theory was introduced by Rosch (1975) and proposes that categories are organized around the most prototypical exemplars, which are central and more "stable." The theory predicts that "prototypical" items, that is, the most typical exemplars of a category, are named more easily and consistently than more "atypical" exemplars and that exemplars that are borderline between categories are associated with the "fuzzy" fringes of the fields. Figure 6.1 illustrates a prototype field for *bird* with the prototype in the middle, some associated, but less central phenomena further out, and a "borderline" phenomenon associated at the fringe.

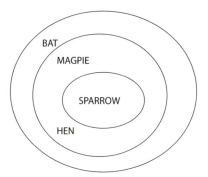

Figure 6.1. A partial prototype field for BIRD (the words in the figure stand for images)

Figure 6.2. Examples of objects: *glass – cup – bowl – plate*

Prototype theory was applied by Whitehouse, Caramazza, and Zurif (1978) (in an experiment designed by Labov, 1973). They found that Broca's aphasics used the same strategies as controls for classifying objects, while anomic aphasics either showed a total inability to name objects systematically or used rules that were too simple. They were also unable to use the added context in a picture as a cue. The task was to determine whether drawn objects were "cups," "plates," or "glasses." Stimuli gradually became more similar and it was noted where each person drew the limits between the different types of objects.

Prototype theory has been combined with considerations of different levels of abstraction in a hierarchical organization of semantic categories into superordinate, basic, and subordinate levels. For example, *animal* is superordinate and *poodle* is subordinate to *dog*, which is a base-level word. It has been claimed that base-level words are more likely to be prototypical, and remain more "robust" for many persons with aphasia. Some aphasic persons also find superordinate and more general categories easier, while subordinate, more specific categories are harder. On the other hand, abstraction is often a problem for aphasic subjects, and moving from a lower to a higher level of abstraction, for example, naming the category that *poodles* and *terriers* both belong to, can be difficult for persons with anomia.

Semantic distinctive features

Semantic distinctive features have been used in descriptions of linguistic categories since antiquity. The idea is that a category can be identified and described with reference to the necessary and sufficient conditions for belonging to that category. This process therefore involves decomposition into more primitive or basic features.

Examples of semantic distinctive features are [+living], [+male], [–adult] for *boy*.

The use of semantic features by normal control subjects and different types of aphasics was studied by Zurif, Caramazza, Myerson, and Galvis (1974). They found

Table 6.1. Semantic features distinguishing some categories denoting humans

	Male	Female	Adult	Child
Man	+	–	+	–
Woman	–	+	+	–
Boy	+	–	–	+
Girl	–	+	–	+

Note that the table can be reduced to two features, adulthood and gender.

that controls used semantic features in a systematic, "technical" way. Broca's aphasics used temporary and conspicuous features and were more dependent on emotional and situational influences. Wernicke's aphasics used indeterminate and deviant features and were generally "out of focus." The words the participants had to classify were *mother, wife, cook, partner, knight, husband, shark, trout, dog, tiger, turtle,* and *crocodile.* The controls tended to classify the words into the *human* and *animal* categories, while Broca's aphasics divided them into *human + dog* versus *other animals.* Controls then sorted the animals according to species, while Broca's aphasics sorted them into more or less dangerous groups.

Semantic fields

Semantic fields or networks are groupings of words according to semantic similarity, or contiguity (co-occurrence), relations. They have been used by several researchers and in a number of different ways. A well-known example is the hierarchical and similarity-based word association network used by Collins and Quillian (1969). The network is based on "is a" relations between words; for example, a *poodle* is a *dog,* a *dog* is an *animal.* Especially for natural kinds, this is a good way of describing paradigmatic, similarity-based relations. Collins and Loftus (1975) presented a model of word meanings based on semantic similarity. Words are activated by spreading activation in the network when related words are aroused. This is the basis for semantic priming of word recognition (i.e., that a word is recognized faster if it has been preceded by a semantically related word). There are, however, also syntagmatic semantic field relations between words, based on contiguity or co-occurrence. Such relations exist between word pairs such as *cat* and *dog, eat* and *food,* or *red* and *light.* Similarity and contiguity relations interact in determining association strength between words. For example, *cat* and *dog* both belong to the same category in a hierarchical, similarity-based field, but they also tend to co-occur in expressions such as *cats and dogs.* Semantic fields can be based on relations between words, which are in turn based on relations between objects, events, and properties in the world.

Semantic word substitutions seem to keep "within category" and resemble "speech errors" made by normal speakers (e.g., *big* becomes *small*) (Buckingham, 1979). Others have studied conceptual organization. Zurif, Caramazza, Foldi, and Gardner (1979) found that both Broca's and Wernicke's aphasics had difficulties in structuring lexical knowledge by conceptual features. The subjects first had to sort words according to thematic relations and common conceptual features. Then they were given a word recognition test in order to see whether these relations were actually used. The words were related in the following ways:

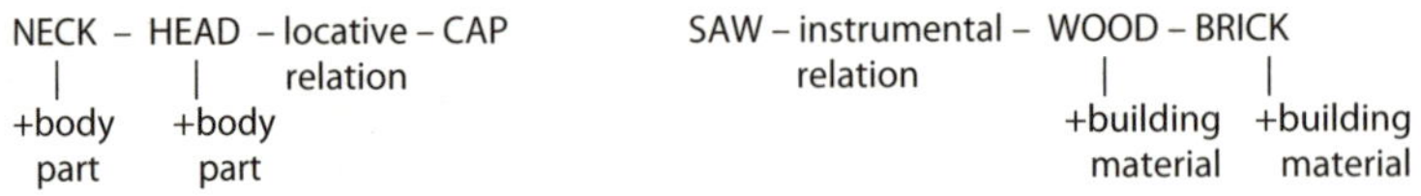

NECK – HEAD – locative – CAP   SAW – instrumental – WOOD – BRICK
 | | relation   relation | |
+body   +body   +building +building
 part   part   material   material

Figure 6.3. Semantic field relations (similarity and contiguity)

Wernicke's aphasics in particular had difficulties in recognizing and using the relations. Luria (1976) claimed that words have graded semantic associative fields. Goodglass and Baker (1976) found that parts of these fields could be damaged selectively
and that object naming was affected by how much of the semantic field was accessible.
They let persons with aphasia name objects and then judge whether other words were
associated with the object names. The speed of recognizing associated words was measured. All subjects had shorter response times for words associated with objects that
they had been able to name. Certain associated words were consistently easier, while
others were harder to recognize. Thus, the semantic association field around a word
seemed to be organized as shown in Figure 6.4:

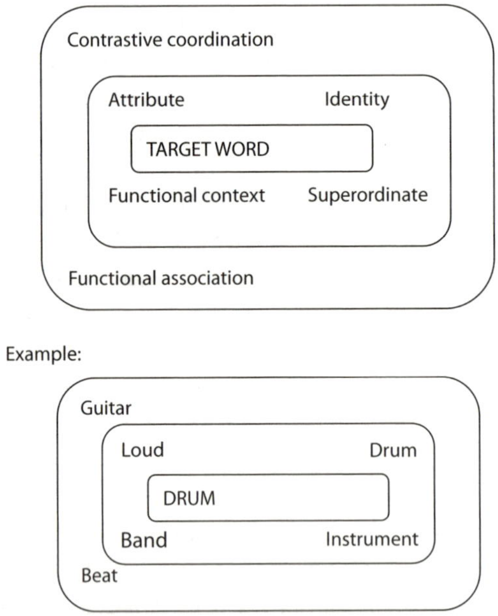

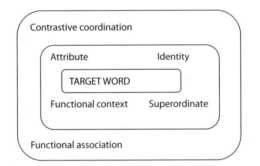

Figure 6.4. Semantic associative fields from Goodglass and Baker (1976)

Derouesné and Lecours (1972) obtained similar results when they made aphasics sort
words which were associated to different degrees. The field of association tended to be
made either smaller or wider by patients with anomia.

The authors of both of these studies claim that they point to a central semantic
disorder. In other experiments, naming therapy for a specific category has been found

to affect the ability to name other categories as well and this is claimed to indicate a disturbance of the access paths and not the semantic field in itself (Rochford, 1971; Seron, Deloche, Bastard, Chassin, & Hermand, 1979; and others). Studies by Kiran and colleagues have shown that there is a semantic complexity effect, in that training on atypical examples of animate and inanimate categories and their semantic features leads to improvement in the naming of more typical exemplars as well, whereas the reverse does not hold (Kiran, Ntourou, Eubanks, & Shamapant, 2005).

Meaning potential and semantic operations

Another perspective is to look at words as having meaning potentials and to have their specific meaning determined by the current context (Allwood 1999, 2003). According to this theory, context determination of meaning is crucial and lexical semantics works by semantic operations on meaning potentials. Semantics and pragmatics are, thus, unified. This perspective is also important when looking at communicative contributions in context (see Chapter 7).

Semantic features and operations in aphasia

As we have seen, an intended target word is very often replaced by a word that is semantically and/or phonologically related to it. The semantic relation can be based on similarity or contiguity (i.e., co-occurrence). Some semantic relations that are often found in these situations are *same semantic category, superordinate, subordinate, part for whole, attribute, spatial relation,* and *functional-causal relation.* This can apply to words denoting objects, functions, processes, and properties. Many semantic substitutions and paraphrases (circumlocutions) describe situational features, indicating a need to contextualize. More substitutions seem to move in the direction from abstract to concrete than in the opposite direction, indicating difficulties with *abstraction* (Allwood & Ahlsén, 1986, 1991).

Examples:

Same category: *cat* for *dog*
Superordinate: *dog* for *poodle*
Subordinate: *poodle* for *dog*
Part for whole: *trunk* for *elephant*
Attribute: *yellow* for *banana*
Spatial relation: *head* for *cap*
Functional causal relation: *kick* for *ball*
Circumlocution: *he had one of those yesterday, the one who picked apples we have one over by the shed* for *ladder*

Further factors to consider in studies of lexical semantics and anomia include modality (visual versus auditory) and factors that may underlie category-specific anomias (see below), such as physical properties versus function.

Sources of data and theories

Some of the main types of evidence used in neurolinguistic theories of lexical semantics have come from certain intriguing syndromes and symptoms in aphasia (see, for instance, Hagoort, 1998).

Deep dyslexia

One source of data for neurolinguistic lexical theories is deep dyslexia and the types of semantic substitutions made by persons with this syndrome when they read (see Chapter 8). Since semantic reading errors are the most typical feature of deep dyslexia, it is naturally interesting to study the nature of these errors and also their combination with visual orthographic errors. An example of a semantic reading error would be reading *school* instead of *university*, while reading *universally* instead of *university* would be a visual error. A hypothetical visual plus semantic error would be reading *generally* instead of *university* (*university* → *universally* → *generally*). Persons with deep dyslexia are usually unable to read by grapheme-to-phoneme conversion (i.e., sound out the words), and therefore have to rely on their visual and semantic abilities to identify words; at the same time, they make these interesting types of errors. Whether this depends on one specific, not yet totally understood disturbance or several disturbances that co-occur for anatomical reasons is not fully known. (See also Chapter 8.)

Category-specific anomia

Another intriguing phenomenon is so-called category-specific anomia, in which a person has an anomia that affects a certain category of words, but leaves other categories unaffected.

One recurring observation is that nouns and verbs can be selectively disturbed in relation to each other. Verbs seem to be more often affected in nonfluent, agrammatic aphasics with frontal lobe lesions. Nouns, on the other hand are more often problematic for persons with anomia, who have temporal-parietal lesions. (We have already observed this difference to some extent in Chapter 5.) The verb disorder can be considered in relation to a possible frontal encoding of verbs of movement and action (cf. Pulvermüller, Shtyrov, & Ilmoniemi, 2005). It may also be related to the role of verbs in grammatical structure. The noun disorder would be more related to the association of sensory features.

Further observations, however, have been made in a number of studies of category-specific disturbances affecting subgroups of nouns.

One such difference is between **concrete** and **abstract** nouns, most often shown as a concreteness effect, namely that concrete nouns are more easily activated. It has been suggested that concrete nouns have richer representational structures in memory, including, for example, a nonverbal image coding (Paivio, 1991), more contextual information (Schwanenflugel, 1991), or a larger set of semantic features (Plaut & Shallice, 1993), but this does not explain why some (albeit few) persons with aphasia activate abstract nouns more easily. Another argument is that concrete nouns are specifically associated with sensorimotor (including perceptual) attributes (Breedin, Martin, & Saffran, 1994). If these attributes are disturbed, abstract nouns would be easier to access than concrete ones.

Another difference — perhaps the best-known one — is between **natural or living objects** and **artifacts**. There are reports of cases of selective disturbances of words for either natural objects (animal, fruits, vegetables) or artifacts (tools, furniture, etc). Such patients may have very vague semantic information about one of the category types, but very detailed semantic information about the other type. Competing interpretations exist, one of which attributes the difference between the two categories to their mainly perceptual/sensory versus mainly functional/motor basis (for natural objects and artifacts, respectively) (e.g., Farah & McClelland, 1991; Warrington & Shallice, 1984). Some support for this interpretation comes from lesion data for known cases (Gainotti, Silveri, Daniele, & Guistolisi, 1995, Gainotti, 1998) and a PET imaging study (Martin, Gagnon, Schwartz, Dell, & Saffran, 1996), where naming of animals resulted in activation in the left medial occipital lobe, while naming of tools activated the left premotor area. (Both groups of stimuli also resulted in bilateral ventral temporal lobe activation.) The other main interpretation claims that we really have more detailed category-specificity in the organization of our mental lexicon; this has been suggested by Caramazza and colleagues (e.g., Caramazza & Hillis, 1990).

A related question is whether there are category-specific semantic disorders, which are also specific to a certain *modality*. This question has not yet been settled, although cases have been presented that might point in this direction. This question is related to the question concerning disrupted access versus central disturbance.

Right-hemisphere lesions and lexical-semantic problems

While semantic problems, such as anomia and semantic substitutions, are common in persons with aphasia as a result of left-hemisphere lesions, they are not as obvious in persons with right-hemisphere damage (RHD). However, RHD subjects also have some lexical-semantic problems, which are of interest. According to Myers (1999), RHD subjects mainly have problems with divergent language tasks. Divergent tasks are typically more "open" than so-called convergent tasks, which require one specific response, and they demand sensitivity to semantic relations. Examples of divergent tasks are verbal fluency tasks, where the subject is asked to name as many members of a category as possible in a minute, naming categories for a number of objects, and determining whether two items are related. Difficulties in performing these tasks have been noted in a number of studies. They seem to point to problems in handling multiple, peripheral, associated meanings, for example, less frequent and primarily connotative meanings. RHD subjects tend to focus on central or prototypical meanings and have problems with, for example, metaphoric meaning and ambiguities, which can lead to language comprehension problems. This points to the right hemisphere as being responsible for more reflective semantic interpretation, involving the interpretation of more peripheral meaning.

Semantic dementia

Semantic dementia is a progressive disorder, which starts out as a selective semantic problem (Hodges, Graham, & Patterson, 1995). The left temporal lobe is affected. This is a specific disorder that affects certain specified semantic information about categories, while superordinate information can still be activated (e.g., *animal* for *dog*). The decline seems to follow the same pattern for both production and comprehension.

Methodological considerations

Group studies versus case studies

Semantic group studies of aphasics were done in the 1970s, as we have seen. They assumed that small groups of aphasics, sorted based on the syndromes of the neoclassical model, could be used for group study comparisons. Later, however, this assumption was strongly questioned, since the syndromes yield groups that are too internally heterogeneous. Another methodology, the extensive case study, has taken over in much of this research. Most of the later studies of lexical semantics in neurolinguistics, including studies of category-specific anomias and deep dyslexia, are case studies.

Central or access disorder

Is anomia a central disorder, affecting certain kinds of representations (or processes) that can be called "the mental lexicon" in itself or is it a disorder affecting *access* to "the mental lexicon"? How one wants to answer this question is closely related to specific assumptions about the nature of "the mental lexicon" in terms of activation-inhibition patterns. It might even be the case that there is no certain way of drawing a line between representations and access processes (cf. Allwood & Ahlsén, 1984, 1986). Much of the research in this area is dependent on which particular process model is chosen.

Mapping of form and meaning

Some of the main questions in lexical-semantic studies have concerned how words are processed, that is, how form and meaning are mapped onto each other in language production and comprehension. Indeed, such questions are no less relevant today.

In relation to process models of different types and to the units studied, how much top-down versus bottom-up processing is assumed to take place? When we understand speech, do we start by mapping words or morphemes to meaning units and construct the meaning of larger units from this mapping, or do we start with expectations and hypotheses about the meaning of a specific word or utterance based on background knowledge, situation, and linguistic context? Or do the two types of processing interact and, if so, how?

Types of process models

What types of process models should be used in the study of lexical semantics? Neurolinguistic studies have played a major role in the design of process models. Many of the earlier studies, and present-day studies as well, are based on serial models, such as Garrett's (1982a,b) or Levelt's (1989) model of speech production (see Figure 6.5 below), or the PALPA model (Kay, Lesser & Coltheart, 1992) (see Figure 3.5) of speech recognition/comprehension, as well as the search and cohort models for visual and auditory word recognition presented below.

Interactive activation models, simulated in artificial neural networks (ANN) are, however, being used more and more, for example, the TRACE model for recognition/ comprehension and the IAM model for production used by Dell and coworkers (e.g., Dell, Schwartz, Martin, Saffran, & Gagnon, 1997) (see below in this chapter and Chapter 13).

Word comprehension

Models: Different models of lexical access have been tried out, such as Forster's *active search model* and Morton's *logogen model,* which posit a passively responsive lexicon where different units are activated by incoming stimuli (Forster, 1976; Morton, 1969);

the *cohort model* proposed by Marslen-Wilson and Tyler (1980); and the *TRACE model* of McClelland and Elman (1986).

In an *active, direct search* lexicon, it is assumed that one searches for matches of an incoming stimulus word in "bins" containing word representations (auditory or visual) which are ordered by some principle, for example, how frequently they have been encountered. The word representations in the "bins" are then linked to a "lexical master file," where phonological and semantic cross-references exist. Similarly, a word can be accessed from a semantic representation in production.

In a *passive, indirect, responsive* model, like the *logogen* model, auditory and visual incoming word stimuli can activate a specific "logogen" (recognition unit) if the stimulus is strong enough (i.e., contains enough activation and not too much inhibition in relation to the features of the logogen to get over its activation threshold). The logogens are also connected to a semantic cognitive lexicon, which can increase or decrease the activation and thus affect which logogen is activated.

A *cohort* model stresses the incremental build-up of activation as, for example, a written word is encountered letter by letter and a particular word is selected at a particular decision point. An early perceptual analysis determines that a set of words are possible candidates and recognition proceeds by eliminating the candidates from left to right.

The *TRACE* model is a highly interactive model for spoken word recognition, emphasizing top-down processing, or dependence on the context, in word recognition. It claims that lexical knowledge helps acoustic perceptual processes.

Data: On-line experiments (lexical decision studies). Lexical organization is often studied in lexical decision experiments. The task in a lexical decision experiment is to determine whether a letter string (or a spoken auditory stimulus) is a real word or not. The stimuli consist of a mix of real words and nonwords that are similar in structure to the real words. Groups of different types of real words are included and compared to each other. The independent variables are, thus, real word versus nonword and type of word. The dependent variable is the reaction time for determining whether a word is a real word or not. Based on differences in reaction times, hypotheses about the processing of different word types are tried out. For example, if a group of very frequent words and a group of infrequent words are included, the decision times will be shorter for the very frequent words.

A possible design for a lexical decision experiment: stimuli.

	Words	Nonwords (made by changing letters in real words)
Frequent bisyllabic nouns	40	40
Infrequent bisyllabic nouns	40	40

A specific instance of the lexical decision task is **semantic priming**, where the relationship between two stimuli is investigated. The first stimulus is presented, followed by the second, which is the target word to decide on (as a real word or a nonword). Semantic priming tasks can establish patterns of association. It has been shown that a semantically related word as prime word facilitates the recognition (lexical decision) of the target word, when compared to a unrelated prime word. For example, the word *orange* is recognized faster as a real word if it has been preceded by the prime word *apple,* than if it has been preceded by, for example, the word *chair.*

All of the above models have to be able to account for a number of effects found in lexical decision tasks, such as the following:

- The frequency effect: The more frequent a word is, the faster it is recognized.
- The length effect: The shorter a word is, the faster it is recognized.
- The concreteness effect: The more concrete a word is, the faster it is recognized.
- The word superiority effect: A letter is recognized faster in a word than if it occurs in isolation.
- The word/nonword effect: Words are identified as words faster than nonwords are identified as nonwords.
- The context effect: words are identified faster in context.
- The degradation or stimulus quality effect: A word that is presented clearly is recognized faster than a word that is blurred in some way (e.g., covered by a grid), if it is presented visually.

They also, of course, have to account for other semantically, visually, and phonologically influenced perception and comprehension errors in normal and pathological data.

Word production

Models: Aphasic word substitutions, like speech errors produced by typical speakers, have been used as evidence for different levels of processing in production. Predictions of levels of representation and processes are made based on what parts of words can be substituted as units and what order different parts of production processes are applied in, as reflected in substituted units.

Garrett's (1982a) production model and Levelt's (1989) model for speaking are examples of influential **serial production models**, while **interactive activation models** have been presented by Dell and coworkers, Harley, and others (e.g., Dell & Reich, 1981; Harley, 1993b). Levelt's model contains the following components:

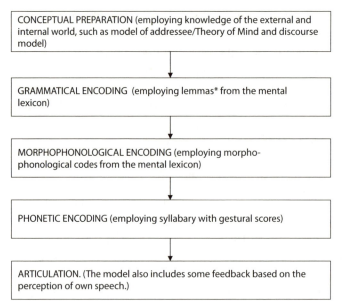

(* a lemma is an entity abstracting over the inflection forms of the same word stem)

Figure 6.5. Levelt's serial production model

Data: Aphasic word substitutions (as well as word substitutions produced by non-aphasic speakers, e.g., so-called Freudian slips) have, however, also provided counter-evidence to serial models (see Butterworth, 1981; cf. Harley, 1993a). So-called blends, where two word forms are combined in the "word" that is finally produced, have inspired models advocating parallel processing and feedback loops between "levels," where lexical semantics and phonology can mutually influence each other. An example of a "blend" is *plower,* combining *plant* and *flower.*

Substitutions where the target and the substitute have both a semantic and a phonological relation (e.g., *cat* for *rat, thumb* for *tongue*) are much more frequent than one would expect if the two levels did not interrelate in some way (e.g., Dell & Reich, 1981; Harley, 1984; Martin et al., 1996). But experiments have also shown that the interaction is limited, so that processing is only semantic at first, while in the last stages phonology seems to dominate (Saffran, Dell, & Schwartz, 2000).

Simulation

Simulations of aphasic word substitutions have been done, using **artificial neural networks** (e.g., Martin, Dell, Saffran, & Schwartz, 1994; Schwartz, Dell, Martin, & Saffran, 1994; Martin et al., 1996), also in this case modeling the interaction between

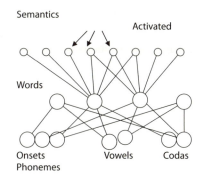

Figure 6.6. How an interactive model with layers for semantics, words, and phonemes might look (simplified)

phonology and semantics. Interactive activation models are nonmodular (i.e., each process is not self-contained). Activation spreads bidirectionally in a continuous flow. In this way, earlier and later "stages of processing" influence each other. A compromise model which is interactive but contains a lexical and a phonological stage was developed by Dell et al. (1997) and can be used as an example. It is a *localist* model, that is, *nodes* correspond to psychological properties (one-to-one). Three levels of nodes are included: *semantic features, known words,* and *phonemes* (see Figure 6.6). All connections between nodes are excitatory and bidirectional. All connections have the same (preset) *weight* and there is a preset *decay* factor (which determines how fast the activation of nodes decays) and normally distributed noise. External updating is used initially by activating the semantic features of the target word. This model allows simulation of dissociations between patients with mostly semantic and mostly phonological errors. Lesions affecting the decay factor produced semantic, mixed, and formal errors. If they were not severe, there was a semantic component in most errors. Lesions affecting connection weight, on the other hand, produced mostly phonological errors. Combinations of the two types of lesions resulted in intermediate, mixed patterns. The model could also simulate longitudinal data for the patients, with the same factors simulating the later stage, only closer to normal values. The model is limited by being too simple to handle all the details of phonological errors, variations in response time, and purely semantic errors that exist in real life.

Simulation models provide new and promising methods for gaining a better understanding of lexical-semantic organization in the brain.

Links to therapy

Lexical-semantic research at the single-word level has inspired a number of therapy methods, which are designed to train word association patterns, for example, Luria's restoration therapy (Luria, 1963), Deblocking therapy (Weigl & Bierwisch, 1970), BOX therapy (Visch-Brink, Bajema, & Van de Sandt-Koenderman, 1997), and Semantic Association therapy (e.g., Martin & Laine, 2000).

Summary

In this chapter, we have looked at lexical semantic aspects of neurolinguistics, starting with the meaning of words. We presented four different theories for analyzing word meaning: prototype theory, semantic distinctive features, semantic fields and meaning potentials with semantic operations, and we related the theories to aphasia. We then turned to four intriguing phenomena that are important sources of data and theories: deep dyslexia, category-specific anomia, lexical-semantic problems following right-hemisphere lesions and semantic dementia. The pervasive nature of lexical-semantic problems and the extensive experimental studies of such problems motivate the sections on experimental methods and models of word processing. Finally, we took a brief look at simulation of lexical semantic problems and links to therapy for disorders affecting lexical semantics.

Further reading

There is an abundance of literature in the area of lexical semantics. The selection below gives a good introduction to the themes that we have examined in this chapter, especially current models and theories in lexical semantics, together with some examples of relevant findings from neurolinguistics . Further literature on specific topics can be found in the references.

Caramazza, A., & Hillis, A. (1991). Lexical organization of nouns and verbs in the brain. *Nature, 349*, 788–790.

Dell, G., Schwartz, M., Martin, N., Saffran, E., & Gagnon, D. (1997). Lexical access in aphasic and nonaphasic speakers. *Psychological Review, 104*, 801–838.

Hagoort, P. (1998). The shadows of lexical meaning in patients with semantic impairments. In B. Stemmer & H. Whitaker (Eds.), *Handbook of neurolinguistics* (pp. 235–248). New York: Academic Press.

Harley, T. (1984). A critique of top-down independent levels models of speech production. Evidence from non-plan-internal speech production. *Cognitive Science, 8*, 191–219.

Harley, T. (1993b). Connectionist approaches to language disorders. *Aphasiology, 7*, 221–249.

Kay, J., Lesser, R., & Coltheart, M. (1992). *Psycholinguistic assessments of language processing in aphasia*. Hove: Lawrence Erlbaum Associates.

Levelt, W. (1989). *Speaking: From intention to articulation*. Cambridge, MA: MIT Press.

Warrington, E., & Shallice, T. (1984). Category specific semantic impairments. *Brain, 107*, 829–854.

Assignments

Look at the following list of semantic word substitutions:

1.   football → balloon
2.   hose → house
3.   poodle → lion
4.   zebra → trunk
5.   donkey → horse
6.   doll → cap
7.   boy → man
8.   spade → garden thing
9.   orange → apple
10. green → purple

Try to explain each substitution:

a.   in terms of semantic fields, prototype theory, or semantic distinctive features;
b.   in terms of one or more diagnoses, indicating in which patients such a substitution might occur;
c.   in terms of what type of model — a serial (Levelt-type) model or an interactive activation (Dell-type) model — you think would best explain the substitution.

Chapter 7

The semantics and pragmatics of communicative contributions in context from a neurolinguistic perspective

Introduction: Objects of study, theories, and sources of data

Objects of study (phenomena) and theories

As we saw in Chapter 6, word-level semantics has been studied in many experiments involving persons with brain damage. But from the point of view of achieving "ecological validity" in relation to everyday language use, it is essential to study how words and utterances are used in context and in real-life interaction, in order to find out more about semantics (meaning in language) and pragmatics (use of language). As we will see in this chapter, semantics and pragmatics are closely interlinked with respect to many of the phenomena that are studied in neurolinguistics.

A number of phenomena can be studied in relation to the semantics and pragmatics of utterances, or communicative contributions in context. Some of these are listed in Table 7.1 below.

The list starts out with the simple extension of semantics to *longer units*, such as *sentences*, *utterances* (since not all utterances are sentences), or *contributions* (since not all contributions in communication are verbal-vocal utterances, for example a head nod can mean "yes").

Contributions should generally be analyzed with respect to their structure and function in relation to the *context* where they occur; for example, how was a contribution related to the previous one and what did it lead to? With respect to function, an utterance can, for example, be analyzed as an action: a *speech act* (Austin, 1962; Searle, 1969). For example, the utterance "hand me a towel" can be described as a request or a command. An indirect speech act has the grammatical form of one speech act while really representing another. For example, "can you hand me the towel?" has the form of a question, but is really also a request. Similarly, communicative interaction can be seen as a *language game* (Wittgenstein, 1953), where the participants make different moves.

A conversation requires the participants to make assumptions about certain *cooperative principles*, if it is to work at all: participants must take each other into cognitive and ethical consideration (Allwood, 1976; Grice, 1975). This means that, unless something else is expressed or expected, we expect each other to maintain quality (say what we believe is true) and quantity (say as much as the listener needs and no more). It also means presenting information that is relevant in an orderly manner. These principles make it possible to joke and use irony, which is done by flouting or breaking them in various ways.

As soon as sequences of utterances occur in monologue or dialogue, things are communicated that are not said in words. The sequencing of utterances follows certain principles and what is mentioned or not mentioned depends on certain *presupposed* common knowledge or the ability to *infer* from the previous context. There are also a number of typical structures used for inference. Some types of inference are linked to a number of phenomena studied primarily under the label of cognitive semantics. Such phenomena include *metaphors* (drawing an analogy between, for example, a strong man and a lion) (Lakoff, 1987) and *deixis* and *anaphora* (both of which refer to something in the environment or in the previous text or conversation, for example, by using a pronoun).

Ways of analyzing meaning in cognitive semantics also include *image schemas* (which are thought to be mental visual-schematic representations of meaning) (Langacker, 1989) and interpreting meaning in terms of the relations between different *mental spaces* (Fauconnier, 1994). We can imagine schemas as spatial representations, especially of words like *into* and *over*. We can also transfer between mental spaces in considering different uses of the same word or phrase, as they are used in metaphors and other semantic figures. We can think of something in a concrete situation or in a more *decontextualized* or abstract sense; for instance, we might think of a particular dog or of dogs in general. We also have to consider *human flexibility and adaptation* and the considerable role they play in the communicative use of language. Communication and language use are highly context-dependent and successful communication demands fast, continuous adaptation to changing circumstances (cf. Penn, 1999). For example, we have to adapt to who is present, what they know, what their attitudes are, where we are, who we are addressing, what happened before, what the topic is now, etc. Some of our communication is probably performed according to fairly holistic patterns.

This leads us to certain phenomena that spotlight real-world interaction even more. In order to communicate with others, we have to form a reasonable *theory of mind* (ToM) about them, that is, a theory about what they know and think that will affect what you say to them and how you say it (cf. Frith, 1989). For example, you need to know how much explicit information you have to give them about a person in order for them to understand your reference. Is *she, my friend, Andy's sister, Tracy, Tracy Anderson,* or *Tracy Anderson who works at the library* the best reference in a given situation?

You also have to make your contributions fit into the context of the interaction by *interactive communication management*, where certain types of utterances require certain other types to follow them (e.g., a question should be followed by an answer in a so-called adjacency pair), or at least certain kinds of utterances fit into a specific context (are *preferred*) better than others. And you need to follow the *turn-taking* pattern of the activity: you must accept, take, keep, or give away "the floor" at appropriate times (Sacks, Schegloff, & Jefferson, 1974). You also have to give *feedback* to show that you are maintaining contact; that you can perceive, understand, and react to what is said by others (Allwood, Nivre, & Ahlsén, 1992). In addition, you have to *manage your own contributions* by *choice* and *change* operations for planning (seen in hesitation, self-interruption, self-correction, etc.) (Allwood, Nivre & Ahlsén, 1990).

We can also describe communication as the interpersonal alignment of different processes in building up coordinated action (Pickering & Garrod, 2004). Participants have to understand and show emotions and attitudes. A considerable amount of human communication in face-to-face interaction consists of communicative gestures and other body communication and actions. Pictures, text, etc., are also used in communication. Everyday communication is, thus, most often *multimodal*. Furthermore, it often makes use of artifacts (computers, phones, photos, microphones, etc.). All these factors have to be handled simultaneously; some of them are more directly linguistic, while others relate to language use. Table 7.1 lists some types of phenomena that are studied in pragmatics or discourse semantics (Ahlsén, 1995; Allwood, 1995).

Table 7.1. Pragmatic and discourse phenomena (relevant objects of study)

Types of phenomena	Study object — labels
Whole utterances/contributions, especially sentences	Sentence semantics — logic, e.g., situation semantics
Whole utterances/contributions in context	Speech acts → Communicative acts / actions, language games
Whole utterances — cooperation	Conversational principles and maxims plus ethics; relevance, manner, quality, quantity; co-construction of meaning
Inferences, sequences of utterances — monological	Inferences, presuppositions, syllogisms, "logico-grammatical structures"
Inferences "conventions of use"	Conversational principles and maxims
Cognitive semantics	Metaphors, etc.
	Deixis — anaphora
	Image schemas, etc.
	Mental spaces
	Contextualization-decontextualization
	Flexibility and adaptation
	Holistic patterns
Interactional phenomena	Theory of mind
	Interactive communication management:
	– Sequences, adjacency pairs, preference organization, etc.
	– Turn-taking
	– Feedback
	Own communication management:
	– Choice and change operations
	Alignment in communication
Gestures, actions (body communication) in interaction and their relation to meaning	Gesture, body communication
	Alignment of body communication and actions

For each type, more specific labels for the study objects are provided in the right-hand column.

The above phenomena are aspects that need to be studied if one aims to get a complete picture of a person's communicative ability, especially in everyday situations of different types, that is, real-life communication. Most of them are usually studied by researchers in the areas of pragmatics or cognitive semantics.

Since neurolinguistics is intimately related to the diagnosis, treatment, and evaluation of communication disorders caused by brain damage, it also has to address these phenomena. For most of them, well-established clinical methods are not generally available, but the area is a dynamic field of research that is developing rapidly.

Sources of data

Interesting findings relating to the phenomena discussed above emerge from the symptoms of different types of brain damage. It seems clear that a better understanding and description of the phenomena per se, together with more extensive studies of their relation to brain damage will give us insights into human communication that we do not have today. It can also give us a better understanding of the communicative problems of different groups of persons with brain damage and hopefully will lead to better ways of helping them to communicate more effectively.

What, then, are the neurolinguistically interesting sources of data?

Aphasia: The scope of the term

The obvious group to study with respect to communication disorders might appear to be persons with aphasia. But we should stop to consider the delimitation and definition of this group, which will be crucial in this chapter, considering the phenomena in question.

Aphasia is typically defined as *a language disorder caused by acquired brain damage*. This definition used to be more restrictive, requiring *focal* brain damage, or even *focal left-hemisphere* brain damage, but these definitions no longer apply today. In some countries, there is a convention that the person said to have aphasia must be an adult or at least older than a specific age (e.g., four years old); otherwise, a language disorder may be referred to by another term such as *dysphasia*. In other places, however, there is no such implicit age limit. The definition of *acquired*, the delimitation of the type of brain damage, and, not least, the definition of *language* all affect what is counted as aphasia. Furthermore, aphasia is typically a *symptom diagnosis*. This means that the presence of symptoms, or in other words, the language disorder, is the main criterion for the diagnosis.

Linguistics has developed and changed in important ways in the last 20 to 30 years. Most importantly, the areas of semantics and pragmatics covered in this chapter are now included and studied in more detail, whereas the focus used to be almost exclusively on phonology and grammar. Since lexical-semantic symptoms are salient in aphasia, they were studied in traditional neurolinguistics, but "language in context" and communicative aspects, body communication, etc., have only recently come to be considered as suitable objects of study. Since pragmatics is a natural part of language and is studied in present-day linguistics, disorders affecting pragmatics should also constitute aphasia, using an up-to-date definition of language (cf. Joanette & Ansaldo, 1999). The end result is that the group of persons defined as having aphasia is much broader than what had traditionally been included under this label.

In the following sections, we will consider different sources of data regarding disorders that could today be labeled aphasia, but which have traditionally been studied under separate labels, due to the more restricted earlier definitions and the greater focus on the etiology (cause) of the brain damage.

(The question of the age of acquisition of the brain damage and the relation to language disorders caused by pre-, peri-, and postnatal brain damage will not be further discussed in this chapter. Chapter 10 contains a section on developmental language disorders from a neurolinguistic perspective.)

In studying the semantics and pragmatics of contributions in communicative interaction, not just language but also other cognitive and social factors become important. Cognitive factors that affect the use of language in communication include attention, memory, sensitivity to and production of emotional expression (e.g., by facial expression or prosody), and the ability to grasp the situation as a whole, selectively attend to what is important, and adapt to changes, including reasonable treatment of the other participants. Problems in these areas can lead to social and communicative difficulties in a number of neurological disorders.

Another important aspect of pragmatic factors is, however, their role in compensation for and rehabilitation from specific disorders of language and communication. A person with aphasia may, for example, be a skilled user of gestures and facial expressions as well as interaction management, and thereby enhance his/her communicative and social possibilities.

Aphasia, especially after left-hemisphere lesions

Pragmatic factors are much less studied than other linguistic aspects of aphasia. Aphasia has not been seen as primarily a pragmatic disorder. But aphasia can involve impaired comprehension of longer utterances and connected texts; difficulties handling logico-grammatical structures; problems with metaphor interpretation, inference, abstraction in general, or decontextualization; and, in some cases, difficulties affecting body communication. Thus, there are plenty of possible sources of semantic-pragmatic dysfunction. Aphasia affecting other aspects of language, such as word finding, word mobilization, and comprehension of words and structures, can also result in more secondary pragmatic problems, such as the apparent violation of conversational principles and conventional patterns of interaction.

The term high-level language (HLL) or subtle language disorders has been used in the description of very subtle language problems which are typically of the semantic-pragmatic kind and affect, for example, inferencing, metaphor comprehension, and logico-grammatical structures (Crosson, 1992). HLL problems occur in mild cases of aphasia and can also be found in traumatic brain injury, early dementia, and to some extent in normal aging.

Right-hemisphere lesions

Right-hemisphere damage (RHD) can result in a number of deficits, which are highly relevant for the use of language in context (see also Myers 1999).

Left neglect, or a reduced awareness of and responsivity toward the left side, most often visually, can interfere with reading, writing, spatial orientation, and the selective direction of attention to the most significant stimuli. Hypo-arousal, that is, a generally reduced responsivity and a narrowed focus of attention, can also reduce general attention. This is, of course, especially true when the neglect is unconscious and accompanied by denial of the deficit. The impact on cognition and communication is relevant for most of the semantic-pragmatic phenomena listed above. Reduced alertness and ability to mobilize intentional attention as well as reduced awareness and selectivity of information can cause difficulties, especially in handling complex communicative situations.

Prosodic deficits can occur, affecting both comprehension and production. Both linguistic and emotional prosody can be disturbed, perhaps more so in the case of the latter. Since many pragmatic cues are prosodic, more monotonous speech production and problems interpreting and producing emotional prosody, can lead to communicative problems. In addition, problems interpreting intonation contours (pitch) and stress in utterances, in particular, naturally lead to comprehension difficulties. A person with RHD has to rely more on other semantic and contextual information.

Lexical-semantic deficits, as discussed in Chapter 6, can cause communication problems, affecting not only the comprehension and production of single words, but also the communication of longer units in interaction. The more "peripheral," connotative, or infrequent meanings used to resolve ambiguities, understand inferences, metaphors, etc., and adapt flexibly to the situation as a whole are vulnerable in RHD persons and this is directly relevant to their semantic-pragmatic ability. Word-finding and word-comprehension problems, of course, also affect interaction patterns.

Emotional information is problematic for many RHD subjects and this can affect both comprehension and production. It is not completely clear why this is so, since these problems seem to be general, affecting not only emotional prosody and facial expression, but also verbal expression of emotions. It is, however, clear that it is not inner emotions per se that are disturbed, just the ability to express and understand their expression. This is, of course, a social handicap in communication and can cause semantic problems of understanding as well as problems affecting interaction patterns.

Discourse deficits have already been mentioned as resulting from the above problems. RHD persons may have problems managing complex communication situations and the difficulties can affect practically all of the types of semantic-pragmatic phenomena discussed above. Problems understanding speaker intentions (e.g., ToM) and communicative acts, especially indirect ones, occur. Attention and integration problems lead to lack of selective focus and integration of information. Alternative meanings, inferences, and metaphors can cause problems. This shows up as problems understanding humor, irony, etc. Social communicative problems often result from these symptoms (cf. Saldert, 2006).

Dementia, especially dementia of Alzheimer type

Dementia is a chronic, progressive, and persistent decline in at least three of the following functions: memory, language and communication, visuospatial skills, personality, and other cognitive abilities such as reasoning and judgment (Cummings, Darkins, Mendez, Hill, & Benson, 1988). Over 50% of all cases are dementia of Alzheimer type (DAT), which is also the type where semantics-pragmatics is most clearly affected.

Other types of dementia with more frontal and subcortical involvement, resulting in poor verbal fluency and reduced speech together with motor speech disorders, are vascular dementia (which often co-occurs with anomia); frontotemporal dementias, such as Pick's disease (characterized by stereotypy, perseveration, and echolalia); and a number of progressive neurological diseases, such as multiple sclerosis, Huntington's disease, amyotrophic lateral sclerosis, progressive supranuclear palsy, Creutzfeldt-Jakob disease, and HIV-associated dementia. For many of these diseases, the symptoms vary depending on the area where the damage is worst. A special case is primary progressive aphasia (PPA), in which other cognitive abilities are relatively spared (Cherrier, Mendez, Cummings, & Benson, 1998). This group of patients is also described as having high-level language or subtle language disorders (see above).

Language and communication in DAT are usually described as going through three stages (cf. Bayles, 1992; Bayles, Tomoeda, & Trosset, 1990; Caramelli, Mansur, & Nitrini, 1998). At the earliest stages, we find anomia and impairment of verbal fluency. Somewhat later, there are also clear semantic-pragmatic problems affecting discourse, which are probably secondary to the temporal lobe damage affecting word retrieval. Typical semantic-pragmatic problems, in addition to anomia, are difficulties in comprehension of complex semantics and syntax, reduction of informational content, increased discourse tangentiality, and referential errors (Chapman & Ulatowska, 1994). Late stages affect language as a whole. In the early stages 30% to 40% of patients exhibit mild anomic aphasia in traditional tests, later they tend to have transcortical sensory aphasia (reduced comprehension but spared repetition), and in the late stages 100% of patients have global aphasia (Faber-Langendoen et al., 1988).

Initially, DAT typically affects the left medial temporal lobe and neocortical areas of the temporal lobe, which is what leads to the problems with word retrieval (Damasio & Damasio, 1989) and the reduction in verbal fluency. Later, we find also damage of the left temporal-parietal-occipital junction area, leading to the symptoms of transcortical sensory aphasia; in the latest stages, the damage extends further into the frontal regions, making the aphasia global. Other key factors behind the language and communication problems in persons with DAT are (a) visuospatial problems, affecting confrontation naming (tactile stimulation and real objects give better results than picture stimuli) (Appel, Kertesz, & Fishman, 1982); and (b) memory problems, affecting both short- and long-term memory.

Traumatic brain injury

Traumatic brain injury (TBI) can be focal, most often affecting the anterior and inferior frontal and temporal lobes, or it may involve more diffuse injury of axons. The result may be reduced frontal lobe "executive control" and judgment, or reduced attention, concentration, memory, initiation, and goal direction. Exaggerated moods and abnormal loquaciousness are also common (McDonald, Togher, & Code, 1999).

All persons with TBI have a "cognitive-communication impairment" and up to 30% or 40% also have problems with a traditional aphasia test, where pragmatics is usually not included. Problems include anomia, seen in impaired confrontation naming, word finding, verbal association, and comprehension. Pragmatic difficulties can be studied using pragmatic analysis, discourse analysis, or conversation analysis. The problems affecting discourse may be of different types. One variant involves disorganized, wandering discourse, often tangential and imprecise, and characterized by word-finding problems. At the same time, hyperverbosity, along with a certain disinhibition, and ineffectiveness in using social and contextual cues may also be found. Another variant consists of sparse speech with many pauses and lack of initiative, associated with difficulties in following extended, rapid, and stressful communication. This group also has problems with abstraction, implicature (i.e., inferencing), and indirect communicative acts. The problems are probably due to cognitive deficits, such as reduced attention and slowed information processing, and to the difficulties with executive functions. Three main types of communicative difficulties in these patients are (a) problems in maintaining coherence and adequate structure and sequencing, (b) comprehension problems caused by reduced sensitivity to inference, and (c) topic drift and problems with cooperation and formulating an adequate ToM of the conversation partner.

Links to therapy

The semantic-pragmatic influence is strong in therapeutic research today and it is being strengthened in everyday clinical work as well, where it does not have a long tradition. Some of the most relevant approaches will be briefly mentioned. *Conversational coaching* (Holland, 1991) prepares the person for interaction in conversation. Coaching can, for example, be based on an analysis of video-recorded interaction, using *Conversation*

Analysis to examine interaction patterns (e.g., Perkins, Whitworth, & Lesser, 1997; Whitworth, Perkins, & Lesser, 1997). It can also be based on *Activity-based Communication Analysis* (Ahlsén, 1995; Allwood, 1995), which analyzes interaction patterns, the use of linguistic means for communication, and critical background factors, such as goals, roles, and the physical circumstances of the activity as such, as well as individual features of the participants. A related approach is *Environmental Needs Assessment* (Hartley, 1992). This brings us to the more explicitly *social approaches*, as presented by Byng, Pound, and Parr (2000) and Simmons-Mackie (2000), which focus on changes in the environment and society to ensure increased participation. Group therapy is also very suitable for the application of pragmatics-based methods (cf. Marshall, 1999). One of the more structured pragmatic methods used in the group context is *Language Game* therapy (Pulvermüller & Roth, 1991). *Supported Communication for Aphasics (SCA)* (Kagan, 1998) is a method of providing support for participation in interaction. Finally, computer support for participation in communication can also be provided (e.g., Todman, Alm, & File, 1999).

Summary

This chapter is an important one, since it deals with fundamental questions of what should be counted as language and how language can be disturbed by brain damage. The chapter stresses the importance of contextual adaptation for successful linguistic communication. Relevant phenomena in aphasia as a symptom diagnosis and also applied to right-hemisphere lesions, dementia and traumatic brain injury are described and some of the many links to and consequences for therapy are discussed.

Further reading

The literature given below covers most of the different semantic-pragmatic theories and therapy methods discussed in this chapter and is important for understanding language use, communication in context, and the various ways in which brain damage can affect proficiency in communication.

Ahlsén, E. (1995). Pragmatics and aphasia — an activity based approach. *Gothenburg Papers on Theoretical Linguistics, 77*. Göteborg University, Department of Linguistics.

Chantraine, Y., Joanette, Y., & Cardebat, D. (1998). Impairments of discourse-level representations and processes. In B. Stemmer & H. Whitaker (Eds.), *Handbook of neurolinguistics* (pp. 261–274). New York: Academic Press.

Joanette, Y., & Ansaldo, A. I. (1999). Clinical note: Acquired pragmatic impairments and aphasia. *Brain and Language, 68*, 529–534.

Levinson, S. (1983). *Pragmatics*. Cambridge: Cambridge University Press.

McDonald, S., Togher, L., & Code, C. (Eds.) (1999). *Communication disorders following traumatic brain injury*. Hove: Psychology Press.

Myers, P. (1999). *Right hemisphere damage — Disorders of communication and cognition*. London: Singular Publishing Group.

Penn, C. (1999). Pragmatic assessment and therapy for persons with brain damage: What have clinicians gleaned in two decades? *Brain and Language, 68*, 535–552.

Stemmer, B., & Whitaker, H. (Eds.) (1998). *Handbook of neurolinguistics*. New York: Academic Press.

Worrall, L., & Frattali, C. (Eds.) (2000). *Neurogenic communication disorders — A functional approach*. New York: Thieme.

The following references specifically cover therapeutic approaches to the kinds of disorders discussed in this chapter.

Byng, S., Pound, C., & Parr, S. (2000). Living with aphasia: A framework for intervention. In I. Papathanasiou (Ed.), *Acquired neurogenic communication disorders: A clinical perspective* (pp. 49–75). London, Whurr.

Hartley, L. (1992). Assessment of functional communication. *Seminars in Speech and Language, 13*, 264–279.

Holland, A., (1991). Pragmatic aspects of intervention in aphasia. *Journal of Neurolinguistics, 6*, 197–211.

Kagan, A. (1998). Supported conversation for adults with aphasia. *Clinical Forum. Aphasiology, 12*, 816–830.

Perkins, L., Whitworth, A., & Lesser, R. (1997). *Conversation analysis profile for people with cognitive impairments*. London: Whurr.

Perkins, M. (2003). Clinical pragmatics. In J. Verschueren, J.-O. Östman, J. Blommaert, & C. Bulcaen (Eds.) *Handbook of Pragmatics*: 2001 Installment (pp. 1–29). Amsterdam: John Benjamins.

Pulvermüller, F., & Roth, V. M. (1991). Communicative aphasia treatment as a further development of PACE therapy. *Aphasiology, 5,* 39–50.

Marshall, R. (1999). *Introduction to group treatment for aphasia: Design and management.* Woburn, MA: Butterworth-Heineman.

Simmons-Mackie, N. (2000). Social approaches to the management of aphasia. In L. Worrall & C. Frattali (Eds.), *Neurogenic communication disorders: A functional approach* (pp. 162–187). New York: Thieme.

Todman, J., Alm, N., & File, P. (1999). Modelling pragmatics in AAC. In F. Loncke, J. Clibbens, H. Arvidson, & L. Lloyd (Eds.), *Augmentative and alternative communication: New directions in research and practice* (pp. 84–91). London: Whurr.

Assignments

1. Discuss why a sentence, an utterance and, a contribution are not necessarily the same thing.

2. Two examples of speech acts or communicative acts are greeting and ordering. How could someone with severe word-finding problems manage these communicative acts? Give concrete examples.

3. Why might a person with semantic-pragmatic problems find it hard to understand the utterance "don't be a baby," uttered by a mother to a child of ten?

4. Deixis is a phenomenon that links semantics and pragmatics. Discuss what the meaning of *you* is in the following three examples, and how it depends on the context:

   a. You have to wear a safety-belt when you drive in Sweden.
   b. Have you seen my shoes?
   c. Have you all got your maps?

5. Choose the study objects from the list in Table 7.1 that you think items (a), (b), and (c) below are probably examples of.

   a. A patient starts to tell a story about a person called Eve and after a while her interlocutor says, "Who's Eve?"
   b. A speech pathologist asks a patient, "Do you have children?" The patient first answers "no" then "yes."
   c. An elderly patient sits in his room in a wheelchair and says "I was just playing football with my father."

Part III

Specific topics in neurolinguistics

Chapter 8

Reading and writing
from a neurolinguistic perspective

The relationship between speech and writing

Reading and writing are interesting in several ways. If we look at language and communication from the evolutionary point of view, the use of written language is a learned ability, secondary to spoken language. The relationship between speech and writing differs for ideographic, syllabic, and alphabetical writing systems. In ideographic systems, most written signs are of some kind of pictorial origin and tend to be associated with whole words. In syllabic writing, each syllable has its own written sign. Finally, in alphabetic writing, the speech sounds are represented more or less directly by letters. Another reason for our interest in the ability to read and write is the fact that many people have problems acquiring these skills. Dyslexia or more general reading and writing difficulties pose a major problem for education in a society that relies on written communication more and more. Understanding the relationship between the processes used for speech and writing and how reading and writing can be disturbed or favored is very important for neurolinguistics.

Reading and writing processes

Reading processes

The most widely used kind of model for reading alphabetical and syllabic writing systems is a dual-route model (e.g., Coltheart, Patterson, & Marshall, 1980; Ellis, 1984), which posits two main strategies for reading:

1. whole word reading,
2. grapheme–phoneme conversion.

Whole word reading means that visual representations of whole words are read, either from the visual word form directly or via the semantic representation of the word. Grapheme–phoneme conversion means moving from letters to phonological representations. Most research on reading focuses on decoding a written word and reading it out aloud.

We can specify the routes or strategies in more detail, with respect to decoding and reading aloud, as follows:

1a. whole word → semantic interpretation → phonological output representation
1b. whole word → phonological output representation

2. grapheme → phoneme

The possibility of reading the letter names aloud in a series also exists, and is sometimes the only possible strategy:

3. grapheme → grapheme naming (or letter-by-letter reading)

When reading comprehension is the focus, the semantic interpretation of the word is much more important. There is a need for more research on text reading.

Most of us are likely to use all of the above strategies and combine them according to our needs for the optimal reading function in each situation. Here are some examples of how this is done:

1a. We apply the semantic interpretation of whole words when we really want or need to understand every word we read, for example, when we are reading something important or difficult that we want to remember.
1b. We use whole word reading, without necessarily understanding everything, when we read stories aloud to children.
2. We use grapheme–phoneme conversion when we need to sound out words, such as when we are learning to read or when we encounter new words or foreign words.

3. We use letter naming when we read a series of letters and have to memorize it, for example, a code.

Writing processes

When we write words, we can have three types of starting points:

1. the semantic lexicon (i.e., when we start from our own thoughts and a specific meaning);
2. written words (when we copy writing);
3. spoken words (when we write from dictation or take notes from a speech or a lecture).

We then need to produce a series of graphemes. This can be done via a word–grapheme output lexicon which can be accessed:

1. directly from the semantic system,
2. from the visual input (possibly via the semantic system).

It can also be accessed:

3. from the visual input and semantic systems via the word pronunciation lexicon and the phoneme level and then phoneme–grapheme conversion.

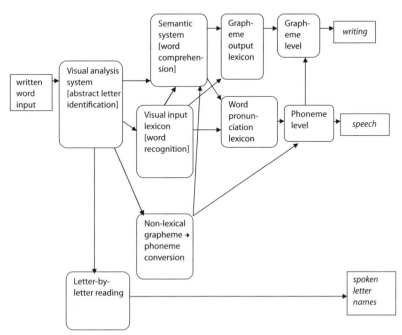

Figure 8.1. Reading and writing processes (Main source: Ellis, 1984)

Acquired disturbances of reading and writing

Acquired dyslexias (alexias)

How can the processes of reading and writing be disturbed? There are several possible disorders or disturbances that can affect the processes, as we can see in the model in Figure 8.1. Different types of disturbance can block different routes in the model and lead to dependence on specific strategies.

For instance, there are patients who can only use *letter-by-letter reading*. In this case, both the whole word reading route and the grapheme–phoneme conversion route seem to be blocked.

Some patients depend on grapheme–phoneme conversion for reading: they read by sounding out the words and then listening to themselves. Such patients have problems reading very long words and words with irregular spelling, since these words are hard to sound out by grapheme–phoneme conversion alone. They do not have access to whole word reading. This type of acquired dyslexia is called *surface* dyslexia (Patterson, Marshall & Coltheart, 1985).

Other patients depend on using whole word reading, because they are unable to sound out words. They cannot read new, unfamiliar words or nonwords (i.e., phonologically regular but nonexistent sound combinations) and they also have problems reading short syncategorematic or function words, such as *and, to, that*. This type of acquired dyslexia is called *phonological dyslexia*.

Deep dyslexia is closely related to phonological dyslexia. Patients with this disorder also rely on whole word reading, and thus have impaired access to grapheme–phoneme conversion. However, deep dyslexia is a challenge to models of acquired dyslexias, since whole word reading is also impaired. Persons with deep dyslexia make the following kinds of mistakes when they read, in addition to being unable to read new words and nonwords:

- visual errors (a visually similar word is substituted, e.g., *cat* becomes *cap*);
- semantic errors (a semantic substitution is made, e.g., *cat* becomes *dog*);
- visual plus semantic errors (e.g., *pivot* becomes *pilot*, then *airplane*);
- derivation errors (e.g., *lovely* becomes *loving*);
- exchanges of function words (e.g., *and* becomes *on*).

For these patients, concrete words with referents that are easy to visualize are easier to read than abstract words. This combination of features has led to two possible interpretations of deep dyslexia: one sees it as a disturbance of more than one route in the model, such that parts of both the grapheme–phoneme conversion process and the whole word reading process are disturbed; another interpretation hypothesizes that the right hemisphere may be taking over reading, using a whole word strategy with some limitations (Coltheart et al., 1980, Coltheart, 2000).

All of these forms of dyslexias are acquired, that is, they occur after brain damage in adults. Acquired forms of dyslexia are sometimes divided into two categories:

Central acquired dyslexias: surface dyslexia, phonological dyslexia, deep dyslexia, and nonsemantic reading (i.e., reading without understanding);

Peripheral acquired dyslexias: letter-by-letter reading, attentional dyslexia (reading disorder caused by a disorder of attention), and neglect dyslexia (reading disorder caused by neglect of one of the visual half-fields, making the patient attend to only one half of the word).

A special case of acquired dyslexia, seen in some persons with aphasia, is the so-called "pure alexia" or "alexia without agraphia." (In describing acquired dyslexia, the two terms *alexia* and *dyslexia* can be used more or less as synonyms, although some researchers prefer to use *dyslexia* for developmental disorders that manifest themselves in early childhood and *alexia* for disorders acquired in adulthood.) Persons with pure alexia can write, but they cannot read, not even something they have just written themselves. They are sometimes able to read single letters and identify words from hearing them spelled aloud; in these cases, they can adopt a letter-by-letter reading strategy. Pure alexia is caused by a lesion which cuts off the input from visual cortex to the left angular gyrus.

Acquired dysgraphias

Acquired dysgraphias are generally described with the same terminology as the acquired dyslexias:

Surface dysgraphia involves using only phoneme–grapheme conversion and the writing process, thus making use of the phonological route.
Phonological dysgraphia involves writing from visual or semantic whole word representations that are transformed into grapheme patterns.
Deep dysgraphia resembles phonological dysgraphia in the same way that deep dyslexia resembles phonological dyslexia.

In most cases, a patient will have both dyslexia and dysgraphia of the same type; the two disorders rarely occur separately.

Acquired dysgraphias can also be divided into central and peripheral types:

Central acquired dysgraphias: surface dysgraphia, phonological dysgraphia, or deep dysgraphia;
Peripheral acquired dysgraphias: disturbances of choice of letter, choice of allograph (letter variant), or motor program.

If the grapheme level is disturbed, this causes problems with spelling in all modalities, whereas if the disturbance is more peripheral, we may find symptoms such as omissions or repetitions of letters or parts of letters, but in this case oral spelling will be correct.

Developmental disorders of reading and writing

Reading and writing disorders and the term "dyslexia"

The expression "developmental reading and writing disorders" is used here in order to include reading and writing problems that are not necessarily specific, in light of different theories of dyslexia and reading and writing disorders.

The term *dyslexia* is used in a number of different ways. One possibility is to define dyslexia according to the discrepancy criterion, which means that the level of reading and writing has to be considerably below the cognitive level or other more general abilities; in other words, there has to be a considerable discrepancy between otherwise "normal" abilities or a "normal" level of development and a much lower level of reading and writing. This is in accordance with the World Health Organization definition of dyslexia. Another way is to define dyslexia as the disturbance of a specific factor, which can occur regardless of the level of other abilities. The most commonly cited specific factor is "phonological ability" or "phonological awareness" (Lundberg, 1994).

While both these possibilities are acknowledged here, our aim is to give an overview of the area of developmental reading and writing disorders in relation to the acquired dyslexias and dysgraphias, so the terms *developmental dyslexia* and *developmental dysgraphia* are not necessarily limited to the two uses mentioned above in this chapter. Instead, they should be interpreted as referring to *developmental reading and writing disorders* in general.

A neurolinguistic perspective

Looking at developmental dyslexias from a neurolinguistic perspective means that the focus is on treating them in the same way as other neurolinguistic disorders. There is an interest in finding the areas of the brain that are involved in the reading and writing processes and localizing and understanding the functional systems and subprocesses involved. Reading and writing problems are seen as symptoms among other linguistic and nonlinguistic symptoms, rather than as a specific phenomenon. This means that they can be viewed in the light of a complex whole (heredity, environment, and development). There is, however, a major difference between our knowledge of acquired and developmental dyslexias in that acquired dyslexias occur when there is a known neurological disorder, whereas the etiology (cause) of developmental dyslexias is less well known.

Various suggestions have been made concerning the causes of developmental dyslexia. It is known that there is a hereditary factor: developmental dyslexia tends to run in the family. Anatomically, for example, a lack of asymmetry between the left and right hemispheres in the area called the planum temporale, which is associated with Wernicke's area and with auditory phonological processing, has been found in subjects with developmental dyslexia. It has also been suggested that the maturation of the brain has been arrested or delayed in certain critical areas, leading to abnormalities in the cell structures of certain layers.

From a neuropsychological point of view, some theories try to find one cognitive factor underlying developmental dyslexia that is critical for reading in particular. Other theories suggest that there is a more general causal factor, which might also affect other kinds of learning (e.g., visuospatial ability, eye movements, iconic memory, or general language disorder). We might hypothesize that there are many different cognitive disorders, that is, several different types of dyslexias, which may be distinct or variable depending on the relations between different cognitive components. The latter alternative bears the different reading strategies and ways of compensating for reading problems in mind. It is also reminiscent of the different forms of acquired dyslexias.

It is possible that the cognitive basis for dyslexia cannot be specific, since reading is an acquired, rather than an "innate" behavior. But the question of whether there is one more general underlying factor or several different ones is still important. There are differences between reading disorders in different individuals. These differences can be explained with reference to their relation to other cognitive problems, such as phoneme discrimination, object naming, etc. Alternatively, they might also be explained with reference to different subcomponents of the reading process (as with acquired dyslexias). It is claimed, however, that one should be cautious in applying models of acquired dyslexias in this context, since developmental dyslexias tend to be associated with broader cognitive disorders. Theories of the normal development of reading have to be considered and may be more relevant than models of word recognition.

Developmental dyslexias and dysgraphias

Despite what was said above, we find forms of developmental dyslexia that seem to correspond to those of acquired dyslexia.

Developmental surface dyslexia is characterized by the use of grapheme–phoneme conversion, good reading of regular words, and regularization in the reading of irregular words. Persons with surface dyslexia seem to have problems establishing and keeping representations in their visual input lexicon. They can be compared to younger children learning to read in the what has been called the "Phoenician" way, that is, sound-by-sound. Another term that has been used for the same phenomenon is *dyseidetic* or *visual dyslexia*.

Developmental phonological dyslexia is characterized by the use of whole word reading, which is not perfect, since visual errors occur. Grapheme–phoneme conversion is not used and nonwords and new words cannot be read. Nonwords (as well as real words) are often read as similar-looking real words; for example, *cheery* becomes *cherry*. The term *dysphonetic* is sometimes used for this group. Their reading resembles that of younger children who learn to read by the so-called "Chinese" method, or whole word strategy.

Developmental deep dyslexia is perhaps not as common in children as the two main types described above, but it does occur, showing reading characteristics similar to those of developmental and acquired phonological dyslexia with added symptoms of acquired deep dyslexia.

In general, it can be said that there is a continuum between developmental phonological and surface dyslexia and that most dyslexic children show mixed strategies and profiles, somewhere in between the two extremes.

As with acquired dysgraphia, types of developmental dysgraphia that correspond to the above-mentioned types of developmental dyslexia also occur.

Yet another developmental reading disorder that should be mentioned is *hyperlexia*, a precocious ability to read words combined with an abnormal fascination with reading, which involves a disturbance of the semantic system (cf. acquired asemantic reading). Hyperlexic children are often developmentally handicapped. They read aloud but without any reading comprehension.

In discussions of developmental dyslexia, subjects have sometimes been divided into auditory and visual dyslexia groups, with the majority showing auditory-phonological problems while a minority group has mainly visual problems. However, it has been claimed that these groups should be treated as one, which is characterized by internal variations in auditory and, to some extent, visual problems (Bryant & Bradley, 1985).

Like acquired dyslexias, developmental dyslexias are also divided into classes affecting more central versus more peripheral orthographic processes.

Summary

In summary, we can say that acquired dyslexias in adults and in children are among the topics traditionally studied in neurolinguistics, with a focus on reading and specifically on the process of single word reading and reading aloud. These studies have resulted in the classification of the different types of dyslexias and dysgraphias described in this chapter, mainly surface, phonological, and deep dyslexia, and their relationship to models of reading and writing. Similar types of dyslexia and dysgraphia seem to be found in children with developmental reading and writing disorders. The term *developmental dyslexia*, used either in the sense of a discrepancy between other cognitive abilities and reading and writing abilities or in the sense of a disturbance of phonological ability or awareness, was discussed. Different distinctions made in classifying dyslexias are acquired versus developmental, central versus peripheral, and auditory versus visual.

Further reading

The book by Ellis gives a more extensive presentation of models and analysis of acquired disorders of reading and writing and the book edited by Hulme and Snowling contains readings on developmental dyslexia. The two papers by Martin and Seymour provide shorter up-to-date overviews of acquired and developmental disorders.

Ellis, A. (1984). *Reading, writing and dyslexia: A cognitive analysis*. London: Lawrence Erlbaum Associates.

Hulme, C., & Snowling, M. (Eds.) (1994). *Reading development and dyslexia*. London: Whurr Publishers.

Martin, N. (1998). Recovery and treatment of acquired reading and spelling disorders. In B. Stemmer & H. Whitaker (Eds.), *Handbook of neurolinguistics* (pp. 560–573). San Diego: Academic Press.

Seymour, P. (1998). Neurolinguistic issues in the treatment of childhood literacy disorders. In B. Stemmer & H. Whitaker (Eds.), *Handbook of neurolinguistics* (pp. 574–585). San Diego: Academic Press.

Assignments

1. Which type of acquired dyslexia would cause each of the following reading errors?
   a. *in* read as *if*
   b. *dog* read as *cap*
   c. *train* read as *bus*

2. Trace the route of reading in deep dyslexia in the model given in this chapter. Where might the various kinds of problems be located, other than grapheme–phoneme conversion?

3. Discuss how (a) phonological dyslexia and (b) surface dyslexia would affect a child's acquisition of reading.

4. What strategies might you use in your everyday reading to overcome or compensate for your problems if you had (a) surface dyslexia or (b) phonological dyslexia?

5. Here are some examples of tasks that are used in measuring linguistic ability as a prerequisite for reading. What abilities do they test and why are these abilities important for reading?

   a. Tell me a word that rhymes with *hot*?
   b. If you take away the first sound of the word *cow*, what is left of the word?
   c. If you reverse the two parts of the word *snowball*, what do you get?
   d. Tell me a word that begins with the same sound that the word *cat* ends with.

6. Return to question 4 about reading processes in the assignments for Chapter 1 and try to give a more specific answer than you did when you first answered it.

Chapter 9

Neurolinguistic aspects of bilingualism

> **In this chapter:**
>
> - *Bilingualism and neurolinguistic questions*
> - *Recovery patterns in bilingual aphasia*
> - *Neurolinguistic questions and hypotheses*

Bilingualism and neurolinguistic questions

If a person knows more than one language, does this affect the way language is processed by that person's brain? How are the different languages kept apart? Do they interfere with each other? These and related questions make bilingualism an interesting subject for neurolinguists to study.

Bilingualism

Bilingualism has given rise to many questions and hypotheses related to brain function. In this chapter, we will briefly review the main questions and findings.

What does *bilingual* mean? We will adopt a simple definition: a bilingual person is someone who knows two languages and is able to keep them apart. This definition does not go further into the questions of what a language is and what it means to know a language. The answer to the first question is, of course, mainly a political question, related to divisions into nations, regions, etc. The second question has attracted some attention and led to the suggestion that there are different subtypes of bilingualism. Such divisions are based on factors such as: (a) age of acquisition of the second language (L2): early L2, late L2, and adult L2; and (b) the fluency or mastery of the two languages: balanced or dominant for one language.

Different types of bilingualism have been proposed. Some of the best-known are the following:

1. **Compound bilingualism**
   The first language (L1) and L2 are learned concurrently before the age of six; often, each language is spoken by one of the person's parents.

2. **Coordinated bilingualism**
   L2 is learned before puberty in the home or some other environment.

3. **Subordinated bilingualism**
   One language, L1, is dominant and L2 is used for mediation; that is, the bilingual person thinks in L1 and then translates into L2.

There is a wide range of possibilities when it comes to how proficient a bilingual individual is in the two different languages and how he/she uses them. But it is probably true that most bilingual individuals are not exactly "balanced"; in other words, they do not know exactly the same things in both languages and they do not use them for exactly the same purposes. It is more common for the two languages to complement each other in the life of a bilingual person; for example, one language may be used at home and another at school or at work. In bilingual societies or situations where most or all of the participants are bilingual, it is also common to code-switch between the languages, that is, to combine both languages in a single utterance.

We will first examine aphasia and bilingualism and then turn to some of the main neurolinguistic questions and hypotheses concerning this topic and the current state of the art.

Recovery patterns in bilingual aphasia

One source of information for neurolinguists interested in bilingualism is the recovery of the different languages by bilingual persons with aphasia. Let us therefore take a closer look at the different recovery patterns found in bilingual aphasia

Parallel recovery of the different languages is by far the most common pattern (see Figure 9.1). Paradis (1977) found that parallel recovery was described in 40% of the case histories he reviewed and points out that the proportion is probably higher than this, since case histories tend to focus on unusual cases.

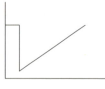   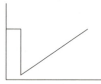

Language A   Language B

Figure 9.1. Parallel recovery

Dissociated recovery is, however, not uncommon and it can show different patterns. There are a number of suggested explanations for dissociated recovery. Pitres first described dissociated recovery in 1895 and *Pitres's law* claims that the *most familiar language* is less impaired and recovers first. *Ribot's law*, on the other hand, claims that *L1* is less impaired and recovers first. Then there is *Minkowski's law,* which claims that the *language with the strongest emotional association* is less impaired and recovers first. Other suggested formulations are that the *more automated or basic language* recovers first. Research has shown, however, that in about 30% of all cases, L2 recovers better than L1.

It has also been hypothesized that different languages are located in different areas of the brain; for example, it has been claimed that the right hemisphere is more involved in the use of L2, as we will see later in this chapter.

Some patterns of dissociated recovery are described below.

Selective recovery is recovery of only one of the languages (Figure 9.2).

Language A   Language B

Figure 9.2. Selective recovery

Differential recovery means that the two languages are not recovered to the same extent (Figure 9.3).

Language A   Language B

Figure 9.3. Differential recovery (L1 and L2 not recovered to the same extent)

Successive recovery means that the two languages are not recovered at the same time, but the recovery of one follows that of the other (Figure 9.4).

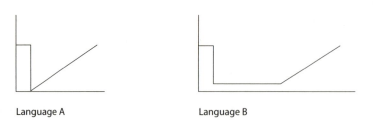

Language A   Language B

Figure 9.4. Successive recovery (L1 and L2 not recovered at the same time)

Alternating antagonism is when only one language recovers or is available at a time, seemingly blocking the other language, and the language that is available for use changes from time to time (see Figure 9.5).

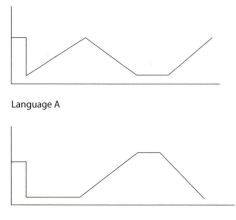

Language A

Language B

Figure 9.5. Alternating antagonism

Mixed recovery involves inappropriate and unrestricted blending of the languages.

The most common kind of dissociated recovery is when L1 recovers better than L2. However, it also seems to be true that the most used language recovers better than less used languages in most cases. Although parallel recovery is the most common situation, the patterns of dissociated recovery have attracted a lot of attention and are quite often found in clinical practice.

Neurolinguistic questions and hypotheses

Neurolinguistic questions related to bilingualism concern which brain structures are involved in language processing by bilinguals and how they are involved. Similarities and differences in comparison with language processing by monolinguals are explored. L1 and L2 processing are compared. Specifically bilingual tasks such as translation are studied. Aphasia in bilinguals and in particular the recovery patterns of aphasic bilinguals have attracted considerable attention, as we have seen above, and attempts have been made to adapt models of language processing to bilingualism.

There have been many hypotheses about how different languages are organized in the brain:

1. One hypothesis claims that all languages are localized in the same areas (Freud, 1891; Minkowski, 1963; Pitres, 1885/1983).
2. The opposite hypothesis claims that different languages are localized in separate areas (Scoresby-Jackson, 1867), for example, that L1 resides in Broca's area and other languages spread forward from there.
3. A third hypothesis suggests that bilinguals develop centers for functions related to bilingualism, such as selection of a language, switching between languages, and translation (Pötzl, 1930). One suggested area for such functions is the supramarginal gyrus in the left hemisphere. This view was criticized by Jakobson (1941) and by Paradis (2004), both of whom claim that these abilities are not really any different from monolingual speakers' ability to handle different *registers* (variants of language used in different situations).
4. A fourth hypothesis claims that all languages are localized in the same areas but have separate neural circuits involving separate nerve cells (e.g., Minkowski, 1963). These nerve cells are located partly in the same area and partly in specific areas. Thus, this hypothesis is a mixture of the previous alternatives, involving a functional explanation of aphasia in bilingualism. It is related to factors such as the role of implicit and explicit memory for the different languages (Fabbro, 2001a, b). This view finds some support in cortical activation studies using fMRI.

The question of the lateralization of language abilities and bilingualism has also attracted some attention, since Albert and Obler wrote *The bilingual brain* in 1978. One hypothesis is that the right hemisphere is more involved in L2 processing than it is in L1 processing. Although L2 processing evokes greater activation of the right hemisphere in PET and fMRI studies (Dehaene et al., 1997), it is claimed that this is probably not the result of L2 having more RH "representation" than L1 (Paradis, 1998). Rather, it is the result of the greater role that pragmatic factors play in compensating for the speaker's poorer proficiency in the use of L2.

Paradis's claim is also in line with the complementary use of the two languages reported above. In a specific test or situation, one language would in many cases be more natural and the other one would require more effort and pragmatic skills to compensate for weaknesses.

There are also different psycho- and neurolinguistic models for interpreting experimental findings in studies of bilingual speakers. One such model is the *Activation Threshold Hypothesis* (Green, 1986, 1998), which claims that the different languages may be activated to different degrees, thereby taking up or requiring more or less of the brain's capacity for processing. A language can be active and ready for use, active but suppressed, or dormant and inactive. Since both activation and suppression of a language require some effort, the resources required for these purposes can be disturbed by neurological illness. This unsettles the balance between activated and suppressed languages.

Another model is the *Competition Model* (formulated by McWhinney and Bates; see, for example, Bates & Wulfeck, 1989; Bates, Wulfeck, & McWhinney, 1991), which claims, in short, that the two languages compete for processing resources and the one that is most activated, for different reasons, wins. (This is on top of the competition that is always present between different alternatives in normal language processing.) When brain damage occurs, it can affect the balance between the state of readiness for activation of each of the languages. It can also affect what these researchers call *cue validity* and *cue cost*. This means how central a linguistic feature or cue, such as word order or noun and verb inflection, is in a language and how much processing capacity it requires. Cue validity and cue cost vary between languages and, for bilingual speakers, also vary depending on their individual history of learning and present proficiency in and use of the two languages.

All this adds up to the realization that bilingualism is a complex phenomenon. Investigating language proficiency in bilinguals with brain damage should be done with some caution and it is especially important to consider the following questions:

1. How comparable are the investigations of the two languages?
2. Are the tests that are used comparable?
3. Have typological considerations, such as potential processing load and differences in cue validity and cue cost, been considered in constructing the tasks?
4. Have cultural, social, and individual factors that might affect the use of the two languages been considered in interpreting the results?

Most of the phenomena reported in the literature, such as dissociated patterns of recovery, language mixing, etc., seem to be possible to explain in terms of disturbances of activation and inhibition patterns, as stated by Paradis, Green, and McWhinney and Bates, in combination with social, cultural, and individual factors affecting activation.

Further reading

Neurolinguistic aspects of bi or multilingualism have only been studied extensively by a few researchers. The references given below are the most important books in this area.

Fabbro, F. (1999). *Neurolinguistics of bilingualism*. Hove: Psychology Press.
Paradis, M. (2004). *A neurolinguistic theory of bilingualism*. Amsterdam: John Benjamins.

Assignments

Try to explain the following cases, using the theories and descriptions of recovery patterns presented in this chapter:

1. A is a 35-year-old Danish sailor, who has been working on ships traveling between many parts of the world. After a stroke, he fluctuates between Danish, English, Spanish, and German and mixes all four languages.

2. B is a retired German professor of Sanskrit. In the acute stage after a stroke, he is diagnosed as having Wernicke's aphasia. When he is asked to read aloud, he utters only Sanskrit or Sanskrit-like words.

3. C was born in Italy and moved to the United States when he was 12 years old. At age 55, he suffers from a stroke and, at first, speaks only Italian (which he has not used since he was a child). He receives language therapy in English and gradually recovers most of his English. Then, however, he can no longer speak Italian.

Chapter 10

On the evolution and development of the brain, communication, and language

> **In this chapter:**
> - *Growing brains, other factors, and human language*
> - *The biological hypothesis versus the social construct hypothesis*
> - *Communication by other primates*
> - *Evolution-based theories in neurolinguistics and acquired language disorders*
> - *Neurolinguistic perspectives on developmental language disorders in children*

Growing brains, other factors, and human language

What is human language and how did we come to develop it? How did our brains evolve and how did this evolution interact with the evolution of the rest of our bodies, our ways of using our arms and legs and our speech organs, our eating habits, and our ways of living? These are intriguing questions that have yet to be answered.

There are different views of how human linguistic communication developed. We can look at the relation between the evolution of the brain and of language by studying the *phylogenetic* development of behavior (especially communication and cognition) and of brain size and structures and areas within the brain. This means looking at how these factors developed in different species during evolution. We can also compare this process with the *ontogenetic* development of the same factors, that is, how they develop in children.

Bigger brains (and bodies)? Brain size and encephalization quotient

The growth in the size of the human brain is one possible explanation of our increased cognitive and linguistic ability. The human brain is large, but some animals, notably elephants, dolphins, and whales, have even larger brains. But we also have to consider the relation of brain size to body size. The measurement used to compare brain (cranial) size in different species is the encephalization quotient (EQ) (Jerison, 1973), which is a relative measure, relating brain size to body size. Old-world monkeys and apes have an EQ of 2.3 to 2.7, leaf-eating colobus monkeys and gorillas have an EQ of around 1.6, and our hypothetical common ancestor is assumed to have had an EQ of 2.5, which is the same as a modern chimpanzee. Modern humans have an EQ of 28.8, according to Stephan (1972). But neither absolute nor relative brain size is a reliable indicator of behavior.

Better speech organs?

Another factor that has been assumed to be critical for human speech is the movement of the larynx further down the throat, which is only present in humans, not for example, in chimpanzees or even in small babies. The ability to speak is thus typically human and might have led to the progress of more advanced human linguistic and cognitive abilities. This theory has been promoted by Philip Lieberman, for example, in his book *Eve spoke* from 1998. Other researchers however, do not give this particular factor as much credit. For example, Noble and Davidson (1996) claim that although the upper airways are used for speech, just as the lower extremities are used for walking, speaking is primarily a way of acting with intention; thus, it is basically cognitive and cannot be separated from thinking. The so called "mother theory of speech perception" is, however, supported by findings related to mirror neurons (see Chapter 10).

Different areas of the brain?

Researchers have been looking for areas of the human brain that differ from those of, for example, the chimpanzee brain. One candidate for such a difference is the asymmetry between the left and right hemispheres. Since the prevalent view is that the left hemisphere is the dominant locus of language in humans, asymmetries between the two hemispheres are interesting. This assumes that specialized structures develop *before* the actual functions that make use of them. Brain asymmetry is, however, quite widespread among other species as well; it is present in both chickens and frogs, for example. So the mere existence of asymmetry is not enough to explain human language. Could it then be explained by the asymmetry of specific areas of the brain? In humans, the right hemisphere extends further forward, while the left hemisphere extends further back, but this is also true of chimpanzees and gorillas (not orangutans, however); possibly a common ancestor had this kind of asymmetry. Humans and other hominids (as evidenced by fossils) have a broader left posterior hemisphere and this could be linked to handedness. Both chimpanzees and gorillas have asymmetrical brains, but they do not seem to have handedness; they use their right and left hands (and feet) equally well. A candidate for a specific area that may be important for language (especially speech comprehension) is the *planum temporale* (an area adjacent to the primary auditory center). As we have already seen, however, localization of language functions is far from simple.

Communication with symbols that stand for something else

If we concentrate on behavior, humans are unique in communicating with symbols (i.e., signs that are arbitrary and conventionalized and stand for things in the world, without resembling or being close to them). One possible critical factor for language is the discovery of *supposition* (in a specific, philosophical sense, i.e., that something can stand for something else). Not only most speech and writing but also symbolic body communication is linguistic in this sense (i.e., conventionalized (Kendon, 1993)), unlike natural, symptom-based body language. Many researchers consider the discovery of symbolic supposition and its usefulness to be the most critical factor in the development of human language.

The biological hypothesis versus the social construct hypothesis

How do individual humans discover supposition and come to use language? According to Noble and Davidson (1996), we learn to be "minded" in a linguistic society, through our interaction with tutors and as a result of a long and fairly continuous evolutionary process. A radically different view is that of Chomsky (1986), who claims that we have an innate mental language organ that matures according to its own program for development, and that this does require exposure to language. These two different views, sometimes referred to as the "social construct story" and the "biological innateness story" of the origins of human language and how it develops, are in competition today. But there are also several intermediate positions.

In the following sections, we will look at some of the theories and descriptions of how human brains and language developed.

The innate linguistic competence hypothesis

The biological innateness view has been presented in different forms, for example, in Steven Pinker's writings such as *The language instinct* (1994). Another fairly recent contribution is Steve Mithen's book *The prehistory of mind* (1996). Linguistic competence is seen as an abstract system that is innate in the human mind. Linguistic competence is the main object of study and is seen as distinct from any given linguistic performance. Language is therefore seen as an abstract entity. According to proponents of the social construct hypothesis, this is an almost mystical view of language as standing outside evolution; it also constitutes a reification of a behavior, that is, making behavior into an abstract entity. Some researchers (Bickerton, 1990; Burling, 1993) propose that a sudden mutation may explain the apparent "gap" between the call systems of primates and human language. Others (e.g., Pinker & Bloom, 1990) suggest that there is a structure only present in humans, which evolution has acted on.

Mithen's description of how cognitive functions evolved in the human brain is a psychological model, which he calls "The mind as a cathedral"; in other words, he thinks of a central "nave" which extends out into surrounding "chapels." The nave starts out containing only general intelligence in Phase 1. In Phase 2, multiple chapels are added around the nave, representing "technical," "linguistic," "social," and "natural history" intelligence, all of which are specialized. In this phase, it is unclear how language is related to other cognitive domains and also whether and how the different domains are connected to each other or to general intelligence. Phase 3 represents increased "cognitive fluidity," which implies open connections between the "nave" and the different "chapels." An alternative view of Phase 3 posits a "superchapel" of meta-representation connected to all of the types of intelligence. This model applies to our hunting and gathering ancestors; other types of intelligence can develop if needed.

Mithen describes a course of evolution, which starts out about 100 thousand years ago. Cognitive flexibility and general and social intelligence increase until about 10 thousand years ago. From apes and australopithecines, via *Homo habilis* and *Homo erectus*, we encounter an increase in modularization (compartmentalization) and the addition of technical and natural history intelligence. This leads us, for example, to the Neanderthals and to a new turn in the development process a few hundred thousand years ago. At this point, there is a move toward increasing fluidity, which emerges in *Homo sapiens sapiens*, our own species, some 10 thousand years ago. (*Homo sapiens sapiens* is thought to have arrived on the scene around 100 or 150 thousand years ago.) Social history intelligence plays an important role in this development; it "invades" other "chapels" and language plays an important part in this process in the later stages of evolution.

The social construct view and evolutionary approaches

The social construct view focuses on linguistic communication as a form of behavior. According to this view, as represented by Noble and Davidson (1996), the brain grew gradually for 2.5 million years, while behavior did not really change very much. The cause of the growth was partly changes in body size, partly a refinement of the function of and motor control over the frontal (or "upper") extremities (i.e., the arms). An important change was bipedalism (walking on two legs), which started about 3.5 million years ago. This made it easier to transport objects and break stones, and this in turn led to improvements in throwing stones. Aiming and pointing intentionally seem to be unique to humans. There may have been a development from throwing to pointing to iconic gestures and then to language (cf. Burling, 1993).

An evolutionary approach to the origin of mind claims that "mindedness" in human terms cannot be separated from the use of language. According to this view, gestures and pictures have a central function in the type of behavior that today is called linguistic. Linguistic behavior is communication using "symbols" (something that represents something else by convention, in Noble and Davidson's definition). Language and thought are not separate. To speak is to pursue an intention. This idea dates back to, for example, de Saussure, Sapir, Wittgenstein, Vygotsky, and Mead. Wittgenstein's view, for example, was that mindedness can only be understood as it is observed in terms of behavior, that the mind is not "private" and that speaking and thinking are linked. This view implies that children learn to be minded through interaction in society; only the ability to learn to be minded is innate. We will return to the concept of "mindedness" and its link to language in discussing communication and language in other primates.

More recent studies of animal (especially bonobo) communication claim that the evolution of linguistic communication was probably fairly continuous and that there was no sudden "leap" to language; rather, it is our inability to understand the communication systems of other primates that led to the assumption of a leap (Savage-Rumbaugh & Lewin, 1994).

Frontal lobe development and "displacement" in the brain

Terence Deacon, in his book *The symbolic species* (1997), compares the human cerebral cortical regional areas to those of a "typical" ape brain with a simulated brain size of a human. He finds that the most important difference is that the prefrontal areas are very much more dominant in the human. He has also traced the development of brain weight in relation to to body weight over the course of evolution and found that the increased human encephalization diverges from that of other mammals. (For example, it makes it necessary to give birth earlier in the development of our offspring, so that human babies are less autonomous than the young of many other species.) The pre-frontal areas control the rest of the brain's activity and this control is very extensive in humans, according to Deacon. Another related aspect of our brain evolution is that over time competing language-related functions have "displaced" each other so that they are now in the cortex of opposite hemispheres; for example, syntax is lateralized in the left hemisphere and prosody in the right.

Communication by other primates

Animals with large brains and supposedly well-developed intelligence, such as whales, dolphins, and above all the primates that are closest to humans in evolutionary terms, such as orangutans and chimpanzees and especially bonobos, are those that have at-tracted most interest from researchers.

So what can we actually learn from studying communication and language-like behavior in other species? Two different approaches have been used in studying chim-panzees and bonobos in particular.

One is the study of the life and communication of primates in their natural setting. Questions about how they live — in trees or on the ground, in large or small groups, as nomads or in one area — are matched with questions about their communication (Goodall, 1986). These might concern how many and what types of distinct "calls" they make; whether these calls are discrete, continuous, or both; and whether there are dif-ferences between male and female communication. We can see a development when we compare more primitive apes to more highly developed primates, for example, orangutans versus chimpanzees, where the lifestyle of the latter seems more human-like in many ways and their communication is more diverse and complex.

The other approach is to raise, for example, bonobos in a human environment including linguistic communication in order to see how much linguistic communi-cation they can pick up or be taught. This approach has been criticized because of its lower ecological validity, but it has also raised important questions about what constitutes language and linguistic communication. The results are much debated and are the focus of the clash between the biological and social construct views (i.e., those who see language as a biologically specific human phenomenon versus those who see it as a result of more gradual evolution). Much of the classical data came from chimpanzees using signed communication; for example, a chimpanzee called Washoe, who was raised by Alan and Beatrice Gardner as a child in their family and taught to sign (Gardner, Gardner, & van Cantfort, 1989) (see also Premack & Wood-ruff, 1978; Premack & Premack, 1983; Premack, 1986). The chimpanzees acquired a number of hand signs, which they used for communication. At the time, the discus-sion of syntactic structure as a central criterion for language raised the question of whether the chimpanzees' signs were simply being produced one after another or actually had syntactic structure, something that was hard to determine, since the chimps used mainly "content word" signs, that is, signs for persons, things, events, and properties. Another chimpanzee, called Lana (Rumbaugh, 1977), was subjected to a more strictly controlled experiment. She was kept in a cage and was able to communicate with her keeper by pressing buttons with signs painted on them. These signs were clearly arbitrary in relation to their meaning (i.e., they had no similarity to what they referred to). In other words, Lana had to press a series of symbols to communicate. Whether her symbol sequences were syntactic or not was, however, also a matter for debate.

The most extensive studies of this type are the ongoing bonobo studies by Sue Savage-Rumbaugh and her coworkers. The best-known bonobo is Kanzi, who has demonstrated many abilities that were generally thought to be specific to humans. Kanzi, his sister Panbanisha, and Panbanisha's son Nyota are the most linguistically accomplished animals studied so far. So what are Kanzi, Panbanisha and Nyota able to do in terms of linguistic communication and the prerequisites for such communication? They seem to comprehend spoken English with some syntactic complexity. They communicate with humans using a keyboard with symbols. Panbanisha has also used drawings of symbols for communication. Kanzi has been reported to produce sounds with some similarity to words in order to communicate. The bonobos have also demonstrated the ability to communicate about events taking place other than "here and now" and they have passed some tests of theory of mind (ToM). In other words, they have demonstrated some ability to understand that others have minds and that their knowledge is not necessarily the same as your own. This ability is critical for important pragmatic aspects of linguistic communication.

The debate about whether the evolution of language featured a sudden leap or continuous development, which is closely linked to the debate about the linguistic abilities of bonobos, remains extremely active. Some of the suggested "critical" factors in language and linguistic communication include the discovery that one thing can "stand for" another in the first place and knowing how this can change dynamically, syntax of a certain complexity, semantics and cognitive schemas, interpersonal construction of joint social perception, "theory of mind," speech (especially tonal patterns), and writing. Bonobos have shown surprising abilities in most of these areas. However, whether there is one critical criterion or deciding factor and, if so, what it might be, are still questions for debate.

One thing, though, does seem to be undisputed: wild primates do not learn the same kind of things as those raised by humans and they do not seem to have moved from nonsymbolic to symbolic communication. Although they show aspects of a capacity for linguistic behavior, their interactive behavior (as we understand it at present) does not seem to require much linguistic or symbolic communication.

Evolution-based theories in neurolinguistics and acquired language disorders

As we have seen above, evolutionary theories emphasize similarities and continuity in development, rather than seeing language as a very specific, modular brain function that is radically different from other cognitive abilities. The principle is that the evolution of abilities that enhance the chance of survival can be tracked and that language is one of these abilities. Communication and language-related abilities in animals such as birds, apes, primates, whales, and dolphins are of interest in studying the prerequisites for language and the similarities and differences between animal communication and human communication. These theories also explain language development in children and acquired language disorders in adults with reference to the parallel evolution and development of brain structures and brain functions and the influence of this development on how language and communication are organized in the human brain.

One of the frameworks for relating brain structures and language functions that developed in the 19th century is the notion of evolution-based or hierarchical theories, introduced by Jackson and von Monakow (see Chapter 2). Jackson described aphasia as a regression, in which automatic language was still available, while propositional language was disturbed. Von Monakow also emphasized the time dimension in language processing and elaborated on its importance. This is a feature that still exists in present-day psycho- and neurolinguistic modeling of language disorders.

Some of the main tenets of this type of framework are:

- that brain structures and cognitive and linguistic functions evolved in parallel;
- that there are parallels between the (phylogenetic) evolution of the species and the (ontogenetic) development of children;
- that acquired language disorders reflect a regression, with increased dependence on evolutionarily older parts of the brain, which the more recently developed cortical structures can no longer inhibit as strongly as usual.

The best-developed present-day theory on this basis perhaps is Jason Brown's microgenetic theory, which originated in the 1970s and has been further developed since then (Brown, 1977, 1980, 1988, 1991). Brown points out parallels not only between phylogenetic and ontogenetic development but also between both these processes and microgenetic development. Microgenesis is the process by which any action, for example, an utterance is produced. According to Brown, every action passes through all the stages of phylogenetic and ontogenetic development, "from the depth to the surface" of the brain. In line with earlier theories, Brown emphasizes the temporal aspect of action, explaining regression as positive and/or negative symptoms. The positive symptoms reflect the more basic level of function that breaks through, while the negative symptoms reflect the lack of control and inhibition on the part of the superimposed levels that are damaged. In Brown's model, structural (neurological) levels are parallel to functional (psychological) levels.

Brown's microgenetic theory is often illustrated with the image of a wave of activity from lower to higher levels of the brain. Another metaphor that is often used to visualize this type of theory is "the brain as an onion" with different superimposed layers.

Brown's structural and functional model of the brain (from 1977) contains four evolutionary levels (Table 10.1): the subcortical *sensorimotor*, the limbic *presentation*, the neocortical *representation*, and the asymmetric neocortical *symbolic* levels.

Table 10.1. Levels in Brown's evolution-based model of brain structure

Level	Sensorimotor	Presentation	Representation	Symbolic
Brain structure	subcortical	limbic	neocortical	asymmetric neocortical
Species	reptile phylogenetic	"older" mammals phylogenetic	"younger" mammals phylogenetic	human ontogenetic

For each level, Brown sets out the related aspects of feeling, thought, perception, and language. Although his terminology can be hard to understand in detail, the model gives a unified picture of language and its relationship to other functions. The model is therefore included in summarized form in Table 10.2, as "food for thought" and as an example of how an evolution-based theory can be described.

Table 10.2. Feeling, thought, perception, and language in Brown's model

Level	Sensorimotor	Presentation	Representation	Symbolic
Feeling	instinct	worry, fear, defense	feelings	Self-awareness
Thought	Body-centered, reflex, instinct, automaticity	semantic operations, image-selection, more distal activity, certain S→R (stimulus-response) delay, paralogic (pre-categorical) thinking	separates object-self, goal direction, certain abstraction, spatial and categorical thinking, generalization, exteriorization	language, voluntariness, "inner space" (introspection, awareness)
Perception	vague pre-object	image	image presentation	symbol, language-related
Language		semantic category	nominal category	phonemic category

Brown also describes disturbances that arise from damage to the different levels (Table 10.3).

There is an anterior and a posterior progression of levels. The *anterior* progression of levels of *speech act differentiation* is:

Table 10.3. Disorders in Brown's model

Level	Sensorimotor	Presentation	Representation	Symbolic
Disorder of thought		psychotic thinking (affect, illusion)	dementia (disorientation, amnesia)	linguistic syndromes
Disorder of perception	disintegration of visuospatial ability and mobility	hallucinations	agnosia	agnosia for complex stimuli
Posterior aphasia		semantic aphasia, semantic paraphasia, semantic jargon "paralogia" (neologistic paraphasia) Wernicke's aphasia	anomia. circumlocution, verbal paraphasia (correct category) anomic aphasia	conduction aphasia (phonematic), phonematic paraphasia
Anterior aphasia		akinetic mutism → transcortical motor aphasia	agrammatism	Broca's aphasia, phonematic-articulatory (anarthria)

motor envelope → differentiation of the speech act (transcortical motor aphasia) → differentiation of global syntactic units (agrammatism) → phonological realization (Broca's aphasia).

The *posterior* progression of *levels of paraphasias* is the following:

asemantic (Wernicke's aphasia/semantic jargon) → associative/categorical/evocative (nominal or anomic aphasia) → phonological (conduction aphasia).

This type of model emphasizes the activating role of the brain stem and subcortical systems, such as the limbic system, which have to do with basic instincts and emotions, versus the more refining, controlling, and inhibiting role of the cortex.

A model like Brown's can be used for many purposes in psycho- and neurolinguistics. In the study of language breakdown, a symptom is defined as the level of disorganization that breaks through. The cognitive structure is "degraded" and the syndrome that is observed is the level of performance that is achieved; in other words, the sum of the loss of functions and pressure from lower levels of the brain is one active level. This is thus a regression hypothesis of language disorders, where the regression is microgenetic: it relates to the unfolding of each instance of an action or a process. Brown stated that his four levels are closed stages of development in the encephalization process; he does not make the transition between levels gradual and continuous.

Brown's view on the differentiation of *cortical* areas is that it proceeds from the more general functions of the cortex to the specification of structure and function in modality-specific association areas and then further specification in the sensory and motor cortex.

There are many more refinements of Brown's microgenetic theory that we will not present in this introductory summary. The interested reader is encouraged to study Brown's more recent books, such as *The life of the mind* from 1988 and *Self and process. Brain states and the conscious present* from 1991.

We can see that Brown uses some of the same terminology for different aphasia types as the classical-neoclassical school, but that his main idea is the progression from more basic to more recent and complex levels of the brain in microgenesis. Current findings on the evolution of communication cannot easily be explained by a purely hierarchical model, at present.

Pragmatics, emotion, and language in context

Proponents of the "innateness" and "social construct" hypotheses concerning the evolution of language have radically different views of pragmatics. The main difference is whether pragmatics is seen as a crucial internal aspect of linguistic communication or as something external and nonlinguistic, not to be included in linguistic analysis. From a social construct or evolutionary point of view, the development of language is intertwined with that of other aspects of cognition. Emotional communication and language use are central driving forces, which determine the meanings and forms of language and communication. This implies a broad view of language with pragmatics as a central component. From a biological innateness perspective, language develops as a separate, modularized ability comprising mainly grammar, and possibly also phonology, whereas other aspects of cognition, emotional communication, and language use are external to this module. Consequently, we have a much more restricted view of what language is, since it excludes pragmatics. We can see that although various aspects of the broader view are included in Brown's model, he still restricts his use of the term "language" to what is also compatible with the biological innateness view. In fact, many researchers are not strong proponents of either one or the other side in this debate, but are looking for some middle way or combination of aspects from both.

Neurolinguistic perspectives on developmental language disorders in children

Developmental language disorders in children have not usually been described in relation to the same frameworks as acquired language disorders in children and adults. It is, however, of considerable interest and importance to try to capture both types of phenomena with the same types of theories. This is especially important if one applies an evolutionary perspective to brain and language. It has traditionally been considered to be "easier" to try to relate brain and language functions in adult brains than in young people's developing brains. Since young brains have considerable plasticity — that is, functions can be transferred from one brain area to another if necessary — and are still developing, one has to be very cautious in ascribing localization of functions to specific brain areas.

For some years, however, explanations in terms of brain dysfunction have been popular in the study of disorders such as *specific (developmental) language impairment (SLI)*, *dyslexia*, and *autism*. This has also led to an increased interest in *acquired language disorders in children*. A few examples can be mentioned: Luria's neuropsychological investigation has been adapted to developmental disorders. Brown's theory and Luria's investigation have also been used for the description of developmental disorders (Sahlén, 1991).

The relationship between acquired and developmental language disorders has been explored in a number of studies. One good example is a paper by Snow and Swisher from 1996, which presents neurobehavioral analogies between syndromes of acquired and developmental language impairments. This study uses traditional accounts of acquired language disorders to construct hypotheses about specific language impairment. By using an analogy, Snow and Swisher assume that there are two main types of SLI with different neuroanatomical bases. Earlier investigations had proposed a bilateral brain substrate for SLI in general, but Snow and Swisher propose a bilateral impairment only for the hypothetical semantic-pragmatic type of SLI, while they posit a unilateral left-hemisphere impairment for the hypothetical phonological-syntactic type of SLI. By using a number of parameters to describe aphasia in adults, aphasia in children, and SLI, they make a comparison that is summarized in Table 10.4 below. The factors mild versus severe, fluent versus nonfluent, persistent versus transient, bilateral versus unilateral, anterior versus posterior, and phonological-syntactic versus semantic-pragmatic have all been used in describing similarities and differences between these disorders. Snow and Swisher combine these factors in making the hypothesis summarized in Table 10.4. The developmental and acquired child-onset language disorders are described in the same way, in terms of brain substrates, bilateral for the fluent and unilateral for the nonfluent syndromes. The adult-onset language disorders, on the other hand, are related to another division of substrates, posterior for the fluent and anterior for the nonfluent syndromes. The age and stage of development, rather than the type of etiology (developmental versus acquired) is therefore hypothesized to be the most important factor.

Table 10.4. A unified theory of child-onset language disorders

	Child-onset language disorders		Adult-onset language disorders	
Syndrome	Nonfluent	Fluent	Nonfluent	Fluent
Substrate	Unilateral	Bilateral	Anterior	Posterior

(Source: Snow & Swisher 1996, p. 465)

Embodiment in communication: The possible role of mirror neurons and alignment

The role of embodiment in communication and its importance for fylogenetic, as well as ontogenetic development and possibly also for microgenesis (i.e. the unfolding of a communicative contribution) and macrogenesis (i.e. conventionalization of communication in society) is attracting increased interest. This interest is, to some extent, caused by hypotheses and findings concerning mirror neurons (cf Arbib, 2005; Gallese & Lakoff, 2005), i.e. neurons that are activated by production as well as perception of, for example, a certain movement of action. Mirror neuron functioning in area F4 for grasping in monkeys (macaques) is well established (Rizzolatti & Arbib, 2005), mirror neurons in humans responding to perceived movements have also been localized (Decety et al. 1997) and auditory mirror neurons have been described (Kohler et al. 2002). Mirror neurons seem to provide a fairly simple mechanism for acting, perceiving, imitating and pantomime, which could be crucial to the development of human communication and language. Mirror neurons in area F4 (and F5) have attracted most attention so far and claims have been made about their role in apraxia and Broca's aphasia, including agrammatism.

Another theory that stresses the role of automatic alignment between two persons as a basis for the evolution, acquisition and processing of language has been proposed by Pickering and Garrod (2004).

Summary

In this chapter we have studied different aspects of the evolution of brain and of language and communication. We have looked at brain size and other anatomical factors in relation to language and we have seen how different hypotheses stress biological innateness or social construction of language. We have also exemplified evolution-based theories in neurolinguistics dealing with acquired as well as developmental language disorders and we have mentioned the possible role of embodiment, mirror neurons and alignment in communication.

Further reading

Arbib, M. A. (2005). From monkey-like action recognition to human language: An evolutionary framework for neurolinguistics. *Brain and Behavioral Sciences* 28(2)(in press).

Brown, J. (1977). *Mind, brain and consciousness*. New York: Academic Press.

Brown, J. (1980). *Language, brain, and the problem of localization*. In D. Caplan (Ed.), *Biological studies of mental processes* (pp. 287–300). Cambridge, MA: MIT Press.

Deacon, T. (1997). *The symbolic species: The coevolution of language and brain*. London: Penguin.

Decety, J., Grèzes, J., Costes, D., Perani, E., Procyk, F., Grassi, M., Jeannerod, F., & Fazio, F. (1997). Brain activity during observation of actions. Influence of action content and subject's strategy. *Brain* 120, 763–1777.

Gallese, V. & Lakoff, G. (2005). The brain's concepts: The role of the sensory-motor system in conceptual knowledge. *Cognitive Neuropsychology, 22* (3/4), 455–479.

Kendon, A. (1993). Human gesture. In K. Gibson & T. Ingold (Eds.), *Tools, language and cognition in human evolution* (pp. 43–62). Cambridge: Cambridge University Press.

Kohler, E., Keysers, C., Umiltà, M. A., Fogassi, L., Gallese, V. & Rizzolatti, G. (2002). Hearing sounds, understanding action: action representation in mirror neurons. *Science* 297, 846–848.

Lieberman, P. (1998). *Eve spoke*. London: W. W. Norton & Company.

Mithen, S. (1996). *The prehistoric mind*. London: Thames & Hudson.

Noble, W., & Davidson, I. (1996). *Human evolution, language and mind*. Cambridge: Cambridge University Press.

Pickering, M., & Garrod, S. (2004). Toward a mechanistic psychology of dialogue. *Behavioral and Brain Sciences*, 27,169–226.

Pinker, S. (1994). *The language instinct: How the mind creates language*. New York: William Morrow.

Rizzolatti, G., & Arbib, M. A. (2005). Language within our grasp. *Trends in Neurosciences* 21, 188–194.

Savage-Rumbaugh, S., Fields, W., & Tagliatela, J. (2001). Language, speech, tools and writing. *Journal of Consciousness Studies, 8*, 273–292.

Savage-Rumbaugh, S., & Lewin, R. (1994). *Kanzi: The ape at the brink of the human mind*. New York: John Wiley.

Assignments

1. Try to design and put into operation a reasonable criterion or set of criteria for ascribing the use of "language" to chimpanzees. What would they have to be able to do and how would you go about finding out if they could do it?

2. Compare the descriptions given of different aphasia types in Brown's model to the corresponding aphasia types in the classical-neoclassical model presented in Chapter 3: With respect to
   a. Wernicke's aphasia, anomic aphasia, and conduction aphasia;
   b. Transcortical motor aphasia, agrammatism, and Broca's aphasia;

   1. Do you find the descriptions compatible? If there are any problems, what are they?

   2. Does Brown's model add or change something in the classical description? If so, what?

   3. What would be the consequence of Snow and Swisher's (1996) hypothesis about fluent and nonfluent disorders in children and adults for the ontogenetic development of the localization of language functions in the brain?

Chapter 11

Multimodality in neurolinguistics

> **In this chapter:**
>
> - *Why is multimodality, including body communication, other gestures, and picture-based communication, important to neurolinguistics?*
> - *Overview of multimodality*
> - *Multimodal communication: Examples of persons who have aphasia or complex communication needs caused by cerebral palsy*
> - *What makes a successful communicator?*
> - *What is multimodal about ordinary face-to-face interaction?*
> - *Restrictions and possibilities including multimodality and communication disorders*
> - *Optimizing multimodal communication for persons with communication disorders and the role of communication aids*

Why is multimodality, including body communication, other gestures and picture-based communication, important to neurolinguistics?

For many persons with language and communication disorders, body communication (BC) seems to play an especially important role in interaction. This chapter discusses some gestures and other body communication in interactions involving persons whose language is severely restricted language due to brain damage. The examples are used as the basis for discussion of what is said, what is shown by body communication and what can be shown by picture-based communication aids in face-to-face interaction. How does multimodality affect, for example, the identification of speech acts, turn-taking, feedback, and sequencing in spoken interaction?

The content and function of communicative contributions in the form of

1. spoken words,
2. spoken words plus gestures and other BC, and
3. simulated "translations" into what can be rendered by a picture-based communication aid

are compared.

The comparisons are then discussed in terms of how to optimize communicative possibilities in different situations, including the use of augmentative and alternative communication (AAC).

Another topic for discussion is how information and communication technology (ICT) tools, such as dialogue systems, can be used by persons with neurolinguistic disorders. In other words, what is the role of multimodality in "accessibility for all"?

Overview of multimodality

Multimodality is important in face-to-face communication for many persons with language and communication disorders. When words fail, gestures, sounds, facial expressions, "acting," etc., can play an important role in managing communication.

This leads us to three questions:

1. How much of ordinary face-to-face communication is managed multimodally and how much is in fact dependent on multimodality.
2. How does the situation regarding multimodal communication differ for persons with communication disorders? We can look at this question from two perspectives: (a) the potential disturbance of certain modalities (speech, gesturing, writing, etc.), and (b) the potential compensatory use of certain modalities, because of a disturbance of others. This means that we can study how the "multimodal space" is distributed between modalities and how changes in this distribution occur and are managed, possibly for purposes of adaptation.
3. How can communication aids for AAC and dialogue systems, which are being used more and more frequently by various public services, best be applied?

If persons with communication disorders are dependent on multimodality in face-to-face communication, how can communication aids best be adapted to this fact and how does this affect the use of communication technologies in society, for example, dialogue systems. The answers to such questions are important in considering the "usability for all" policy, which many public services espouse and which is meant to ensure maximal participation in society by persons with communication disorders.

We will start by considering some examples of persons with aphasia and communication disorders caused by cerebral palsy. We will then turn to the question of what makes a successful communicator and discuss it in relation to different dimensions of communication. These dimensions are then related to the examples of communication disorders, in discussing restrictions on and possibilities for the use of multimodality in communication. The role of multimodality in ordinary face-to-face interaction will be discussed briefly, before we turn to the question of communication aids and dialogue systems.

Multimodal communication: Examples of persons who have aphasia or complex communication needs caused by cerebral palsy

Many persons with aphasia, who have severely restricted speech output and sometimes also apraxia affecting the intentional movement of their arms and hands, are nevertheless intuitively judged to be good communicators because of their spontaneous compensatory use of multimodal communication (Ahlsén, 1985, 1991, 2002, 2003; Feiereysen, 1987, 1991; Lott, 1999; see also Chapter 7 of this book).

Consider the following examples.

Example 1

A person with aphasia is asked what her previous job was. Because of her word-finding problems (severe anomia), she is unable to produce nouns, proper names, and most verbs. In this situation, she points in the direction of her previous workplace, she smiles and utters phrases such as *oh, it was fun*, she looks around the room for a newspaper, when she finds one she points to it, she gets it and opens it to find an advertisement for the shop where she used to be employed.

Example 2

Another person with aphasia is asked by her interlocutor where she was going the other day when they met at the corner of the street. She has fairly severe dysarthria, making her speech hard to understand. In this situation, she "draws" a corner on the table and points into it, thereby providing gestural support for her speech, indicating that she went back inside the house on the corner.

Example 3

A third person with aphasia is asked about his son's occupation. He tries to pronounce the word *theater*, but is unable to say it clearly, because of his literal paraphasias, that is, substitutions of speech sounds. The interlocutor looks slightly puzzled, which leads the aphasic speaker to say *now I him* and then he gets up and moves around making very expressive facial expressions and gestures, impersonating an actor.

The interlocutor of a person with aphasia often also uses multimodal communication, more or less spontaneously, in order to be understood by the aphasic subject, as in example 4.

Example 4
A speech and language therapist asks a person with aphasia about the age of her children by saying are they older than ten, then clarifies, when asked what she said, by changing the word *older* to *bigger,* emphasizing it heavily, and showing the height of a ten-year-old with her hand (Ahlsén, 1993).

Severe speech and motor impairment may prevent children with cerebral palsy both from pronouncing words clearly and from pointing and making other gestures or movements. Adding different channels of communication may be necessary in order to express a wish, as in example 5.

Example 5
A six-year-old girl with severe cerebral palsy is having a meal. She is spoon-fed by her caregiver and the interaction is focused on eating. Still, she manages to initiate another topic (a film) by directing her caregiver's attention to a videotape on a table nearby. She does this by making sounds while directing her eye gaze with a certain intensity (Ferm, Ahlsén, & Björck-Åkesson, 2005).

All these examples tell us about the use of channels other than speech as compensatory support when speech and/or arm and hand movements are not enough to allow the conversational partner share a certain content. All the examples tend to involve specific factual content such as names, entities, places, assertions, questions, and topics of discussion. Iconic gestures, pantomime, pointing, eye gaze, drawing, and pointing to pictures are especially important in this respect.

But other aspects of face-to-face interaction are probably just as important. Apart from conveying specific factual information, it involves the communication of feelings and attitudes and also communication regulating the interaction itself. There is good reason to believe that these aspects are crucial for spoken interaction. They also involve multimodality to a high degree, usually being in large part conveyed by other means than just words. Facial expression, gestures and other body communication, and prosody, or the intonation of words and phrases, play an important part here.

If we return to interactions involving persons with aphasia, we can, for example, observe multimodality being used in:

1. the frequent use of smiling, facial expressions, head movements, movements of arms, hands, and legs (such as clenching one's fist or stamping one's foot), changes

of body posture and gaze, prosodic markers, and sounds such as sighing, laughing, and smacking, all of which convey emotions and attitudes

2. enhanced use of body posture, leaning forward to indicate interested participation and leaning backward to indicate that a topic (or an interaction as a whole) should be finished or that communication is being left up to the interlocutor

3. increased use of head nods and head shakes, as well as hand gestures and gaze, to regulate communication, that is, provide feedback concerning contact, perception, comprehension, and attitudes and regulate who has the turn (right to contribute), as well as to indicate one's own production problems.

We can also use the term *aphasia* in accordance with present-day conceptions of "language," which means that we include persons with disorders that do not really primarily affect words and grammar, but rather the use of facial expressions, gestures, etc., as in the case of persons with acquired right-hemisphere lesions. Thus, we must deal with not only the disturbance of speech and the compensatory nature of multi-modality, but also with the disturbance of other modalities. An example could be a lack of the contextually appropriate emotional prosody and facial expression to go with an utterance expressing sympathy or happiness. Another example would be problems understanding a joke or an ironic comment. In these cases, maybe more emotional or attitudinal information could be expressed by words, in order to compensate for the lack of nonverbal modalities.

What makes a successful communicator?

Expression

As we have seen from the examples above, we have a wide range of means of expression at our disposal and these can normally be used freely in face-to-face interaction, supplementing each other in sequence or, more commonly, in simultaneous use.

The successful combination of different means of communication, to optimize the interactive flow of information and co-construct meaning by using multimodality in a given situation makes a good communicator. The situation includes the social activity being undertaken, the goals, the participants and their roles, the physical circumstances, and the use of artifacts, such as different media (phone, speech synthesis, etc.). All of these factors interact in determining the optimal way of communicating (Ahlsén, 1995, 2005; Allwood, 1976, 1995, 2000, 2001).

Content

What must be communicated? As we have seen above, three main types of communication have to take place: factual information has to be conveyed or co-constructed, interaction has to be regulated, and feelings and attitudes have to be communicated (Allwood, 2002).

Degrees of conscious control and intentionality

Modalities. While most of our words are produced with a fairly high degree of conscious control, gestures, facial expressions, and body movements are generally produced more automatically.

Types of information. Factual information is more likely to be communicated with greater control and intentionality than communication regulation (of one's own communication and interaction) and emotions or attitudes.

Degree of intentionality: Indicate, display, and signal. A useful way of describing degrees of intentionality in communication is to distinguish between indicating, which is done without intentionality (e.g., **indicating** that one is embarrassed by blushing); **displaying,** where one shows something intentionally (e.g., by pointing); and **signaling**, where one shows that one is showing something (e.g., most language use) (cf. Allwood, 2002).

Type of sign: Icon, index, and symbol. Another useful trichotomy is Peirce's semiotic distinction between three types of signs. An *icon* refers to something by a *similarity* relation; for example, a picture is similar to what it represents. An *index* refers to something by a *contiguity* relation, either in space or in time, such as an arrow pointing to a place. Finally, a *symbol* refers to something in an *arbitrary* way; for example, most words have no natural relationship to what they stand for (which is why different languages usually have completely different words for the same category of objects.) (Peirce, 1931). In this trichotomy, symbolic communication is considered to require a high degree of conscious control.

What is multimodal in ordinary face-to-face interaction?

If we look at ordinary face-to-face interaction, much of what goes on is not expressed in words but is handled by other modalities. This is especially true of interaction-regulating information, which depends on body communication, such as body posture, gesture, and gaze, as well as on intonation and voice quality. It also applies to communication of emotions and attitudes, where facial expression, sounds, tone of voice, and

Table 11.1. Types of information and degrees of intentionality and control in ordinary face-to-face interaction

	Factual	Communication-regulating	Emotional/Attitudinal
Indicate	x	X	X
Display	x	X	X
Signal	X	x	x

X = is used most often
x = can be used

body communication in general are important. Indicated and exposed information are often dependent on multimodality, where body communication and prosody play an important role.

If we look at Table 11.1 (cf. Allwood, 2002), we can see how the type of information is often related to the degree of intentionality.

Finally, indexical and iconic signs are mixed with symbolic expression in ordinary face-to-face interaction.

To sum up, we know that multimodality is the usual situation, but how necessary is it? We may have the feeling that we communicate more efficiently in face-to-face interaction and that the risk of misunderstanding is smaller than in long-distance communication. This is probably at least partly due to the multimodality of face-to-face communication, which makes us able to express more finely tuned nuances, including information that we do not necessarily want to express in words; by the same token, we can take in such information from our conversation partner. The sensation of greater ease and pleasure in communicating face-to-face and the widespread feeling that some types of important discussions should preferably take place face-to-face point to the importance of multimodality. On the other hand, other factors also affect which types of communication we prefer for different purposes; sometimes communication by phone or in writing is preferred. In this way, multimodality may sometimes be avoided in order enhance control of primarily factual communication.

In most cases, then, we are probably not truly dependent on multimodality, even though it has advantages for many purposes and can enhance the efficiency of communication.

Restrictions and possibilities concerning multimodality and communication disorders

As we have seen, full-fledged multimodality in face-to-face interaction involves many dimensions and possibilities. Different activity factors can restrict or increase the use of multimodality in different ways. We will consider two types of restrictions and possibilities: those imposed by communication disorders and those imposed by communication aid devices.

Factual information

Many communication disorders involve problems in producing the words, phrases and sentences needed in order to convey factual information, as we saw in the examples above. In some cases, the ability to use symbolic communication as a whole seems to be affected, thus making it necessary to compensate by using iconic or indexical communication. In other cases, it is mainly the words and grammar per se that are affected and it should be possible to express similar factual content by using other modalities, for example, iconic gestures or pointing to objects or pictures of objects, actions, and qualities. In both cases, body communication of indexical and iconic information is important, as is indicated and exposed information. Both these conditions require visual communication, even though communication aids where pointing is used may generate synthetic speech to reduce this dependence somewhat.

This means that face-to-face communication is the best condition for people with such communication disorders and that communication aids have to be used so that they are adapted to the total communication situation by (a) allowing face-to-face interaction, and (b) being used in a way that combines different modes of communication. A relevant question here is how much of the various dimensions of communication can be put into the communication aid. So far, it is mainly factual information at the iconic and sometimes the indexical and symbolic levels that is included, and this type of information seems best suited for the purpose. The use of communication aids is largely dependent on a high degree of control and intentionality, and consequently signals are used most. Pictures, words (and texts), and intermediate sign systems such as Bliss are among the tools used.

For many people with, for example, cerebral palsy, some aspects of what is usually communicated by gestures, facial expressions, and prosody are affected by the disorder and thus have to be communicated in a more "signaling" way, for example, by using pictorial representations of feelings, etc. Usually, however, spontaneous indicating and indexical communication is also available and must be closely attended to by these subjects' interlocutors.

Interaction-regulating information

In informal interaction, communication is most often regulated by indicating or displaying, rather than signaling. It is also regulated almost exclusively by body communication, prosody, etc., and not by words and sentences. This means that interaction regulating can best be done in a natural way using multimodal communication; the same is true of persons with communication disorders. There are, however, complicating factors. One is timing. Many persons with communication disorders are slow communicators, who make long pauses. Others speak too fast or with an irregular speech rhythm. And the use of communication aids affects the pacing of communication profoundly, potentially making it hard for users to claim and keep a turn (i.e., the right to speak), give feedback of the right type at the right time, and participate in finely tuned sequences of communication. The use of a communication aid by one party changes the pacing and interaction regulation of the whole interaction, if this person is a full participant. There is reason to believe that interaction regulation is extremely dependent on multimodality in face-to-face interaction. In a phone conversation or Internet chat, the modalities available to all participants are reduced. Interaction regulation is therefore facilitated in one sense; on the other hand, it is also made harder by the lack of face-to-face contact.

Emotion/Attitudes

Emotions and attitudes are mostly conveyed and shared by means of body communication such as posture, facial expressions, smiles, different sounds such as sighs, etc. Thus, they tend to be mainly indicated and exposed, rather than signaled. The result is that multimodality is crucial for this purpose.

Since interaction-regulating and emotional/attitudinal communication is, to a great extent, used spontaneously to compensate for problems and make it easier to "navigate through" the interchange of factual information, we can conclude that multimodality and face-to-face interaction will be particularly important for persons with communication disorders.

Multimodality makes it possible to use different modalities to strengthen the communication of specific content. It also makes it possible to use the modalities that one has better mastery of, instead of those that are more affected, in communicating a message.

Intermodal relations

One aspect of multimodality that is especially relevant from a neurolinguistic perspective is the interrelation between different modalities in the acquisition, retention, and processing of language. Much remains to be found out about these relations. Some of the relevant phenomena are:

- that the learning/encoding and processing of words of different types seem to be related to different features which rely more on one or another modality; for example, many words for objects seem to rely mostly on visual-perceptual features, whereas words for physical actions, handling tools, etc., seem to rely more on motor or functional features;

- that similar relations seem to exist for gestures;
- that category-specific anomias exist, which seem to provide more clues about these types of relations;
- that different areas of the brain are more active in relation to different types of words, for example, the parietal-temporal-occipital area for objects and the frontal lobes for motion verbs (Pulvermüller, Shtyrov & Ilmoniemi, 2005);
- that disturbances of language and gesture seem to show parallels in that word-finding problems in children with semantic problems may be accompanied by a lack of specificity and complexity in gestures (Månsson, 2004);
- that a difference between spontaneous and controlled production can affect gestures and speech in a similar way (Ahlsén, 1985).

Intermodal relations, thus, relate semantic content, structural complexity, and localization of brain activity for words and gestures and possibly also for other modalities (Ahlsén, 1985; Caramazza & Shelton, 1998; Månsson, 2004; Pulvermüller, Shtyrov, & Ilmoniemi, 2005; Warrington & Shallice, 1984,).

Optimizing Multimodal Communication for Persons with Communication Disorders and the Role of Communication Aids

Although there have been great hopes for ICT aids for persons with communication disorders, some lingering drawbacks have also been noted (cf. Ahlsén, 1994). Communication aids have not proven as easy to use, as useful for communication, or as widely available as one might have expected. There are many different reasons for this situation. One of the main ones was the unavailability of small, attractive, portable computers with AAC systems including, for example, pictures and synthetic speech, until quite recently. Another reason was that, again until recently, most people were not used to handling computers in their everyday life. Obviously, most of these obstacles have gradually been removed, although they still have to be considered in many individual cases. For the first time, we have the technical and social possibility of trying out small and flexible communication aids in everyday life.

The most serious challenge, however, to the use of ICT aids is gaining a better understanding of how multimodality works naturally and spontaneously in face-to-face interaction and how this knowledge can be applied to improve communication aids for everyday communicative interactions. There is good reason to believe that the failure to make ICT aids attractive to users is directly related to a gap in the naturalness and immediacy of communication in face-to-face communication with and without the aids. There is a long-standing focus on factual information in AAC systems. However, some attempts have been made to include more types of information and to work on total communication (e.g., Todman & Alm, 1998). There is also an increased interest in studying pragmatics and nonverbal communication in relation to communication disorders, and although this is not usually linked to a direct interest in ICT aids, it is possible to combine these efforts (e.g., Todman & Alm, 1998).

But we still have a long way to go. Consideration of all the dimensions of communication mentioned above is important for this purpose. A certain ingenuity in inventing multimodal communication methods that are complex but at the same time natural is also needed. The two main problems of timing –not being too slow for the flow of normal conversation — and search strategies –efficient ways to find what you want to express in the system — which are, of course, related, still remain largely unsolved.

Dialogue systems

As we saw above, dialogue systems — that is, computer programs that can hear and understand what users say and respond to them — are mainly intended for communicating factual information, communication regulation, and emotional/attitudinal information are increasingly taken into consideration. We also saw that our society is becoming more and more dependent on dialogue systems and that persons with communication disorders, who often also have motor disorders, are a group that could be especially dependent on using dialogue systems to handle different devices, such as cars and robots.

What, then, needs to be considered in the development of dialogue systems? There are certainly many aspects to consider. The questions below represent an attempt to summarize some of these aspects and provide food for thought and discussion.

- What modality or modalities can be used? Are there alternatives?
- What are the time restrictions?
- How hard to understand are the contributions of the system? How long are they?
- What types of contributions are accepted from the user? How set or flexible are the requirements?
- Is the system robust to phenomena such as hesitation, self-interruption and self-repetition, and articulation problems? What are the repair possibilities?
- Is there an option involving a human instead of the system?
- Is it possible to add more multimodality in order to simplify and provide more options?

- Is it possible to prepare and pre-store one's contributions (e.g., by using one's own computer and then simply outputting the right contribution at the right time, when talking to the dialogue system)?

One of the purposes of introducing speech-based dialogue systems is to make interaction with the system simpler and more natural for ordinary users. It is important to consider whether we are also making the interaction simpler and more natural for users with communication disorders and, if we suspect that we are not, whether and how we can enhance the accessibility of the systems for these users.

Two ways in which we can find out more about how to design and adapt dialogue systems for persons with communication disorders are (a) to conduct studies involving these kinds of users in contact with dialogue systems and have user reference groups to try out new designs; (b) to work on the design of dialogue interfaces to specific aids, such as robots, for persons with communication and motor disorders, thereby learning more about specific cases, which can be generalized in further design.

Summary

This chapter addressed the topic of multimodality in face-to-face communication, especially in the case of persons with language and communication disorders caused by aphasia or cerebral palsy. It has been claimed that ordinary face-to-face interaction involves multimodality to a great extent, and that persons with communication disorders are often even more dependent on multimodality in order to compensate for problems in finding or producing specific words. Different dimensions of communication, such as modality of expression, type of information, and type of sign were introduced and related to communication disorders. Multimodality was then considered in relation to information and communication technologies, especially communication aids. Potential problems and possibilities were discussed with respect to optimizing communication involving ICT.

Further reading

There are many aspects of multimodality and neurolinguistics, some of them related to the origin of speech and gestures, some to the use of drawing, picture communication, and gestures by persons with brain damage and language and communication disorders. The recommended literature has its main focus on the third aspect,

Ahlsén, E. (2003). Communicative contributions and multimodality — Reflections on body communication, communication aids for persons with language disorders and dialogue systems. In P. Paggio, K. Jokinen, & A. Jönsson (Eds.), *Proceedings of the 1st Nordic Symposium on Multimodal Communication*. CST Working Papers, Report No. 6, pp. 129–140.

Allwood, J. (2002). Bodily communication — Dimensions of expression and content. In B. Granström, D. House, & I. Karlsson (Eds.), *Multimodality in language and speech systems* (pp. 7–26). Dordrecht: Kluwer Academic Publishers.

Feyereisen, P. (1991). Communicative behaviour in aphasia. *Aphasiology, 5*, 323–333.

Lott, P. (1999). *Gesture and aphasia*. Bern: Peter Lang.

Todman, J., & Alm, N. (1998). Talk boards: Social conversation for text users without speech. *Closing the Gap, 17*, 16.

Assignments

1. Imagine (a) a shopping scene
    (b) a family dinner

    For each of these scenarios, try to identify actions that are usually carried out by spoken communication.
    If you had a severe speech disorder, how would you try to perform the same actions with the help of multimodal communication? (Think of other modalities, iconic and indexical communication.)

2. How could a dialogue system for train schedules be designed in order to rely less on spoken and written language, including numbers, and more on other modalities?

Part VI

Resource chapters

Chapter 12

Methods of investigating the brain

> **In this chapter:**
>
> - *Methods that were used extensively in the past*
> - *Methods that are often used in neurolinguistic studies today*
>   - *Static recording: Brain imaging*
>   - *Dynamic recording: Electrical activity*
>   - *Dynamic recording: Brain imaging*

Introduction

This chapter presents a short overview of different techniques that have been used to investigate the brain. Questions such as which area in the brain has been damaged by a particular lesion (related to specific behavioral symptoms), what would happen to a specific type of behavior if a certain part of the brain was lesioned (e.g., by an operation), what has happened to the vascular system of the brain, which areas of the brain are active in responding to a certain type of stimulus or performing a specific type of action, and how this activation pattern is changed when there is a lesion of a particular area, can all be addressed by various techniques. Most of them involve more or less direct registration or imaging of brain structures or of dynamic activation patterns in the brain. Techniques such as radiography, measurements of electrical currents, blood flow, and metabolic changes, and magnetic resonance imaging related to the synaptic activity of brain cells are used.

Most of these methods involve fairly complex and indirect measurements and calculations, which will not be described in any detail here. The aim is mainly to give a general overview of the various types of methods and the main principles involved in each.

Methods that were used extensively in the past

Autopsy of brains for lesion analysis

The classical studies of Broca, Wernicke, and others in the late 19th century were based on the observation of linguistic symptoms in patients and post-mortem autopsies of their brains to identify characteristics of different areas of the brain. This method was used extensively for a long time. Nowadays, as we shall see, lesion analysis (i.e., comparing lesioned brain structures to characteristics of a patient's behavior) is most often based on imaging techniques.

Wada test (intracarotid sodium amytal test)

The intracarotid sodium amytal (amobarbital) test (ISA) has been used since the 1940s, when it was described by Wada (1949). It is used to study inter- and intra-hemispheric differences, for example in handling language functions. If one injects amobarbital into one of the carotid arteries, the brain areas supplied by that artery are temporarily anesthetized. This makes it possible to study how each of the hemispheres handles language functions separately. This is important, since it mimics the effects that a lesion or a surgical procedure might induce. The technique has been used especially for checking hemispheric functions before major surgery to one hemisphere, for example, in cases of epilepsy.

Cerebral angiography (radiography)

This method has been in use for a long time. It is a radiological technique for evaluating the cerebral vascular structure and can thus be used for diagnosing malformations, aneurysms, etc., affecting the blood vessels. A contrast substance is injected through a catheter into the carotid artery and the blood vessels become visible in the angiogram. A certain risk of stroke is involved in this procedure.

Methods that are often used in neurolinguistic studies today

Static recording: Brain imaging

Computed tomography (CT). Computed tomography is a radiographic method in which a narrow beam of X-rays examines the brain in very thin slices. The X-ray beam rotates around the head, passes through it, and is recorded by detectors on the other side that measure the quality and quantity of the beam. From these detectors, we obtain images with shades of white, gray, and black for the various areas, depending on the X-ray attenuation (reduction in intensity). Data regarding absorbed photons from the X-ray are processed into a two-dimensional image of the slice of the brain. This is a complex mathematical procedure that makes it possible to study density, which provides information about lesions, etc. Hemorrhages and aneurysms can be seen as high-density lesions and cerebral infarctions, edemas, and cysts can be seen as low-density lesions. Tumors can be either high- or low-density. Contrast is sometimes enhanced by injecting contrast-enhancing agents into the intravascular space. The CT of a lesion tends to change over time, reflecting the different stages in its life. CT has been used in many neurolinguistic studies since the 1970s.

Magnetic resonance imaging (MRI). MRI measures the magnetic activity of the atomic nuclei of hydrogen (in water molecules). This is done by placing the brain in an external magnetic field. This makes the hydrogen atoms align themselves in a single plane. By transmitting signals from an external radio frequency transmitter, extra energy is provided to the atoms and makes them rearrange themselves in different patterns. After the signal, they return to their earlier position, but first discharge electromagnetic signals. These signals are recorded and the computer converts them into images in shades of white, gray, and black, representing different strengths of the signals. This is a non-invasive method that does not even use X-rays. It also gives very clear images, with a somewhat better quality than CT images.

Dynamic–recording: Electrical activity

Electroencephalography (EEG). EEG depicts electrical activity generated by brain cells. It represents the potential differences between two points on the scalp surface caused by the brain waves (electrical potentials) from the cortex below them. A number of metal electrodes (8 to 16) are placed on the scalp. In this way, brain waves can be recorded from areas in the different lobes of the two hemispheres. The patterns are graphically represented and can then be compared for different areas.

Spontaneous cortical activity is generated by the synaptic activity of the axons on the dendrites and thus there is more activity in areas where there are many dendrites, especially from pyramidal cells. The different frequency ranges of electrical activity are represented by the Greek letters alpha, beta, gamma, theta, and delta. The waves can be between 25 and 200 microvolts with a frequency of 0.5 to 35 cycles per second. During an epileptic seizure, however, amplitudes as high as 1,000 microvolts may occur. Abnormal patterns may be irregular, with high spikes or reversed waves. Altered levels of consciousness can easily be detected and EEG has proven to be a very useful diagnostic tool.

Evoked or event-related potentials (ERP). When the central nervous system reacts to sensory stimulation, the electrical activity is referred to as evoked potentials. These potentials can be fairly small in amplitude (1 to 5 microvolts). They are recorded by electrodes in the same way as for EEG. But since EEG is very sensitive to factors such as blinking, moving the head, etc., the small response specific to a stimulus might not be detected on its own. Consequently, an averaging technique is used in ERP measurement, that is, the EEG is averaged over many events with the same stimulus, which eliminates disturbances, and reveals the actual response. The ERP is a typical series of positive and negative peaks, representing earlier and later stages of information processing. Negative peaks are named with an "N" plus the number of milliseconds from the stimulus onset, for example, N280. Positive peaks are named with a "P" plus the number of milliseconds from the stimulus onset, for example, P600. Peaks can also have sequence numbers, such as N1 or P3. The advantages of using ERPs for neurolinguistic (and other) research are that the technique is inexpensive and noninvasive, and that it allows fine temporal measurements of cognitive processing.

Dynamic recording: Brain imaging

Regional cerebral blood flow measurement (rCBF). This was the first technique to give computerized pictures or maps of areas of activity during dynamic language use, such as when a subject is naming objects, reading aloud, etc. The technique measures how fast the blood passes through the different areas of the brain. When a specific area of the brain is active, blood flows through this area faster — in other words, the blood flow is increased — since the blood is needed to provide the additional metabolic energy that is required. A short-lived radioactive isotope is dissolved in a solution and injected into an artery or inhaled. It can then be tracked with a gamma-ray camera with multiple scintillation detectors, which measures attenuated radiation around the head. A computer then maps the surface of the brain, with different colors for different levels of activity. Important findings from rCBF studies from the 1960s to 1980s include the fact that there is prefrontal activity during rest and bilateral activity in speech activities.

Positron emission tomography (PET). PET is another isotope technique, which registers physiological changes in brain cells by tagging radioactive positron isotopes with water molecules or glucose and injecting them into the body. Then the spatial distribution of positron (radiation) emitting radioisotopes and their dissipated energy can be measured. When an injected positron collides with an electron, they are both annihilated and two photons (gamma rays) are emitted, which travel in opposite directions. These photons are detected by detectors circling the brain. Computer images are generated, where oxygen or glucose metabolism reflects the physiological changes in brain cells in patterns of neural activity representing cognitive activity. The spatial and temporal resolution is not optimal, but the technique is constantly being improved and has proven very valuable. One important finding made with this method was that focal brain damage causing aphasia also results in changes in the functioning of other, more distant areas.

Single photon emission tomography (SPECT). SPECT measures rCBF by using a technology similar to of the one used in PET. A radiotracer substance tagged with a radiopharmaceutical is injected and the distribution of the radiopharmaceutical is measured. This is done with gamma-ray detecting cameras and tomographic techniques and the signal in this case is a single gamma ray. SPECT uses the point of gamma-ray emission and its trajectory. It provides three-dimensional rCBF images.

Functional magnetic resonance imaging (fMRI). Functional MRI is a dynamic imaging technique, which can detect changes in regional blood oxygen levels associated with cortical neuronal activity, by using magnetic resonance imaging. For example, the so-called BOLD (Blood Oxygenation Level — Dependent) effect results in increased fMRI signals when activation (synaptic firing) increases in a particular region. Dynamic activation patterns can thus be studied when a subject is performing a linguistic task. Like MRI, this technique creates images with relatively high resolution. fMRI is faster than PET, which means that it can register a large number of separate measurements of functionally significant signals during a short time span, but it is still slower than electrophysiological techniques. Rather complex calculations involving the correlation of so-called "voxels" (elementary volume units of the image matrix) which, it is assumed, reflect neural responses to stimuli, have to be done. This helps to overcome the strong background noise involved and the high sensitivity to factors such as heart rate, head motion, etc. In other dynamic methods (e.g., ERP), these kinds of factors, but not the background noise, are otherwise usually dealt with through subtraction, that is, statistical comparison of the stimulation condition and the resting state, to identify the actual effects of the stimuli.

Magnetoencephalography (MEG). MEG has high temporal resolution (like ERPs) and high spatial resolution as well, that is, it can localize neurophysiological events in small cerebral regions with some precision (better than ERPs). It is completely non-invasive (involving no radioactive tracers) and measures electrical activity related to neural transmission more directly than metabolism or blood flow data. It is also more suited for single-subject measurements and the study of individual variation, since it does not require group averaging (which is often used in PET and fMRI studies).

The neuromagnetometer used for MEG records very small changes in the magnetic fields which are generated in the brain (cortex) in response to a particular stimulus (localized precisely in time). A SQUID (Superconducting Quantum Interference Device) is connected to the magnetometer (both are in liquid helium at a temperature close to absolute zero). Different configurations of magnetic coils are used in order to reduce the influence of environmental magnetic sources, enhancing the spatial precision. Averaging over repeated stimulus presentations is also used and recorded as EMFs (evoked magnetic fields). The number of detector arrays can be as high as 24 to 72 simultaneously; the detectors record EMFs from the whole surface of the head.

Further reading

Bhatnagar, S. (2002). *Neuroscience for the study of communicative disorders*. Second Edition. Philadelphia: Lippincott Williams & Wilkins.

Stemmer, B., & Whitaker, H. (Eds.) (1998). *Handbook of neurolinguistics*. San Diego: Academic Press.

Chapter 13

Modeling the brain

> **In this chapter:**
>
> - *Basic ideas: Symbol processing and neural network models*
> - *Making an ANN model*
> - *Representations in ANN models*
> - *Learning in ANN models*
> - *Connectionist models of language production*

Introduction

This chapter introduces some basic information about modeling language processing in artificial neural networks. It presents some basic ideas behind symbol processing models of the types that we can see in other chapters of the book (Chapters 3, 6 and 8) and neural network models. It takes a simple ANN model as example and then turns to an account of how representations can be treated in ANN models. On the basis of this information, we then take a look at learning in ANN models and, specifically, at examples of connectionist models of language production. Since ANN modeling is becoming increasingly popular in neurolinguistics, this basic information can hopefully be of some help in understanding studies using ANN techniques.

Basic ideas: Symbol processing and neural network models

Models of language processing are important and useful for neurolinguists. By means of simulation, or constructing a "suitably analogous apparatus on a computer," a neurolinguistic model can be evaluated. Thus, empirical evidence leads to the construction of a model, which is then simulated on the computer, providing more empirical evidence, and the process continues (Eikmeyer & Schade, 1991).

There are two main types of modeling: *symbol processing* and *neural network modeling*. For a long time, symbolic mechanisms were assumed in neurolinguistic modeling and most models were symbolic. But now, as an alternative, artificial neural (ANN) network models — also called connectionist, PDP (parallel distributed processing), or subsymbolic models — can be used to model cognitive functions below the symbol level as well.

How, then, can we describe the main differences between the two types of modeling? In conceptualizing the brain and its functions, they differ in terms of their levels of conceptual abstraction and formal realization.

1. While symbol processing models view the brain as a physical symbol system, ANNs see it as a network of (formal) interlinked neurons.
2. Representation in symbol processing is done according to the computer metaphor, in a yes-no fashion. The dynamic flow of activation is, however, emphasized in ANN, using a brain metaphor, which, although coarse, is closer to neuroanatomical/ neurophysiological reality, and working with representations of degree.
3. Yet another important difference is that symbol processing models assume a central processor that performs the symbol manipulations, while ANNs have many processors which interact through the flow of activation. This approach assumes that cognition or intelligence emerges and can be modeled from the simultaneous interaction of many small, interconnected units with many connections (like neurons). ANNs are, thus, "brainlike" (Chapman, 1991, pp. 35–40) in that they are made up of a great many components.

So-called hybrid models, combining features of symbolic and ANN modeling, also exist, as do suggestions for the combination of different symbolic and ANN models to handle different components of language processing (e.g., Pinker, 1996).

The main reason for developing ANN models was that traditional symbolic models did not perform well on certain tasks that the brain seems to handle easily, such as speech comprehension and face recognition. The collective, parallel, and interactive workings of many simple elements seem to be able to perform the complex computations needed for these functions. Other reasons are that learning is possible through differing wiring of the connections between the simple units (perhaps the most important feature of ANNs), that networks are more noise-resistant, and that they can be self-organizing.

Some of the aspects of how the brain works are certainly relevant for modeling and especially for ANN models:

1. There are many simple processing elements (nodes), capable of transferring a one-dimensional type of information, called activation.

2. Each of the nodes is connected to many others. The structure of the connecting network and the efficiency of individual connections (weights) determine the network's functioning.

3. The connections are the most important aspect of the model. The structure of the network is mostly fixed, but the efficiency of connections can often be modified by learning rules, which enable the network to learn new tasks.

Making an ANN model

Models exist at different levels of abstraction; *neurobiological models* keep the closest to biological reality, while *application-oriented models*, on the other hand, are very much abstracted from biology. The models that we are concerned with here, *functional models* (or *Interactive Activation Models, IAM*), are intermediate in abstraction; they resemble biological processes but are also structured on the basis psychological assumptions.

Some of the relevant facts about neurons are the following:

- that neurons collect electrochemical pulses and, if the sum of pulses is strong enough, generate an action potential;
- that the brain is assumed to contain about 10^{11} neurons, each of which is connected to many other components (about 10^4) and performs some relatively simple computation, mainly on the basis of information it receives from its local connections; 20% of these neurons are in the neocortex;
- that cortical neurons have an average of 4,000 connections to other neurons;
- that this gives 3.2×10^{13} connections in the neocortex alone;
- that roughly 2.8×10^{13} connections are modifiable.
  (Murre & Sturdy, 1995)

What processes, then, are relevant to model in a functional model of this type? The general feature of having a large number of simple processing elements (nodes) which can transfer activation is important, as are rich network interconnections between the nodes. How the network structure looks is of great importance and how the weights are assigned to individual connections is a key feature. An important question is how the network can learn to perform tasks based on the change of weights.

Modeling a neuron

What do neurons in the brain and nodes in artificial neural networks have in common and how do they differ?

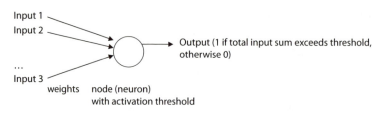

Figure 13.1. Formal neuron

ANN models are based, in a rough and simplified way, on the local structure of nervous systems. This means that they do not aim to be direct models of real nervous systems and that not all aspects of such systems are modeled. The main similarity of nodes in these mathematical-computational models to the neurons in the central nervous system is that excitatory and inhibitory activation signals from connections with other cells or nodes are summed up to decide whether or not a cell or node should be activated and pass on activation to the next cell. A threshold activation value has to be passed in order for activation to take place.

In a neuron, activation is collected by the dendrites and sent on as voltages to the soma. If the activation threshold is exceeded, the axon passes the output current to the synapse, where a chemical connection to dendrites of other cells takes place.

A formal or modeled neuron (or node) has an activation strength and receives input activations which are added up; if the threshold value of 1 is exceeded, an activation or inhibition of 1 is passed on to the next node. The synapse is simulated as a weight, that is, a number.

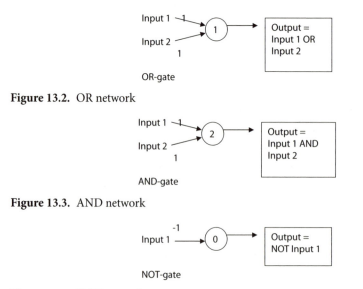

Figure 13.2. OR network

Figure 13.3. AND network

Figure 13.4. NOT network

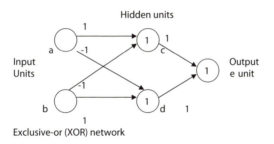

Figure 13.5. XOR network
(Figures 13.2 to 13.5 adapted from Franklin, 1999)

There are, however, several differences between real neurons and formal neurons; for example, there are different neurotransmitters in the brain, which have different effects, whereas the artificial networks only activate or inhibit the subsequent neuron, and they simulate the magnitude of the output instead of the firing rate.

A very basic kind of ANN is the XOR network in Figure 13.5 above, which illustrates how a network can function.

What are the dynamics of how an ANN system functions? According to Murre and Goebel (1996), single nodes operate by:

- Propagation: they calculate net input (sum from other nodes);
- Activation: they transform net input into current activation value;
- Output: they transform their current activation value into the current output value of the node.

There are different possible **activation functions**, such as linear or threshold functions; if so-called backpropagation is used, there is often a logistic function (an S-shaped activation curve). Most networks have recurrent connections, resulting in interactive stimulation. This means that node A activates node B, which in turn activates node A again. A decay parameter can be used to regulate how fast activation will recede. The output function is often a simple linear function.

Activations can be updated according to three main activation schedules:

1. Asynchronous random (at each iteration, a single node is selected randomly and only its activation is updated);
2. Synchronously (activations of all nodes are updated simultaneously);
3. Sequentially, or feedforward (all nodes within a given layer are updated synchronously, but layers themselves are updated in a strict order from input layer to output layer — there cannot be recurrent connections).

In addition, there are other patterns such as "winner takes all" activation.

We can illustrate this by means of a simple network for word recognition, which is able to distinguish between three different words. If we imagine a network for word recognition, with nodes at the letter level and the word level, it might work as follows. We have three possible words — HIT, BIT, and BIG — represented by nodes at the word level. There are nodes at the letter level for H and B in word-initial position, I in word-medial position, and T and G in word-final position. The input letters presented to the network are B, I, and T. The first thing that happens is that the letter nodes for initial B, medial I, and final T are activated. They send activation to the word nodes, which compete for enough activation to pass their threshold level. Finally, the word node for BIT wins by receiving the most activation and the word BIT is the output of the network.

The network works according to the Hebbian learning rule:

> When an axon of cell A is near enough to excite a cell B and repeatedly or persistently takes part in firing it, some growth process or metabolic change takes place in one or both cells such that A's efficiency, as one of the cells firing B, is increased. (Hebb, 1949, p. 62 (traced back to William James))

This can explain the formation of cell assemblies, or attractor-like configurations of densely connected nodes. Cell assemblies are important aspects of how activation of brain cells works, how memory and learning can take place, and how language can be handled by the brain.

Representations in ANN models

Representations are handled in different ways in different types of networks. The basic types are local or distributed representations, while an intermediate alternative is feature representation.

1. In a *local representation*, one unit represents one object, one concept, or one hypothesis. We have a one-to-one correspondence between units and items to be represented. This is easy to understand and modeling can be done at the fully cognitive level. For example, if we want to model the dynamics of thoughts, we can use one unit for each "concept." (There is no symbol manipulation via rules and no stored program, as we would have in a symbolic computer model.)
2. Networks can have *distributed representation*. This means that each unit (node) may participate in the representation of several items and conversely each item is represented by a pattern of activity over several different units. Distributed representation is much more computationally compact than local representation. This type of model represents at the subcognitive level, since individual units are not interpreted. Cognition emerges only at the whole system level. An advantage of this method is that all nodes carry some of the burden in representing an item. An item can only be found less directly; since it is more dynamically coded, it

can more elegantly engage in dynamic processes and it does not have to be coded manually, but is the result of learning (Eikmeyer & Schade, 1991).

3. *Featural representation* can be seen as something between local and distributed representation. Individual items are represented distributively by patterns of activity over sets of units and the individual units also locally represent features of the given item. Features can either be programmed into the system or arise during the training process. This can lead to spontaneous generalization. The model can be said to represent at the microcognitive level. At the conceptual level, patterns of activation interact in complex ways. Thoughts are activation vectors. Units can, however, still be interpreted and inferences can sometimes be discerned. The cognitive level is emergent.

Some of the useful features of ANN models in general are the following:

-   They do not need a central executive, but work with distributed control and all decisions are made based on local information. (Thus, no effort is spent on gathering global information and arriving at global decisions.)
-   Default assignments are automatic: an input gives an output, that is, the network always does something.
-   They give complete patterns, which allows content addressability. Databases can be small.
-   They have graceful degradation (i.e., if a system degrades, it continues to operate at a lower level instead of failing completely), and this makes them less brittle.
-   They model spontaneous generalization. They induce global behaviors beyond the scope of any of their individual units, that is, emergent behaviors.
-   Learning is possible.

Learning in ANN models

We will now consider how learning can be achieved in ANN models. The output of a unit (node) is its activation. The pattern of activation at time t is the network's configuration at t. (This corresponds to short-term memory, or what is represented at t, where t is a specific point in time.) The pattern of weights (like long-term memory) represents what the network knows and determines how it responds to a given input. Learning takes place via the changing of weights.

An ANN is built on a directed graph (or digraph), which is called the architecture of the network. The units of the network are the nodes of the digraph, while the weighted links are the arcs of the digraph. The set of all its possible weight matrices comprises its weight space. For example, the XOR network in Figure 13.5 has the weight space specified in Figure 13.6 below.

$$
\begin{array}{c}
\begin{array}{ccccc}
\text{a} & \text{b} & \text{c} & \text{d} & \text{e}
\end{array} \\
\begin{array}{c}
\text{a} \\ \text{b} \\ \text{c} \\ \text{d} \\ \text{e}
\end{array}
\left(
\begin{array}{ccccc}
0 & 0 & 1 & -1 & 0 \\
0 & 0 & -1 & 1 & 0 \\
0 & 0 & 0 & 0 & 1 \\
0 & 0 & 0 & 0 & 1 \\
0 & 0 & 0 & 0 & 0
\end{array}
\right)
\end{array}
$$

Figure 13.6. A weight matrix representing the weight space for an XOR network

Learning involves a search problem in the weight space, where the network tries to find the matrix that will do what is required in the best way. (This can be compared to the search for a path through state space in symbolic artificial intelligence).

There are different ways to make networks learn. Learning can be *supervised* or *unsupervised*. *Supervised learning* uses hard-wired weights and connections specified by a human designer and can be used when there is a carefully thought-out model that works. Unsupervised learning can, for example, use self-organizing networks (see below).

Error correction (supervised practice) means that responses are compared to target output and the weights are adjusted to give an output that approaches the target output. An example of this is *backpropagation*, where a layered, feedforward network (i.e., a network of layers of units where each unit sends output only to units in the subsequent layer) is trained on a corpus of input-output exemplars. Each output is compared with the desired output of the exemplar and the error is calculated. The error is then propagated back through network and used to modify the weights so as to reduce the error.

Reinforcement (graded learning) calculates a numerical score over a sequence of trials, which is the value of a cost function; the weights are then adjusted to lower the cost. (The cost function comes from the designer; in human brains, it might be assumed to have evolved.) This type of learning works rather like the "getting hot, getting cold" game.

Stochastic learning means that random or Hebbian weight change is accepted if the cost decreases or by some probability distribution. It uses trial and error, trying out random weight changes and checking the cost to see if it has decreased. If it has, the network accepts the change; otherwise, it goes back again. It can also apply a Hebbian weight change. (Hebb's (1949) rule: increase the synaptic strength between any two connected neurons that fire almost simultaneously.)

Self-organization involves weights being modified in response to the input. For example, the network can see which output was the strongest for a particular input and strengthen these connections even more while weakening neighboring connections a little. Repetition then takes place and the process recurs. Self-organizing maps, developed by Kohonen (1989), are an important approach to learning in neural networks. They are similar to modularity in that they translate delimiting constraints into neural network architectures. They are based on local inhibition but also involve topological organization of the inhibitory connections. When networks are trained with stimuli that have spatial relations, these tend to be reproduced by the maps. They also have some similarity to primary visual areas. Another example is speech recognition, where the network produces a phonotopic map, in which similar speech sounds are grouped together. The spoken word becomes a trajectory activating areas on the map (Murre & Goebel, 1996).

Connectionist models of language production

We now turn to some other examples of how language production can be modeled in ANN, building largely on the work of Eikmeyer and Schade (1991). Some studies that exemplify this method are those by Dell and Reich (1981) and Dell (1986). (See also the section on simulation in Chapter 6 of this book.)

In a local network, linguistic items can be represented by single nodes. The nodes can be organized in layers representing linguistic levels; in other words, they contain linguistic items of the same size and type, such as words, syllables, syllable types, or phonemes. The network has excitatory links connecting nodes from different levels in part-whole relations, which can be bidirectional (i.e., provide feedback). Inhibitory connections within levels can be used and competition can be modeled in this way by lateral inhibition between items on the same level. The decay rate of activation for nodes can also be used to model, for example, features of aphasia, such as anomia and agrammatism. At certain points in time, a node with the highest activation on all levels is selected for production and these choices model linguistic sequentialization (Eikmeyer & Schade, 1991; Murre & Goebel, 1996).

In artificial intelligence models using interactive activation networks with local symbol representations, nodes can be identified with linguistic units in the input to the network. The input causes a flow of interacting activations until the network stabilizes. The end configuration is then the basis for a solution, recognition, or response. This type of model does not include learning algorithms; the process is only studied after learning is completed.

PDP (Parallel Distributed Processing) models were pioneering network models developed by Rumelhart and McClelland in the 1980s, which focused on the learning process itself and learning algorithms, for example, in studies of visual letter perception and the simulation of children's acquisition of verb tense inflection (Rumelhart & McClelland, 1986).

Modeling lesions

In neurolinguistics, it is of some interest to build or use models of some part of language processing and then to model lesions in the network in order to examine specific features of neurolinguistic disorders. There are two basic ways of doing this:

1. some nodes can be removed (if it is a distributed network);
2. the interchange or flow of activation among the nodes can be distorted or even interrupted.

There are a number of ways to impede the flow of activation:

- the activation interchange within the semantic layer can be manipulated;
- the excitatory links between semantic layer and the word layer can be reduced in strength;
- phonological encoding can be obstructed by manipulating the connections among the word layer, the syllable layer, the phoneme layer, and the layer of phonological features.

Lesions in the semantic layer result in the selection of non-intended concepts (which can be spelled out correctly). Lesions affecting the connection between semantics and words on a general level reduce the strengths of all connections, which leads to word-finding problems. Slower activation and more noise interference increase the risk that the wrong word will be activated. Phonological cues can also affect this. Lesions affecting the connection between semantics and words on a specific level reduce the strengths of some connections, which produce sound associates as output. Lesions below the word layer lead to phonological problems. Slower activation means that not all the sounds of words are activated; some come out right, some wrong, and some not at all. The result is neologistic jargon. In distributed networks, there are more degrees of freedom.

Some examples of how lesions affecting language functions can be simulated can be found in Eikmeyer and Schade (1991, pp. 163–167). According to Eikmeyer and Schade, the proper procedure in simulating language processes in neural networks is to relate the simulation to a program, which is then related to empirical evidence; this is necessary in order to evaluate the model. Modeling is thus a "circular" procedure, based on a theory and/or empirical observations, and evaluated against data and theoretical claims. (See also Chapter 6, where lesion/symptom simulations by Dell and colleagues are reported.)

Further reading

Arbib, M. (Ed.) (1998). *The handbook of brain theory and neural networks*. Cambridge, MA: MIT Press.

Franklin, S. (1999). *Artificial minds*. Cambridge, MA: MIT Press.

Murre, J., & Goebel, R. (1996). Connectionist modeling. In T. Dijkstra & K. de Smedt (Eds.), *Computational psycholinguistics* (pp. 49–81). London: Taylor & Francis.

Chapter 14

Some basic concepts in neuroscience

> **In this chapter:**
>
> - *Gross neuroanatomy*
> - *Neurophysiology*
> - *Cellular organization (cytoarchitecture):*
>   *Brodmann areas*

Introduction

This chapter is intended to be a guide to some of the basics of the anatomy and physiology of the brain that the reader needs to understand the subject matter of this book.

The focus is on both general information and information that is specifically important for language functions, mostly higher mental functions relevant for language and cognition in communication. The most important brain structures in this regard are presented in a very selective summary.

Gross neuroanatomy

The central nervous system (CNS) consists of the brain and spinal cord, while the peripheral nervous system (PNS) comprises the peripheral nerves between the CNS and other body parts

Cerebrum

If we look at the surface of the brain, we basically see the **cerebrum**, which is covered by the **cortex**; the cortex consists of a layer of gray matter, that is, nerve cells or neurons, about one centimeter thick. Underneath the cortex, we find white matter, or fibers connecting different parts of the brain. There are also many **subcortical**

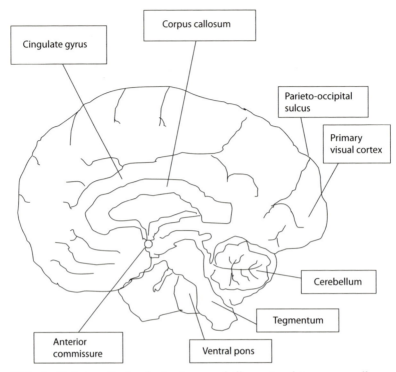

Figure 14.1. Sagittal view: Cortex, brain stem, cerebellum, cingulate, corpus callosum, anterior commissure

structures, such as the cingulate, various nuclei, and the **brain stem.** At the back of the brain, we find the **cerebellum.**

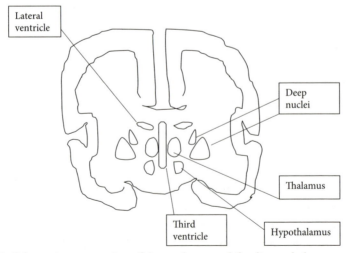

Figure 14.2. Schematic cross-section of the cerebrum and the diencephalon

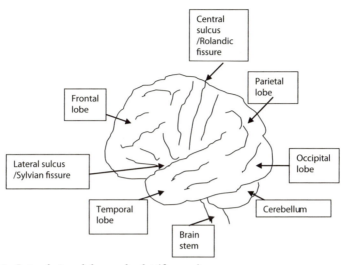

Figure 14.3. Lateral view: lobes and sulci (fissures)

The brain is divided into two halves or **hemispheres**, the left and the right. They look quite similar, but there are many differences in function; specific functions may be lateralized more to one hemisphere or the other, and there are also some differences in the two hemispheres' anatomy.

The two hemispheres are connected by fibers of white matter, most importantly the **corpus callosum**, but also the **anterior commissure**.

Each of the hemispheres can be divided into four major lobes: the **frontal lobe**, the **temporal lobe**, the **parietal lobe**, and the **occipital lobe**.

The cortex of the lobes is "folded" into **convolutions** or **gyri** and in between the gyri there are **sulci** or **fissures**. Two fissures are particularly noticeable: the **Rolandic** (or **central**) **fissure** divides the frontal lobe from the parietal lobe, while the **Sylvian** (or lateral) **fissure** separates the frontal lobe from the temporal lobe. The gyri form a specific pattern, which makes it possible to use them for gross orientation. For example, you can refer to the first temporal gyrus or the third frontal gyrus, the prerolandic or motor gyrus, the postrolandic or somatosensory gyrus, the angular, or the supramarginal gyrus. All of these terms are often used in neurolinguistic descriptions.

A major division can also be made between the **anterior** (or frontal) and the **posterior** (parietal-temporal-occipital) parts of the brain. Furthermore, deep or **subcortical** structures, which are more ancient in development and more "basic," can be separated from surface or **cortical** structures.

In neurolinguistics, the distinctions among the lobes and the divisions between anterior and posterior, left and right, and subcortical and cortical are often used for reference, as are the areas defined by the gyri and fissures.

Some of the major functional features of these brain areas are:

- Frontal lobes: planning, decision-making, initiative, motor functions;
- Parietal lobes: somatosensory perception;
- Occipital lobes: visual perception;
- Temporal lobes: auditory perception;
- Anterior parts: more active, productive;
- Posterior parts: more receptive, analytical;

In the anterior parts of the brain, the motor cortex has been fairly well described; it is often diagrammed in the form of a "homunculus" (a miniature human), that is, with the different areas of function (i.e., body parts) projected with the size of each one proportional to how fine-grained its function is. Other areas have less anatomically specified functions.

In the posterior parts, the cortical sensory centers (auditory, visual, and somatosensory) have also been more clearly localized and described (the somatosensory area is also presented as a homunculus based on the tactile sensation related to the different body parts). The association areas between the primary sensory centers have functions that are less clearly localized.

Some of the functions that are suggested to be localized to one hemisphere or the other are related to the less specified areas of the anterior and posterior parts of the brain. For example, many aspects of language and speech, especially grammar and phonology, seem to be more lateralized to the left hemisphere, while, for example, tonal patterns and visuospatial orientation seem to be more lateralized to the right hemisphere.

The earlier developed, subcortical structures of the brain are essential for consciousness and attention (the reticular formation of the brain stem), as well as basic instincts and emotions (the limbic system), which activate the brain. The cortex contains more controlled and specified higher cognitive functions, which partly inhibit the more "primitive" functions.

Blood supply

The most important blood vessel supplying the brain from the point of view of language, is the cerebral medial artery, which is in turn supplied by the carotid artery. It spreads out like a tree over most of the more important cortical areas for language and speech (around the Sylvian fissure). Other important blood vessels are the posterior and superior cerebral arteries, which meet the "tree" of the cerebral medial artery in the so-called "watershed areas," where the thinnest vessels at the periphery of the "tree" are very vulnerable to brain damage, since small coagulated blood clots can easily deprive them of blood supply. Lesions affecting language functions are very often caused by *stroke*, most often by *infarction*: coagulated blood seals off part of the blood supply and thereby deprives an area supplied by the blood vessel of oxygen, causing cell death after a while. An *embolism* involves a small piece of coagulated blood coming loose from a bigger clot and getting stuck in a narrow blood vessel. A *hemorrhage*, whereby the wall of a blood vessel bursts and blood is pumped out of the blood vessel, is another type of lesion affecting the blood supply.

Cerebellum

The cerebellum (see Figure 14.1) handles the coordination of movements. A lesion affecting the cerebellum can lead to *ataxia*, that is, a lack of coordination of movement, for example when the patient tries to change directions while walking. Such coordination problems can also affect articulation. Imaging studies of brain activation show that other speech and language functions also require participation from the cerebellum.

Deep and subcortical structures

The role of subcortical structures for language and speech is less mapped out than that of the cortical structures, but several such structures do seem to play important roles. The **limbic area**, which comprises the **cingulate gyrus** (a deep medial cortical area), handles basic instincts and emotions. It is therefore vital for motivation, affect, etc., in language and communication, as in other areas of activity. (See Figure 14.1.)

The **brain stem** regulates consciousness and cortical tone, and is therefore essential for being awake and aroused enough to communicate.

The **thalamus** acts as a "switchboard" between nerve fibers from the brain and different areas of the body. It consists of a variety of nuclei with different functions, some of which are important for language and speech functions.

Neurophysiology

The nerve cells or **neurons** constitute the gray matter of the cortex. There are also so-called **glia cells**, which fulfill more supportive functions. Neuronal activity consists of neurons being activated in patterns for different functions.

The nerve cell (neuron)

Each **neuron** has a **body** or **soma**, which contains the core of the cell. **Dendrites** branch out from the soma. The dendrites and the soma can receive activation from other cells. The cell also has one major "outgoing" process, called the **axon**, through

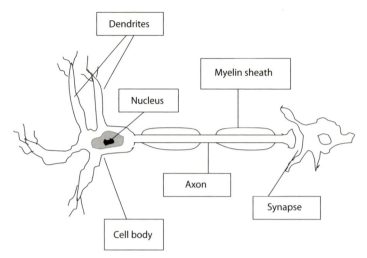

Figure 14.4. Neuron

which activation can be transmitted to another cell. The axon is surrounded by a sheath of **myelin** in sections. The electrical nerve signal can be speeded up by the conducting features of the myelin.

The bodies and dendrites of neurons can be grouped together into a **nucleus**. They also form **layers** which make up the surface of the brain, the cortex or gray matter. Nerve fibers run in tracts of so-called white matter (because of the white myelin).

The synapse

A synapse is the actual transmission of activation between neurons. At the end of each axon there is an **end plate (terminal bouton)**. The end plate adjacent to another cell can, when it is activated through the axon, release a **neurotransmitter substance** and activate or inhibit activation from the end plate over the synaptic cleft to the next cell. There are a number of different transmitter substances, such as acetylcholine. Activation is therefore a chemical process as well as an electrical one. As a transmitter substance is emitted from the end plate, the body or dendrite of the next cell reacts by becoming receptive for activation (its membrane becomes permeable to the transmitter substance).

A neuron can receive activation from a number of axons from different neurons. Each cell has a certain **threshold** that determines the level of activation which is needed for the cell to actually be activated. The incoming activation (and inhibition) from different axons is constantly being summed up; when activation reaches the threshold level, the cell is activated and fires activation through its own neuron on to another cell.

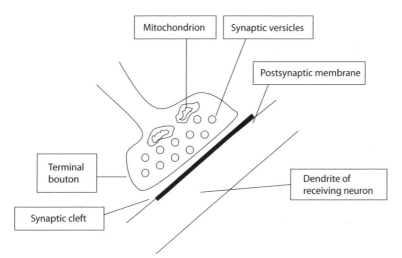

Figure 14.5. Synapse

In this way, patterns of activation arise for different activities of the brain. Activation is also sent through nerve fibers to the muscles in the rest of the body, while incoming signals received from different parts of the body via nerve fibers activate nerve cells in the brain. Signals from the different sensory channels are projected onto specific areas of the cortex.

Cellular organization (cytoarchitecture): Brodmann areas

Based on the organization of the cortex in six cellular layers with different architectures, as seen under the microscope, Brodmann (1909) identified 50 different regions. The Brodmann area numbers are used to refer to specific areas.

Important Brodmann areas for language and communication:
Primary sensory cortex (postcentral gyrus): 1, 2, 3
Primary motor cortex (precentral gyrus): 4
Primary visual cortex (medial occipital lobe): 17
Primary auditory cortex (Heschl's gyrus): 41, 42
Sensory association cortex (superior parietal lobe): 5, 7
Association language cortex, Wernicke's area (superior temporal gyrus): 22
Motor speech cortex, Broca's area (lower third frontal convolution): 44, 45
Supramarginal gyrus: 40
Angular gyrus: 39
Occipital-temporal lobe border: 37

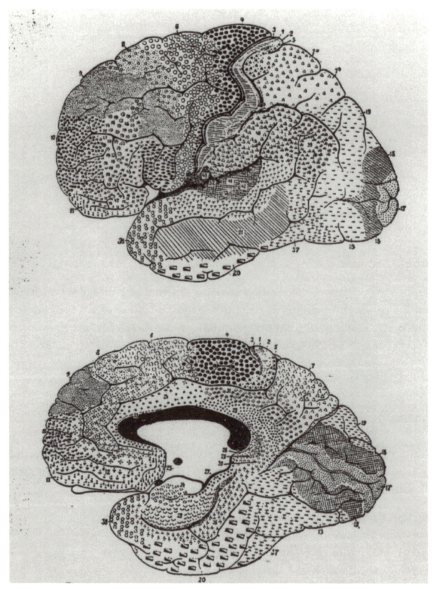

Figure 14.6. Brodmann map

Hearing

The central auditory area is situated in the first temporal gyrus. Adjacent to this area is a larger area that further analyzes the content of what is perceived auditorily, for instance, speech.

Vision

The central area for vision lies at the back of the occipital lobe. Adjacent to the visual cortex is an area that further analyzes what is perceived visually, such as pictures or printed letters.

Sensation

Sensations from different parts of the body are projected onto the somatosensory cortex in the postrolandic gyrus of the parietal lobe. This area also has adjacent areas for further analysis, for example, an area next to the area for sensations from the articulatory organs of the mouth (the lips, tongue, etc.) can evaluate speech movements of the mouth.

Motor system

The nerve signals for the activation of muscles in different parts of the body are sent out from the motor cortex in the prerolandic gyrus of the frontal lobe. Immediately anterior to this area are areas for the control and "programming" of movements. Large areas of the frontal lobes also monitor activity more holistically and control the work of the rest of the brain.

Further reading

Bhatnagar, S. (2002). *Neuroscience for the study of communicative disorders*. Second Edition. Philadelphia: Lippincott Williams & Wilkins.

Webster, D. (1999). *Neuroscience of communication*. Second Edition. London: Singular Publishing Group.

References

Ahlsén, E. (1985). *Discourse patterns in aphasia. Gothenburg Monographs in Linguistics, 5.* Göteborg University, Department of Linguistics.

Ahlsén, E. (1991). Body communication and speech in a Wernicke's aphasic — A longitudinal study. *Journal of Communication Disorders, 24*, 1–12.

Ahlsén, E. (1993). Conversational principles and aphasic communication. *Journal of Pragmatics, 19*, 57–70.

Ahlsén, E. (1994). Aphasia as a challenge to AAC. In J. Brodin & E. Björck-Åkesson (Eds.), *Proceedings from the Third ISAAC Research Symposium in Augmentative and Alternative Communication*, Kerkrade, Oct. 14–15, 1994, pp. 34–40.

Ahlsén, E. (1995). Pragmatics and aphasia — An activity based approach. *Gothenburg Papers on Theoretical Linguistics, 77.* Göteborg University, Department of Linguistics.

Ahlsén, E. (2002). Speech, vision and aphasic communication. In P. McKevitt, S. O'Nualláin, & C. Mulvihill (Eds.), *Language, vision and music* (pp. 137–148). Amsterdam: John Benjamins.

Ahlsén, E. (2003). Communicative contributions and multimodality — Reflections on body communication, communication aids for persons with language disorders and dialogue systems. In P. Paggio, K. Jokinen, & A. Jönsson (Eds.), *Proceedings of the 1st Nordic Symposium on Multimodal Communication.* CST Working Papers, Report No. 6, pp. 129–140.

Ahlsén, E. (2005). Argumentation with restricted linguistic ability: Performing a role play with aphasia or in a second language. *Clinical Linguistics and Phonetics, 19*, 433–451.

Albert, M., Goodglass, H. & Helm, N. (1973). Melodic intonation therapy for aphasia. *Archives of Neurology, 29*, 130–131.

Albert, M., & Obler, L. (1978). *The bilingual brain. Neuropsychological and neurolinguistic aspects of bilingualism.* Berlin: Springer.

Allwood, J. (1976). *Linguistic communication as action and cooperation. Gothenburg Monographs in Linguistics, 2.* Göteborg University, Department of Linguistics.

Allwood, J. (1981). On the distinctions between semantics and pragmatics. In W. Klein & W. Levelt (Eds.) Crossing the boundaries in linguistics. (pp- 177-189). Dordrecht: Reidel.

Allwood, J. (1995). An activity based approach to pragmatics. *Gothenburg Papers in Theoretical Linguistics, 76.* Göteborg University, Department of Linguistics.

Allwood, J. (1999). Semantics as meaning determination with semantic-epistemic operations, In J. Allwood & P. Gärdenfors (Eds.), *Cognitive semantics* (pp. 1–17). Amsterdam: John Benjamins.

Allwood, J. (2000). An activity based approach to pragmatics. In H. Bunt & B. Black (Eds.), *Abduction, belief and context in dialogue: Studies in computational pragmatics* (pp. 47–80). Amsterdam: John Benjamins.

Allwood, J. (2001). Cooperation and flexibility in multimodal communication. In H. Bunt & R. J. Beun (Eds.), *Cooperative multimodal communication. Lecture notes in computer science, 2155* (pp. 1–16). Berlin: Springer.

Allwood, J. (2002). Bodily communication — Dimensions of expression and content. In B. Granström, D. House, & I. Karlsson (Eds.), *Multimodality in language and speech systems* (pp. 7–26). Dordrecht: Kluwer.

Allwood, J. (2003). Meaning potential and context. Some consequences for the analysis of variation in meaning. In H. Cuyckens, R. Dirven & J. Taylor (Eds.) *Cognitive approaches to lexical semantics* (pp. 29–65). Berlin: Mouton de Gruyter.

Allwood, J., & Ahlsén, E. (1984). *Afasi och semantik* [Aphasia and semantics]. *Gothenburg Papers in Theoretical Linguistics, S5.* Göteborg University, Department of Linguistics.

Allwood, J., & Ahlsén, E. (1986). *Semantic aspects of aphasic word substitution. Gothenburg Papers in Theoretical Linguistics, 51.* Göteborg University, Department of Linguistics.

Allwood, J., & Ahlsén, E. (1991). Semantic operations and aphasia. In H. A. Sigurdsson (Ed.), *Papers from the Twelfth Scandinavian Conference of Linguistics* (pp. 1–13). Reykjavik, University of Iceland, Linguistic Institute.

Allwood, J., Nivre, J., & Ahlsén, E. (1990). Speech management — On the nonwritten life of speech. *Nordic Journal of Linguistics, 13,* 3–48.

Allwood, J., Nivre, J., & Ahlsén, E. (1992). On the semantics and pragmatics of linguistic feedback. *Journal of Semantics, 9,* 1–26.

Appel, J., Kertesz, A., & Fishman, M. (1982). A study of language functioning in Alzheimer patients. *Brain and Language, 23,* 159–166.

Arbib, M. (Ed.) (1998). *The handbook of brain theory and neural networks.* Cambridge MA: The MIT Press.

Arbib, M. (2005). From monkey-like action recognition to human language: An evolutionary framework for neurolinguistics. *Brain and Behavioral Sciences, 28,* 105–124.

Austin, J. (1962). *How to do things with words.* Oxford: OUP.

Bates, E., & Wulfeck, B. (1989). Comparative aphasiology: A cross linguistic approach to language breakdown. *Aphasiology, 3,* 111–142.

Bates, E., & Wulfeck, B. (1989). Crosslinguistic studies of aphasia. In B. MacWhinney & E. Bates (Eds.), *The crosslinguistic study of sentence processing* (pp. 328–371). New York NY: Cambridge University Press.

Bates, E., Wulfeck, B., & MacWhinney, B. (1991). Cross linguistic studies of aphasia: An overview. *Brain and Language, 41,* 123–148.

Bay, E. (1962). Aphasia and non-verbal disorders of language. *Brain, 85,* 411–426.

Bayles, K. (1992). Relation of linguistic communication abilities of Alzheimer's patients to stage of disease. *Brain and Language, 42,* 454–472.

Bayles, K., Tomoeda, C., & Trosset, M. (1990). Naming and categorical knowledge in Alzheimer's disease: The process of semantic memory deterioration. *Brain and Language, 39,* 498–510.

Bertalanffy, L. V. (1968). *General systems theory. Foundations, development, applications.* London: Allen Lane.

Bhatnagar, S. (2002). *Neuroscience for the study of communicative disorders.* Second Edition. Philadelphia PA: Lippincott Williams & Wilkins.

Bickerton, D. (1990). *Language and species.* Chicago IL: University of Chicago Press.

Blevins, J. (1995). The syllable in phonological theory. In J. A. Goldsmith (Ed.), *The handbook of phonological theory* (pp. 206–235). Cambridge: Blackwell.

Blumstein, S. (1973). *A phonological investigation of aphasic speech.* The Hague: Mouton.

Blumstein, S. (1994). Impairments of speech production and speech perception in aphasia. *Philosophical Transactions of the Royal Society of London B, 346,* 29–36.

Bouillaud, J. (1825). Recherches clinique propres a démontrer que la perte de la parole correspond à la lésion del lobules antèrieurs du cerveau. *Archives Générale del a Médicine, 8,* 25–45.

Breedin, S. D., Martin, N., & Saffran, E. (1994). Category-specific semantic impairments: An infrequent occurrence? *Brain and Language, 47,* 383–386.

Broca, P. (1861). Perte de la parole. *Bulletin de la Sociéte d'Anthropologie de Paris, 2,* 219–237.

Broca, P. (865). Remarques sur la siège de la faculté du langage articulé. Bulletin del la *Société d'Anthropologie de Paris, 6,* 330–357.

Brodmann, K. (1909). *Vergleischende Lokalisationslehre der Grosshirnrinde.* Leipzig: Barth.

Brown, J. (1977). *Mind, brain and consciousness.* New York NY: Academic Press.

Brown, J. (1980). *Language, brain, and the problem of localization.* In D. Caplan (Ed.), *Biological studies of mental processes* (pp. 287–300). Cambridge MA: The MIT Press.

Brown, J. (Ed.) (1981). *Jargon aphasia.* New York NY: Academic Press.

Brown, J. (1988). *The life of the mind.* Hillsdale NJ: Lawrence Erlbaum Associates.

Brown, J. (1991). *Self and process. Brain states and the conscious present.* New York NY: Springer.

Bryant, P., & Bradley, L. (1985). *Children's reading problems.* Oxford: Blackwell.

Buckingham, H. (1979). Semantic paraphasia. *Journal of Communication Disorders, 12,* 197–209.

Buckingham, H. (1980). On correlating aphasic errors with slips of the tongue. *Applied Psycholinguistics, 1,* 199–220.

Buckingham, H. (1981). Where do neologisms come from? In J. Brown (Ed.), *Jargon aphasia* (pp. 39–62). New York NY: Academic Press.

Burling, R. (1993). Primate calls, human language and nonverbal communication. *Current Anthropology, 34,* 1–37.

Butterworth, B. (1979). Hesitation and the production of verbal paraphasias and neologisms in jargon aphasia. *Brain and Language, 8,* 133–161.

Butterworth, B. (1981). Speech errors: Old data in search of new theories. *Linguistics, 19,* 627–662.

Butterworth, B. (1992). Disorders of phonological encoding. *Cognition, 42,* 261–286.

Byng, S., Pound, C., Lindsay, J., & Swinburn, K. (2001). *The aphasia therapy file.* Hove: Psychology Press.

Byng, S., Pound, C., & Parr, S. (2000). Living with aphasia: A framework for intervention. In I. Papathanasiou (Ed.), *Acquired neurogenic communication disorders: A clinical perspective* (pp. 49–75). London: Whurr.

Caplan, D. (1982) Lecture series. Linguistic Institute, University of Maryland.

Caplan, D. (1987). *Neurolinguistics and linguistic aphasiology: An introduction.* Cambridge: CUP.

Caplan, D. (1992). *Language: Structure, processing, and disorders.* Cambridge: CUP.

Caramazza, A. (1984). The logic of neuropsychological research and the problem of patient classification in aphasia. Brain and Language, 21, 9-20.

Caramazza, A., & Hillis, A. (1990). Where do semantic errors come from? *Cortex, 26,* 95–122.

Caramazza, A., & Hillis, A. (1991). Lexical organization of nouns and verbs in the brain. *Nature, 349,* 788–790.

Caramazza, A., & Shelton, J. (1998). Domain specific systems in the brain: The animate-inanimate distinction. *Journal of Cognitive Neuroscience, 10,* 1–34.

Caramazza, A., & Zurif, E. (1976). Dissociation of algorithmic and heuristic processes in language comprehension: Evidence from aphasia. *Brain and Language, 3,* 572–582.

Caramelli, P., Mansur, L., & Nitrini, R. (1998). Language and communication disorders in dementia of the Alzheimer type. In B. Stemmer & H. Whitaker (Eds.), *Handbook of neurolinguistics* (pp. 463–473). New York NY: Academic Press.

Carlomagno, S. (1994). *Pragmatic approaches to aphasia (Promoting Aphasics' Communicative Efficiency).* London: Singular.

Chantraine, Y., Joanette, Y., & Cardebat, D. (1998). Impairments of discourse-level representations and processes. In B. Stemmer & H. Whitaker (Eds.), *Handbook of neurolinguistics* (pp. 261-274). New York NY: Academic Press.

Chapman, D. 1991. *Vision, instruction and action.* Cambridge MA: The MIT Press.

Chapman, S. B., & Ulatowska, H. (1994). Differential diagnosis in aphasia. In R. Chapey (Ed.), *Language intervention in adult aphasia* (pp. 121–131). Baltimore MD: Williams & Wilkins.

Cherrier, M., Mendez, M., Cummings, J., & Benson, D. F. (1998). Language and communication in non-Alzheimer dementias. In B. Stemmer & H. Whitaker (Eds.), *Handbook of neurolinguistics* (pp. 447–461). New York NY: Academic Press.

Chomsky, N. (1965). *Aspects of the theory of syntax.* Cambridge MA: The MIT Press.

Chomsky, N. (1986). *Knowledge of language.* New York NY: Praeger.

Chomsky, N. (1992). *A minimalist program for linguistic theory. MIT Working Papers in Linguistics, 1,* MIT.

Christensen, A. -L. (1974). *Luria's neuropsychological investigation.* Copenhagen: Munksgaard.

Christman, S. S. (1992). Uncovering phonological regularity in neologisms: Contributions of sonority theory. *Clinical Linguistics and Phonetics, 6,* 219–247.

Clements, G. N. (1990). Target related neologism formation in jargonaphasia. *Brain and Language, 46,* 109–128.

Collins, A., & Loftus, E. (1975). A spreading-activation theory of semantic processing. *Psychological Review, 82,* 407–428.

Collins, A., & Quillian, M. (1969). Retrieval time from semantic memory. *Journal of Verbal Learning and Verbal Behavior, 8*, 240–247.

Coltheart, M. (2000). Deep dyslexia is right hemisphere reading. *Brain and Language, 71*, 299–309.

Coltheart, M., Patterson, K., & Marshall, J. (Eds.) (1980). *Deep dyslexia*. London: Routledge and Kegan Paul.

Crosson, B. (1992). *Subcortical functions in language and memory*. New York NY: Guilford Press.

Crystal, D., Fletcher, P., & Garman, M. (1976). *The grammatical analysis of language disability*. London: Edward Arnold.

Cummings, J., Darkins, A., Mendez, M., Hill, M., & Benson, D. F. (1988). Alzheimer's disease and Parkinson's disease: Comparison of speech and language alterations. *Neurology, 38*, 680–684.

Damasio, H., & Damasio, A. (1989). *Lesion analysis in neuropsychology*. New York NY: Oxford University Press.

Danly, M, Cooper, W., & Shapiro, B. (1983). Fundamental frequency, language processing, and linguistic structure in Wernicke's aphasia. *Brain and Language, 19*, 1–24.

Dax, M. (1865). Lésions de la moitié gauche de l'encéphale coincident avedl'oubli des signes de la pensée. Montpellier, 1836. *Gaz. Hebdom., S2,* 11, 259–260.

Deacon, T. (1997). *The symbolic species: The coevolution of language and brain*. London: Penguin.

Decety, J., Grèzes, J., Costes, D., Perani, E., Procyk, F., Grassi, M., Jeannerod, F., & Fazio, F. (1997). Brain activity during observation of actions. Influence of action content and subject's strategy. *Brain* 120, 763–1777.

Dehaene, S., Dupoux, E., Mehler, J., Cohen, L., Paulesu, E., Perani, D., et al. (1997). Anatomical variability in the cortical representation of first and second language. *Neuroreport, 8*, 3809–3815.

Dell, G. (1986). A spreading activation theory of retrieval in language production. *Psychological Review, 93*, 283–321.

Dell, G., & Reich, P. (1981). Stages in sentence production: An analysis of speech error data. *Journal of Verbal Learning and Verbal Behavior, 20*, 611–629.

Dell, G., Schwartz, M., Martin, N., Saffran, E., & Gagnon, D. (1997). Lexical access in aphasic and nonaphasic speakers. *Psychological Review, 104*, 801–838.

Derouesné, J., & Lecours, A. (1972). Two tests for the study of semantic deficits in aphasia. *International Journal of Mental Health, 1*, 14–24.

Descartes. R. (1974*). Œvres de Descartes*. C. Adam & P. Tannery (Eds.) (tome XI, pp. 301–497) Paris: Vrin.

Dogil, G. (1989). The phonological and acoustic form of neologistic jargon aphasia. *Clinical Linguistics and Phonetics, 4*, 265–279.

Eikmeyer, H.-J., & Schade, U. (1991). Sequentialization in connectionist language production models. *Cognitive Systems, 32*, 128–138.

Ellis, A. (1984). *Reading, writing and dyslexia: A cognitive analysis*. London: Lawrence Erlbaum Associates.

Fabbro, F. (1999). *Neurolinguistics of bilingualism*. Hove: Psychology Press.

Fabbro, F. (2001a). The bilingual brain: Bilingual aphasia. *Brain and Language, 79*, 201–210.

Fabbro, F. (2001b). The bilingual brain: Cerebral representation of languages. *Brain and Language, 79*, 211–222.

Faber-Langedoen, K., Morris, J., Knesevich, J., LaBarge, E., Miller, J., & Berg, L. (1988). Aphasia in senile dementia of the Alzheimer type. *Annals of Neurology, 23*, 365–370.

Farah, M., & McClelland, J. (1991). A computational model of semantic memory impairment: Modality-specificity and emergent category-specificity. *Journal of Experimental Psychology: General, 120*, 339–357.

Fauconnier, G. (1994). *Mental spaces. Aspects of meaning construction in natural language*. Cambridge: CUP.

Ferm, U., Ahlsén, E., & Björck-Åkesson, E. (2005). Conversational topics between a child with complex communication needs and her caregiver at mealtime. *Augmentative and Alternative Communication, 21*, 19–40.

Ferrier, D. (1886). *The functions of the brain*. London: Smith, Elder & Co.

Feyereisen, P. (1987). Gestures and speech, interactions and separations: A reply to McNeill (1985). *Psychological Review, 94*, 493–498.

Feyereisen, P. (1991). Communicative behaviour in aphasia. *Aphasiology, 5*, 323–333.

Fillmore, C. (1968). The case for case. In E. Bach & T. R. Rrms (Eds.) Universals in linguistic theory (pp-.1-90). New York: Holt, Rinehart & Winston.

Finkelnburg, K. M. (1870). Asymbolie und Aphasie. *Berliner Klinishes Wochenschrift, 7*, 449–450, 460–462.

Flourens, P. (1824). *Recherches expérimentales sur les proprétés et les fonctions du système nerveux dans les animaux vertèbres*. Paris: Baillière

Forster, K. (1976). Accessing the mental lexicon. In T. Wales & E. Walker (Eds.), *New approaches to language mechanisms* (pp. 139–174). Amsterdam: North Holland.

Franklin, S. (1999). *Artificial minds*. Cambridge MA: The MIT Press.

Freud, S. (1891). *Zur Auffassung der Aphasien. Eine kritische Studie*. Leipzig and Vienna: Franz Deutiche.

Friedmann, N. (2001). Agrammatism and the psychological reality of the syntactic tree. *Journal of Psycholinguistic Research, 30*, 71–90.

Friedmann, N., & Grodzinsky, Y. (2000). Split inflection in neurolinguistics. In M.-A. Friedemann & L. Rizzi (Eds.), *The acquisition of syntax: Studies in comparative developmental linguistics* (pp. 84–104). Geneva: Longman Linguistics Library Series.

Frith, U. (1989). A new look at language and communication in autism. *British Journal of Disorders of Communication, 24*, 123–150.

Fromkin, V. (1971). The non-anomalous nature of anomalous utterances. *Language, 47*, 27–52.

Gainotti, G. (1998). Category-specific disorders for nouns and verbs. In B. Stemmer & H. Whitaker (Eds.), *Handbook of neurolinguistics* (pp. 3–11). New York NY: Academic Press.

Gainotti, G., Silveri, M., Daniele, A., & Guistolisi, L. (1995). Neuroanatomical correlates of category-specific semantic disorders: A critical survey. *Memory, 3*, 247–264.

Gall, F. & Spurzheim, G. (1810–1819). *Anatomie et physiologie du système nerveus en général et du cerveau en particulier*. Paris: Schoell.

Gallese, V. & Lakoff, G. (2005). The brain's concepts: the role of the sensory-motor system in conceptual knowledge. Cognitive Neuropsychology, 22 (3/4), 455-479.

Gandour, J. (1998). Phonetics and phonology. In B. Stemmer & H. Whitaker (Eds.), *Handbook of neurolinguistics* (pp. 207–219). New York: Academic Press.

Gardner, R., Gardner, B., & van Cantfort, T. (1989). *Teaching sign language to chimpanzees*. New York: State University of New York Press.

Gardner, H., Zurif, E., Berry, T., & Baker, E. (1976). Visual communication in aphasia. *Neuropsychologia, 14*, 275–292.

Garrett, M. (1982a). Production of speech: Observations from normal and pathological language use. In A. W. Ellis (Ed.), *Normality and pathology in cognitive functions* (pp. 19–76). London: Academic Press.

Garrett, M. (1982b). Remarks on the relation between language production and language comprehension systems. In M. Arbib, D. Caplan, & J. C. Marshall (Eds.), *Neural models of language processes* (pp. 209–224). New York NY: Academic Press.

Geschwind, N. (1965). Disconnection syndromes in animals and man. *Brain, 88*, 237–294 and 585–644.

Goldstein, K. (1948). *Language and language disturbances*. New York NY: Grune & Stratton.

Goodall, J. (1986). *The chimpanzees of Gombe*. Cambridge, MA: Harvard University Press.

Goodglass, H. (1976). Agrammatism. In H. Whitaker & H. A. Whitaker (Eds.), *Studies in neurolinguistics, Vol. 2* (pp. 237–260). New York NY: Academic Press.

Goodglass, H., & Baker, E. (1976). Semantic field, naming and auditory comprehension in aphasia. *Brain and Language, 3*, 359–374.

Goodglass, H., & Kaplan, E. (1973). *The assessment of aphasia and related disorders*. Philadelphia PA: Lea & Febiger.

Green, D. (1986). Control, activation and resource. *Brain and Language, 27*, 210–223.

Green, D. (1998). Mental control of the bilingual lexico-semantic system. *Bilingualism, Language and Cognition, 1*, 67–81.

Green, E. (1969). Phonological and grammatical aspects of jargon in an aphasic patient: A case study. *Language and Speech, 12*, 103–118.

Grice, P. (1975). Logic and conversation, In P. Cole & J. L. Morgan (Eds.), *Syntax and semantics, Vol. 3: Speech acts* (pp. 41–58). New York NY: Seminar Press.

Grodzinsky, Y. (1984). The syntactic characterization of agrammatism. *Cognition, 16*, 99–120.

Grodzinsky, Y. (1986). Language deficits and the theory of syntax. *Brain and Language, 26*, 35–59.

Grodzinsky, Y. (1990). *Theoretical perspectives on language deficits*. Cambridge MA: The MIT Press.

Grodzinsky, Y. (1995). A restrictive theory of agrammatic comprehension. *Brain and Language, 51*, 26–51.

Grodzinsky, Y. (1998). Comparative aphasiology: Some preliminary notes. In E. Visch-Brink & R. Bastiaanse (Eds.), *Linguistic levels in aphasiology* (pp. 175–192). London: Singular.

Hagoort, P. (1998). The shadows of lexical meaning in patients with semantic impairments. In B. Stemmer & H. Whitaker (Eds.), *Handbook of neurolinguistics* (pp. 235–248). New York NY: Academic Press.

Harley, T. (1984). A critique of top-down independent levels models of speech production. Evidence from non-plan-internal speech production. *Cognitive Science, 8,* 191–219.

Harley, T. (1993a). Phonological activation of semantic competitors during lexical access in speech production. *Language and Cognitive Processes, 8,* 291–309.

Harley, T. (1993b). Connectionist approaches to language disorders. *Aphasiology, 7,* 221–249.

Harris, J. (1998). Phonological universals and phonological disorders. In E. Visch-Brink & R. Bastiaanse (Eds.), *Linguistic levels in aphasiology* (pp. 91–118). London: Singular.

Hartley, L. (1992). Assessment of functional communication. *Seminars in Speech and Language, 13,* 264–279.

Head, H. (1926). *Aphasia and kindred disorders of speech.* Cambridge: CUP.

Hebb, D. (1949). *The organization of behavior.* New York: Wiley.

Hécaen, H., & Lanteri-Laura, G. (1977). *Évolution des connaissances et des doctrines sur les localisations cérébrales.* Paris: Desclée de Brouwer.

Helm-Estabrooks, N., Fitzpatrick, P. M., & Barresi, B. (1982). Visual action therapy for global aphasia. Journal of Speech and Hearing Disorders, *47(4),* 385–389.

Henschen, S. (1926). On the frunction of trhe right hemisphere of the brain in relation to the left in speech, music and calculation. *Brain, 49,* 110–123.

Hodges, J., Graham, N., & Patterson K. (1995). Charting the progression in semantic dementia: Implications for the organization of semantic memory. *Memory, 3,* 463–495.

Holland, A. (1991). Pragmatic aspects of intervention in aphasia. *Journal of Neurolinguistics, 6,* 197–211.

Howard, D., & Hatfield, F. M. (1987). *Aphasia therapy: Historical and contemporary issues.* London: Lawrence Erlbaum Associates.

Howard, D., & Patterson, K. (1992). *The pyramids and palm trees test.* Thames Valley Test Company.

Hulme, C., & Snowling, M. (Eds.) (1994). *Reading development and dyslexia.* London: Whurr Publishers.

Jackson, J. Hughlings (1932). Selected Writings. J. Taylor (Ed.) London: Hodder & Stoughton.

Jakobson, R. (1941). *Kindersprache, Aphasie und Allgemeine Lautgesetze.*Uppsala: Unitersitetets Årsskrift.

Jakobson, R. (1964). Towards a linguistic typology of aphasic impairments. In A- V- S. de Rueck & M. O'Connor (Eds.) *Disorders of language.* London: Churchill.

Jeannerod, M. (1997). *The cognitive neuroscience of action.* Oxford: Blackwell.

Jerison, H. (1973). *The evolution of brain and intelligence.* New York: Academic Press.

Joanette, Y., & Ansaldo, A. I. (1999). Clinical note: Acquired pragmatic impairments and aphasia. *Brain and Language, 68,* 529–534.

Just, M., & Carpenter, P. (1992). A capacity theory of comprehension: Individual differences in working memory. *Psycholinguistic Review, 99,* 122–149.

Kagan, A. (1998). Supported conversation for adults with aphasia. *Clinical Forum. Aphasiology, 12,* 816–830.

Kagan, A., & Saling, M. (1988). *An introduction to Luria's aphasiology: Theory and application.* Johannesburg: Witwatersrand University Press.

Kay, J., Lesser, R., & Coltheart, M. (1992). *PALPA: Psycholinguistic assessments of language processing in aphasia.* Hove: Lawrence Erlbaum Associates.

Kean, M.-L. (1977). The linguistic interpretation of aphasic syndromes: Agrammatism in Broca's aphasia, an example. *Cognition, 5*, 9–46.

Kendon, A. (1993). Human gesture. In K. Gibson & T. Ingold (Eds.), *Tools, language and cognition in human evolution* (pp. 43–62). Cambridge: CUP.

Kiran, S., Ntourou, K., Eubanks, M., & Shamapant, S. (2005). Typicality of inanimate category exemplars in aphasia: Further evidence for the semantic complexity effect. *Brain and Language, 95*, 178–180.

Kleist, K. (1916). Über Leitungsaphasie und die grammatisches Störungen. *Monatsschrift für Psychiatrie und Neurologie, 40*, 118–199.

Kohler, E., Keysers, C., Umiltà, M. A., Fogassi, L., Gallese, V. & Rizzolatti, G. (2002). Hearing sounds, understanding action: action representation in mirror neurons. *Science 297*, 846–848.

Kohn, S. (1993). Segmental disorders in aphasia. In G. Blanken, J. Dittman, H. Grimm, J. C. Marshall, & C.-W. Wallesch (Eds.), *Linguistic disorders and pathologies: An international handbook* (pp. 197–209). Berlin: Walter de Gruyter.

Kohonen, T. (1989). *Self-organization and associative memory,* 3rd edition. Berlin: Springer.

Kolk, H. (1987). A theory of grammatical impairment in aphasia. In G. Kempen (Ed.), *Natural language generation: New results in artificial intelligence, psychology, and linguistics* (pp. 388–391). Dordrecht: Martinus Nijhoff.

Kolk, H. (1998a). Disorders of syntax in aphasia. In B. Stemmer & H. Whitaker (Eds.), *Handbook of neurolinguistics* (pp. 249–260). San Diego CA: Academic Press.

Kolk, H. (1998b). The malleability of agrammatic symptoms and its implications for therapy. In E. Visch-Brink & R. Bastiaanse (Eds.), *Linguistic levels in aphasiology* (pp. 193–210). London: Singular.

Kolk, H., & Heeschen C. (1992). Agrammatism, paragrammatism and the management of language. *Language and Cognitive Processes, 7*, 89–129.

Kussmaul, A. (1876). *Die Störungen der Sprache.* H. Gutzmann (Ed.) 1910. Leipzig: Vogel.

Labov, W. (1973). The boundaries of words and their meanings. In C.-J. Bailey & R. Shuy (Eds.), *New ways of analyzing variations in English* (pp. 340–373). Washington DC: Georgetown University Press.

Lakoff, G. (1987). *Women, fire and dangerous things.* Chicago IL: University of Chicago Press.

Langacker, R. (1989). *Foundations of cognitive grammar, 1: Theoretical prerequisites.* Stanford CA: Stanford University Press.

La Peyronie, F. (1741). Mémoire contenant plusieurs observations sur les maladies du cerveau, par lesquelles on tâche de découvrir le véritable lieu du cerveau dans lequel l'âme exerce ses fonctions. *Mém. Acad. des Sciences, 39*, 199–218.

Lashely, K. (1933). Integrative functions of the cerebral cortex. *Psychological Review, 13*, 1–42.

Lashley, K. (1950). In search of the engram. *Symposia of the Society for Experimental Biology, 4*, 454–482.

Lecours, A. R., & Lhermitte, F. (1979). *L'Aphasie*. Paris: Flammarion.

Lenneberg, H. E. (1967). *Biogical foundations of language*. New York NY: Wiley.

Lesser, R. (1978). *Linguistic investigations in aphasia*. London: Edward Arnold.

Lesser, R., & Milroy. L. (1993). *Linguistics and aphasia: Psycholinguistic and pragmatic aspects of intervention*. London: Longman.

Levelt, W. (1989). *Speaking: From intention to articulation*. Cambridge MA: The MIT Press.

Levinson, S. (1983). *Pragmatics*. Cambridge: CUP.

Lichtheim, L. (1885). Über Aphasie. *Deutsches Archiv für klinishcer Medizin, 36*, 204–268.

Lieberman, P. (1998). *Eve spoke*. London: W. W. Norton & Company.

Linebarger, M. (1998). Algorithmic and heuristic processes in agrammatic language comprehension. In E. Visch-Brink & R. Bastiaanse (Eds.), *Linguistic levels in aphasiology* (pp. 153–174). London: Singular.

Linebarger, M., Schwartz, M., & Saffran, E. (1983). Sensitivity to grammatical structure in so-called agrammatic aphasics. *Cognition, 13*, 361–393.

Linell, P. (1982). The written language bias in linguistics. *Studies in Communication, 2*. Linköping University, Department of Communication Studies.

Lott, P. (1999). *Gesture and aphasia*. Bern: Peter Lang.

Lundberg, I. (1994). Reading difficulties can be predicted and prevented: A Scandinavian perspective on phonological awareness and reading. In C. Hulme & M. Snowling (Eds.), *Reading development and dyslexia*. London: Whurr Publishers.

Luria, A. R. (1963). *Restoration of brain functions after brain trauma*. Oxford: Pergamon Press.

Luria, A. R. (1966). *Higher cortical functions in man*. London: Tavistock.

Luria, A.R. (1970). *Traumatic aphasia*. The Hague: Mouton.

Luria, A. R. (1973). *The working brain: An introduction to neuropsychology*. Hove: Basil Haigh.

Luria, A. R. (1976). *Basic problems in neurolinguistics*. The Hague: Mouton.

Marie, P. (1906) La troisème circonvolution frontale gauche ne joue aucun rôle spécial dans la fonction du langage. *Semaine Médicale, 26*, 241–247.

Månsson, A.-C. (2004). *Gesture and meaning. Gothenburg Monographs in Linguistics, 23*. Göteborg University, Department of Linguistics.

Marshall, R. (1999). *Introduction to group treatment for aphasia: Design and management*. Woburn MA: Butterworth-Heinemann.

Marslen-Wilson, W., & Tyler, L. (1980). The temporal structure of spoken language understanding. *Cognition, 8*, 1–71.

Martin, N. (1998). Recovery and treatment of acquired reading and spelling disorders. In B. Stemmer & H. Whitaker (Eds.), *Handbook of neurolinguistics* (pp. 560–573). San Diego CA: Academic Press.

Martin, N., Dell, G., Saffran, E., & Schwartz, M. (1994). Origins of paraphasias in deep dysphasia: Testing the consequence of a decay impairment in an interactive spreading activation model of lexical retrieval. *Brain and Language, 47*, 609–660.

Martin, N., Gagnon, D., Schwartz, M., Dell, G., & Saffran, E. (1996). Phonological facilitation of semantic errors in normal and aphasic speakers: Evidence for interaction of semantic and phonological representations from a picture naming task. *Brain and Language, 47*, 349–351.

Martin, N., & Laine, M. (2000). Effects of contextual priming on impaired word retrieval. *Aphasiology, 14*, 53–70.

McClelland, J., & Elman, J. (1986). The TRACE model of speech perception. *Cognitive Psychology, 18*, 1–86.

McDonald, S., Togher, L., & Code, C. (Eds.) (1999). *Communication disorders following traumatic brain injury*. Hove: Psychology Press.

Menn, L., & Obler, L. (1990a). Cross-language data and theories of agrammatism. In L. Menn & L. Obler (Eds.), *Cross-language agrammatic source book* (pp. 1369–1389). Amsterdam: John Benjamins.

Menn, L., & Obler, L. (Eds.) (1990b). *Cross-language agrammatic source book*. Amsterdam: John Benjamins.

Meynert, T. (1885/1968). *Pshychiatry, a Clinical treatise of diseases of the forebrain based upon a study of its structure, functions and nutritions*. New York NY: Hafner.

Miceli, G., Mazzuchi, A., Menn, L., & Goodglass, H. (1983). Contrasting cases of Italian agrammatic aphasia without comprehension disorder. *Brain and Language, 19*, 65–97.

Miceli, G., Silveri, M. C., Romani, C., & Caramazza, A. (1989). Variation in the pattern of omissions and substitutions of grammatical morphemes in the spontaneous speech of so-called agrammatic patients. *Brain and Language, 26*, 447–492.

Minkowski, M. (1963). On aphasia in polyglots. In L. Halpern (Ed.), *Problems of dynamic neurology*. Jerusalem: Hebrew University.

Mithen, S. (1996). *The prehistoric mind*. London: Thames & Hudson.

Moen, I., & Sundet, K. (1996). Production and perception of word tones (pitch accents) in patients with left and right hemispere damage. *Brain and Lanugage, 53*, 267–281.

Morton, J. (1969). Interaction of information in word recognition. *Psychological Review, 76*, 165–178.

Murre, J., & Goebel, R. (1996). Connectionist modeling. In T. Dijkstra & K. de Smedt (Eds.), *Computational psycholinguistics* (pp. 49–81). London: Taylor & Francis.

Murre, J., & Sturdy, D. (1995). The connectivity of the brain: Multilevel quantitative analysis. *Biological Cybernetics, 73*, 529–545.

Myers, P. (1999). *Right hemisphere damage — Disorders of communication and cognition*. London: Singular.

Nespoulous, J.-L., Lecours, A. R., & Joanette, Y. (1982). La dichotomie "phonetique-phonemique," a-t-elle une valeur nosologique? Unpublished manuscript.

Nespoulous, J.-L., & Moreay, N. (1998). Repair strategies and the production of segmental errors in aphasia. In E. Visch-Brink & R. Bastiaanse (Eds.), *Linguistic levels in aphasia* (pp. 133–146). London: Singular.

Nielsen, J. (1947). *Agnosia, apraxia, aphasia. Their value in cerebral localization*. New York NY: Paul B. Hoeber.

Noble, W., & Davidson, I. (1996). *Human evolution, language and mind*. Cambridge: CUP.

Paivio, A. (1991). *Mental representation: Dual-coding hypothesis*. New York NY: Harvester Wheatsheaf.

Paradis, M. (1977). Bilingualism and aphasia. In H. Whitaker & H. A. Whitaker (Eds.), *Studies in neurolinguistics, Vol. 3* (pp. 65–121). New York NY: Academic Press.

Paradis, M. (1998). Language and communication in multilinguals. In B. Stemmer & H. Whitaker (Eds.), *Handbook of neurolinguistics* (pp. 418–431). San Diego CA: Academic Press.

Paradis, M. (2004). *A neurolinguistic theory of bilingualism*. Amsterdam: John Benjamins.

Patterson, K., Marshall, J., & Coltheart, M. (Eds.) (1985). *Surface dyslexia: Cognitive and neuropsychological studies of phonological reading*. Hillsdale NJ: Lawrence Erlbaum Associates.

Pavlov, I. (1949). *Complete collected works*, vols 1–6. Moscow: Izd. Akad. Nauk. (/Russian)

Peirce, C. S. (1931). *Collected papers of Charles Sanders Peirce, 1931–1958*, 8 vols. Edited by C. Hartshorne, P. Weiss, & A. Burks. Cambridge MA: Harvard University Press.

Penn, C. (1999). Pragmatic assessment and therapy for persons with brain damage: What have clinicians gleaned in two decades? *Brain and Language, 68*, 535–552.

Perkins, L., Whitworth, A., & Lesser, R. (1997). *Conversation analysis profile for people with cognitive impairments*. London: Whurr. (CAPPCI)

Perkins, M. (2003). Clinical pragmatics. In J. Verschueren, J.-O. Östman, J. Blommaert, & C. Bulcaen (Eds.) *Handbook of Pragmatics*: 2001 Installment (pp. 1–29). Amsterdam: John Benjamins.

Pickering, M., & Garrod, S. (2004). Toward a mechanistic psychology of dialogue. *Behavioral and Brain Sciences, 29*, 169–225.

Pinker, S. (1994). *The language instinct: How the mind creates language*. New York NY: William Morrow.

Pinker, S. (1996). Rules of language. In H. Geirson & M. Losonsky (Eds.), *Readings in language and mind* (pp. 558–569). Oxford: Blackwell.

Pinker, S., & Bloom, P. (1990). Natural selection and natural language. *Behavioral and Brain Sciences, 13*, 707–784.

Pitres, A. (1885/1983). Aphasia in polyglots. In M. Paradis (Ed.), *Readings on aphasia in bilinguals and polyglots* (pp. 26–49). Montreal: Didier.

Plaut, D. C., & Shallice, T. (1993). *Connectionist neuropsychology: A case study*. Mahwah NJ: Lawrence Erlbaum Associates.

Pulvermüller, F., Shtyrov, Y., & Ilmoniemi, R. J. (2005). Brain signatures of meaning access in action word recognition. *Journal of Cognitive Neuroscience, 17(6)*, 884–892.

Pollock, J. Y. (1989). Verb movement, Universal Grammar and the structure of IP. *Linguistic Inquiry, 20*, 365–424.

Pötzl, O. (1930). Aphasie und Mehrsprachigkeit. *Zeitschrift für die gesamte Neurologie und Psychiatrie, 12*, 145–162.

Premack, D. (1986). *"Gavagai," or the future history of the animal language controversy*. Cambridge MA: The MIT Press.

Premack, D., & Premack, A. (1983). *The mind of an ape*. New York NY: W. W. Norton.

Premack, D., & Woodruff, G. (1978). Does the chimpanzee have a theory of mind? *Behavioral and Brain Sciences, 4*, 515–526.

Pulvermüller, F., & Roth, V. M. (1991). Communicative aphasia treatment as a further development of PACE therapy. *Aphasiology, 5*, 39–50.

Pulvermüller, F., Shtyrov, Y., & Ilmoniemi, R. (2005). Brain signatures of meaning access in action word recognition. *Journal of Cognitive Neuroscience, 17*, 884–892.

Rizzolatti, G. & Arbib, M. A. 2005. Language within our grasp. *Trends in Neurosciences* 21, 188–194.

Rochford, G. (1971). A study of naming errors in dysphasic and in demented patients. *Neuropsychologia, 9,* 437–443.

Romani, C., & Calabrese, A. (1998). Syllabic constraints on the phonological errors of an aphasic patient. *Brain and Language, 64,* 83–121.

Rosch, E. (1975). Cognitive representations of semantic categories. *Journal of Experimental Psychology (General), 104,* 192–233.

Rumbaugh, D. (Ed.) (1977). *Language learning by a chimpanzee: The Lana project.* New York NY: Academic Press.

Rumelhart, D., & McClelland, J. (1986). *Parallel distributed processing: Explorations in the microstructure of cognition, Vol. 1. Foundations.* Cambridge MA: The MIT Press.

Sacks, H., Schegloff, E., & Jefferson, G. (1974). A simplest systematics for the organization of turn-taking for conversation. *Language, 50,* 695–735.

Saffran, E., Dell, G., & Schwartz, M. F. (2000). Computational modeling of language disorders. In M. Gazzaniga (Ed.), *The new cognitive neurosciences* (pp. 933–948). Cambridge MA: The MIT Press.

Saffran, E., Schwartz, M., & Marin, O. (1980). The word order problem in agrammatism. I. Comprehension. *Brain and Language, 10,* 263–280.

Sahlén, B. (1991). *From depth to surface. A case study approach to severe developmental language disorders.* Lund: Studentlitteratur.

Saldert, C. (2006). *Inference and conversational interaction. Gothenburg Monographs in Linguistics, 31.* Göteborg University, Department of Linguistics.

de Saussure, F. (1916). *Cours de linguistique génerale.* Paris: Payot.

Savage-Rumbaugh, S., Fields, W., & Tagliatela, J. (2001). Language, speech, tools and writing. *Journal of Consciousness Studies, 8,* 273–292.

Savage-Rumbaugh, S., & Lewin, R. (1994). *Kanzi: The ape at the brink of the human mind.* New York NY: John Wiley.

Schwanenflugel, P. J. (1991). Why are abstract concepts hard to understand? In P. J. Schwanenflugel (Ed.), *The psychology of word meaning* (pp. 223–250). Mahwah NJ: Lawrence Erlbaum Associates.

Schwartz, M., Dell, G., Martin, N., & Saffran, E. (1994). Normal and aphasic naming in an interactive spreading activation model. *Brain and Language, 47,* 391–394.

Schwartz, M., Saffran, E., Fink, R., Myers, J., & Martin, N. (1993). Mapping therapy: A treatment program for agrammatism. *Aphasiology, 8,* 19–54.

Scoresby-Jackson, R. E. (1867). Case of aphasia with right hemiplegia. *Edinburgh Medical Journal, 12,* 696–706.

Searle, J. (1969). *Speech acts.* Cambridge: CUP.

Seron, X., Deloche, V., Bastard, G., Chassin, G., & Hermand, N. (1979). Word finding difficulties and learning transfer in aphasic patients. *Cortex, 15,* 149–155.

Seymour, P. (1998). Neurolinguistic issues in the treatment of childhood literacy disorders. In B. Stemmer & H. Whitaker (Eds.), *Handbook of neurolinguistics* (pp. 574–585). San Diego CA: Academic Press.

Simmons-Mackie, N. (2000). Social approaches to the management of aphasia. In L. Worrall & C. Frattali (Eds.), *Neurogenic communication disorders: A functional approach* (pp. 162–187). New York NY: Thieme.

Slobin, D. I. (1966). The acquisition of Russian as a native language. In F. Smith & G. A. Miller (Eds.), *The genesis of language: A psycholinguistic approach* (pp. 129–148). Cambridge MA: The MIT Press.

Snow, D., & Swisher, L. (1996). Neurobehavioral analogies between syndromes of acquired and developmental language impairment: Hypotheses for research. *Aphasiology, 10,* 453–468.

Söderpalm, E. (1979). *Speech errors in normal and pathological speech.* Malmö: CWK, Gleerup.

Stark, H., & Stark, J. (1990). Syllable structure in Wernicke's aphasia. In J.-L. Nespoulous & P. Villiard (Eds.), *Morphology, phonology and aphasia* (pp. 213–234). New York NY: Springer.

Stemmer, B., & Whitaker, H. (Eds.) (1998). *Handbook of neurolinguistics.* San Diego CA: Academic Press.

Stephan, H. (1972). Evolution of primate brains: A complete anatomical investigation. In R. Tuttle (Ed.), *The functional and evolutionary biology of primates* (pp. 155–174). Chicago IL: Aldine Atherton.

Todman, J., & Alm, N. (1998). Talk boards: Social conversation for text users without speech. *Closing the Gap, 17,* 16.

Todman, J., Alm, N., & File, P. (1999). Modelling pragmatics in AAC. In F. Loncke, J. Clibbens, H. Arvidson, & L. Lloyd (Eds.), *Augmentative and alternative communication: New directions in research and practice* (pp. 84–91). London: Whurr.

von Monakow, C. (1911). Localization of brain functions. In G. von Bonin (Ed.) *Some papers on the cerebral cortex.* Springfield IL: Charles C. Thomas.

von Monakow, C. (1914). *Die Lokalisation im Grosshirn.* Wiesbaden: Bergmann

Visch-Brink, E., Bajema, I., & Van de Sandt-Koenderman, M. (1997). Lexical-semantic therapy: BOX. *Aphasiology, 11,* 1057–1078.

Visch-Brink, E., & Bastiaanse, R. (Eds.) (1998). *Linguistic levels in aphasia.* London: Singular.

Vygotsky, L. (1970). *Thought and language.* Boston MA: The MIT Press.

Wada, J. (1949). (A new method for the determination of the side of cerebral speech dominance. A preliminary report of the intra-carotidinjection of sodium amytal in man.) *Igaku to Seibutsugaki, 14,* 221–222.

Warrington, E., & Shallice, T. (1984). Category specific semantic impairments. *Brain, 107,* 829–854.

Webster, D. (1999). *Neuroscience of communication.* Second Edition. London: Singular.

Weigl, E., & Bierwisch, M. (1970). Neuropsychology and linguistics. *Foundations of Language, 6,* 1–18.

Weisenburg, T., & McBride, K. (1935). *Aphasia.* New York NY: Hafner.

Wernicke, C. (1874). *Der Aphasische Symptomencomplex.* Breslau: Cohn and Weigert.

Whitaker, H. A. 1971. *On the representation of language in the human brain.* Edmonton: Linguistic Research.

Whitaker H. A, & Whitaker H. (Eds.) (1976a). *Studies in neurolinguistics*, Vol 1, New York NY: Academic Press.

Whitaker H. A, & Whitaker H. (Eds.) (1976b). *Studies in neurolinguistics*, Vol 2, New York NY: Academic Press.

Whitaker H. A, & Whitaker H. (Eds.) (1977). *Studies in neurolinguistics*, Vol 3, New York NY: Academic Press.

Whitaker, H. (Ed.) (1999). *Agrammatism*. New York NY: Academic Press.

Whitehouse, P., Caramazza, A., & Zurif, E. (1978). Naming in aphasia: Interacting effects of form and function. *Brain and Language, 6*, 63–74.

Whitworth, A., Perkins, L., & Lesser, R. (1997). *Conversation analysis profile for people with aphasia*. London: Whurr. (CAPPA).

Whitworth, A., Webster, J., & Howard, D. (2005). *A cognitive neuropsychological approach to assessment and intervention in aphasia. A clinician's guide*. Hove: Psychology Press.

Willis, T. (1664). *De cerebri anatome qui accessit nervorum descriptio et usus*. Londines.

Willis, T. (1672). *De anima brutorum*. Londines: R. Davis.

Wittgenstein, L. (1953). *Philosophical investigations*. Oxford: Blackwell.

Worrall, L., & Frattali, C. (Eds.) (2000). *Neurogenic communication disorders — A functional approach*. New York NY: Thieme.

Zurif, E., Caramazza, A., Foldi, N., & Gardner, H. (1979). Lexical semantics and memory for words in aphasia. *Journal of Speech and Hearing Research, 22*, 456–467.

Zurif, E., Caramazza, A., Myerson, R., & Galvis, J. (1974). Semantic feature representations for normal and aphasic language. *Brain and Language, 1*, 167–187.

Index